Shakespeare Theatre, Folger Library, Washington, D. C.
Replica of a typical theatre of Shakespeare's time.

THE TRAGEDY OF HAMLET,
PRINCE OF DENMARK

All the unsigned footnotes in this volume are by the writer of the article to which they are appended. The interpretation of the initials signed to the others is: I. G. = Israel Gollancz, M.A.; H. N. H.= Henry Norman Hudson, A.M.; C. H. H.= C. H. Herford, Litt.D.

PREFACE

By Israel Gollancz, M.A.

THE EARLY EDITIONS

The authorized text of *Hamlet* is based on (i) a Quarto edition published in the year 1604, and (ii) the First Folio version of 1623, where the play follows *Julius Cæsar* and *Macbeth*, preceding *King Lear*. The Quarto of 1604 has the following title-page:—

"THE | Tragicall Historie of | HAMLET, | *Prince of Denmarke*. | By William Shakespeare. | Newly imprinted and enlarged to almost as much | againe as it was, according to the true and perfect | Coppie. | AT LONDON, | Printed by I. R. for N. L. and are to be sold at his | shoppe vnder Saint Dunston's Church in | Fleetstreet. 1604" (*vide* No. 2 of *Shakespeare Quarto Facsimiles*, issued by W. Griggs, under the superintendence of Dr. Furnival).

A comparison of the two texts shows that they are derived from independent sources; neither is a true copy of the author's manuscript; the Quarto edition, though very carelessly printed, is longer than the Folio version, and is essentially more valuable; on the other hand, the Folio version contains a few passages which are not found in the Quarto, and contrasts favorably with it in the less important matter of typographical accuracy (*vide* Notes, *passim*).

The two edition· represent, in all probability, two distinct acting versions of Shakespeare's perfect text.

Quarto editions appeared in 1605, 1611, *circa* 1611–1637, 1637; each is derived from the edition immediately preceding it, the Quarto of 1605 differing from that of 1604 only in the slightest degree.

THE FIRST QUARTO

The 1604 edition is generally known as the Second Quarto, to distinguish it from a remarkable production which appeared in the previous year:—

"The | Tragicall Historie of | HAMLET | *Prince of Den-marke* | By William Shake-speare. | As it hath been diuerse timis acted by his Highnesse ser- | uants in the Cittie of London: as also in the two V- | niuersities of Cambridge and Oxford, and else-where | At London printed for N: L. and John Trundell. | 1603."

No copy of this Quarto was known until 1823, when Sir Henry Bunbury discovered the treasure in "a small Quarto, barbarously cropped, and very ill-bound," containing some dozen Shakespearean plays. It ultimately became the property of the Duke of Devonshire for the sum of £230. Unfortunately, the last page of the play was missing.

In 1856 another copy was bought from a student of Trinity College, Dublin, by a Dublin book-dealer, for one shilling, and sold by him for £70; it is now in the British Museum. In this copy the title-page is lacking, but it supplies the missing last page of the Devonshire Quarto.[1]

In connection with the publication of the 1603 Quarto, reference must be made to the following entry in the *Stationers' Register*:—

[1] In 1858 a lithographed facsimile was issued by the Duke, in a very limited impression. The first serviceable edition, and still perhaps the best, appeared in 1860, together with the Quarto of 1604, *"being exact Reprints of the First and Second Editions of Shakespeare's great Drama, from the very rare Originals in the possession of his Grace the Duke of Devonshire; with the two texts printed on opposite pages, and so arranged that the parallel passages face each other. And a Bibliographical Preface by Samuel Timmins.* . . . Looke heere vpon this Picture, and on this." Lithographic reprints were also issued by E. W. Ashbee and W. Griggs; the text is reprinted in the Cambridge Shakespeare, *etc.*

> "[1602] xxvj ^{to} Julij.
>
> *James Robertes.* Entered for his Copie vnder the handes of master *Pasfield* and master *Waterson* Warden A booke called *'the Revenge of* HAMLETT *Prince [of] Denmarke' as yt was lateli Acted by the Lord Chamberleyne his servantes* . . . vjd."

James Robertes, the printer of the 1604 edition, may also have been the printer of the Quarto of 1603, and this entry may have had reference to its projected publication; it is noteworthy that in 1603 "the Lord Chamberlain's Servants" became "The King's Players," and the Quarto states that the play had been acted "by His Highness' Servants." On the other hand, the entry may have been made by Robertes to secure the play to himself, and some "inferior and nameless printer" may have anticipated him by the publication of an imperfect, surreptitious, and garbled version, impudently offering as Shakespeare's such wretched stuff as this:—

> *"To be, or not to be, I there's the point,*
> *To Die, to sleepe, is that all: I all?*
> *No, to sleepe, to dreame, I mary there it goes,*
> *For in that dreame of death, when wee awake,*
> *And borne before an e'erlasting Judge;*
> *From whence no passenger ever return'd,*
> *The undiscoured country, at whose sight*
> *The happy smile, and the accursed damn'd."*

The dullest poetaster could not have been guilty of this nonsense: a second-rate playwright might have put these last words in Hamlet's mouth:—

> *"Mine eyes haue lost their sight, my tongue his vse:*
> *Farewell Horatio, heaven receive my soule"*:

"The rest is silence"—Shakespeare's supreme test is here.

A rapid examination of the first Quarto reveals the following among its chief divergences:—(i) the difference in length; 2,143 lines as against 3,719 in the later Quarto; (ii) the mutilation, or omission, of many passages "distinguished by that blending of psychological insight with imagination and fancy, which is the highest manifestation of Shakespeare's genius"; (iii) absurd misplacement and maiming of lines; distortion of words and phrases: (iv) confusion in the order of the scenes; (v) difference in characterization; *e. g.* the Queen's avowed innocence ("But as I have a soul, I swear by heaven, I never knew of this most horrid murder"), and her active adhesion to the plots against her guilty husband; (vi) this latter aspect is brought out in a special scene between Horatio and the Queen, omitted in the later version; (vii) the names of some of the characters are not the same as in the subsequent editions; *Corambis* and *Montano*, for *Polonius* and *Reynaldo*. What, then, is the history of this Quarto? In the first place it is certain that it must have been printed without authority; in all probability shorthand notes taken by an incompetent stenographer during the performance of the play formed the basis of the printer's "copy." Thomas Heywood alludes to this method of obtaining plays in the prologue to his *If you know not me, you know no bodie:*—

> "(This did throng the Seats, the Boxes, and the Stage
> So much, that some by Stenography drew
> The plot: put it in print: (scarce one word trew)."

The main question at issue is the relation of this piratical version to Shakespeare's work. The various views may be divided as follows:—(i) there are those who maintain that it is an imperfect production of an old *Hamlet* written by Shakespeare in his youth, and revised by him in his maturer years; (ii) others contend that both the First and Second Quartos represent the same version, the difference between the two editions being due to carelessness and incompetence; (iii) a third class holds, very strongly, that the First Quarto is a garbled version of an old-fashioned play of *Hamlet*, written by some other dramatist, and revised to a certain extent by Shakespeare about the year 1602; so that the original of Quarto 1 represented Shakespeare's *Hamlet* in an intermediate stage; in Quarto 2 we have for the first time the complete metamorphosis. All the

evidence seems to point to this third view as a plausible settlement of the problem; there is little to be said in favor of
the first and second theories.

THE LOST HAMLET

There is no doubt that a play on the subject of *Hamlet*
existed as early as 1589, in which year there appeared
Greene's *Menaphon*, with a prefatory epistle by Thomas
Nash, containing a summary review of contemporary literature. The following passage occurs in his "talk" with
"a few of our triviall translators":—

"It is a common practice now a daies amongst a sort
of shifting companions, that runne through every arte and
thrive by none to leave the trade of *Noverint* (*i. e.* attor-
ney) whereto they were borne, and busie themselves with
the endevours of art, that could scarcelie latinize their
neck verse if they should have neede; yet English Seneca
read by candle-light yeeldes manie good sentences, as
Bloud is a beggar, and so forth: and if you intreate him
faire in a frostie morning, he will afoord you whole *Hamlets*, I should say Handfulls of tragical speaches. But O
grief! *Tempus edax rerum;* what is it that will last always? The sea exhaled by drops will in continuance be
drie; and Senaca, let bloud line by line, and page by page,
at length must needs die to our stage." The play alluded
to by Nash did not die to our stage till the end of the century; in Henslowe's *Diary* we find an entry:—"9. of June
1594. . . .   R[eceive]d at hamlet. viijs:"
the play was performed by the Lord Chamberlain's men,
the company to which Shakespeare belonged.

"[Hate Virtue is] a foul lubber," wrote Lodge in *Wit's
Miserie, and the World's Madness,* 1596, "and looks as pale
as the wisard of the ghost, which cried so miserally at the
theater, like an oyster-wife, *Hamlet revenge.*" [1]

[1] Several other allusions occur during the early years of the seventeenth century, evidently to the older Hamlet, *e. g.* Dekker's *Satrio-
mastix,* 1602, ("My Name's Hamlet revenge"); *Westward Hoe,* 1607

In all probability Thomas Kyd was the author of the play alluded to in these passages; his probable authorship is borne out by Nash's subsequent allusion to "the Kidde in Æsope's fable," as also by the character of his famous *Spanish Tragedy*.[1] *Hamlet* and *The Spanish Tragedy* may well be described as twin-dramas;[2] they are both dramas of venegeance; the ghost of the victim tells his story in the one play as in the other; the heroes simulate madness; a faithful Horatio figures in each; a play-scene brings about the catastrophe in *The Spanish Tragedy*, even as it helps forward the catastrophe in *Hamlet;* in both plays Nemesis involves in its meshes the innocent as well as the guilty,—the perpetrators of the wrong and the instruments of vengeance. To this same class of drama belongs *Titus Andronicus*, and it is interesting to note that early in his career Shakespeare put his hand to a Hamletian tragedy. Nash's reference to the Senecan character of the lost *Ham-*

("Let these husbands play mad *Hamlet,* and cry *revenge*"); Rowland's *The Night Raven,* 1618 ("I will not cry *Hamlet Revenge*"), *etc.* There is a comic passage in *The Looking Glass for London and England,* written by Lodge and Greene, probably before 1589, which strikes me as a burlesque reminiscence of the original of *Hamlet,* Act I. Sc. ii. 184–240; Adam, the smith's man, exclaims thus to the Clown:—"Alas, sir, your father,—why, sir, methinks I see the gentleman still: a proper youth he was, faith, aged some forty and ten; his beard rat's colour, half black, half white; his nose was in the highest degree of noses," *etc.*

[1] *The Spanish Tragedy* and Kyd's other plays are printed in Dodsley's *Old Plays.* An interesting point in Kyd's biography (*vide Dict. Nat. Biog.*) is that his father was in all probability a sort of *Noverint.*

[2] So much so was this the case that "young Hamlet," and "old Hieronimo," were often referred to together, and the parts were taken by the same actors, *cp.* Burbadge's elegy:—

> "Young Hamlet, old Hieronimo,
> King Leir, the grieved Moore, and more beside
> That liv'd in him, have now for ever died":

Occasionally the two plays were, I think, confused: thus, Armin in his *Nest of Ninnies* (1608) writes:—"There are, as Hamlet saies, things cald whips in store"; Hieronimo certainly says so in the most famous passage of *The Spanish Tragedy.*

let receives considerable confirmation when one remembers that Kyd translated into English, from the French, Garnier's Senecan drama entitled *Cornelia,* and it is possible that even in Shakespeare's *Hamlet* we can still detect the fossil remains of Senecan moralizations which figured in the older play, and which were Kyd's reminiscences of Garnier.[1]

THE GERMAN HAMLET

It is possible that although the pre-Shakespearean *Hamlet* has perished, we have some portion of the play preserved in a German MS. version bearing the date, "Pretz, October 27, 1710," which is probably a late and modernized copy of a much older manuscript. The play, entitled *"Der Bestrafte Brudermord oder: Prinz Hamlet aus Dännemark"* (*Fratricide Punished, or Prince Hamlet of Denmark*) was first printed in the year 1781, and has been frequently reprinted; the text, with an English translation, is given in Cohn's fascinating work, *"Shakespeare in Germany in the Sixteenth and Seventeenth Centuries: An account of English Actors in Germany and the Netherlands, and of the Plays performed by them during the same period"* (London, 1865). The "English Comedians" in all probability carried their play to Germany towards the end of the XVI Century, when a rough German translation was made; but the earliest record of a performance of *Hamlet a Prinz in Dennemarck,* by "the English actors," belongs to the year 1626.[2]

---

[1] *e. g.* A thoroughly Senecan sentiment is the Queen's

> *"Thou know'st 'tis common; all that lives must die.*
> *Passing through nature to eternity";*

It occurs almost verbatim in *Cornelia.*

[2] In connection with the subject of *Hamlet* one must not forget the visit of Lord Leicester's servants to Denmark in 1585; Kempe, Bryan, and Pope, three of the company, subsequently joined the Chamberlain's company, and were actors in Shakespeare's plays. Shakespeare's remarkable knowledge of Danish manners and customs may have been derived from these friends of his.

The intrinsic value of *Fratricide Punished* is small indeed, but two points of historical interest are noteworthy:—(i) Polonius, as in the First Quarto, is here represented by Corambus, and (ii) a prologue precedes the play, the persons represented therein being *Night, Alecto, Thisiphone, Miegera.* A strong case can, I think, be made out for the view that this thoroughly Senecan Prologue represents a fragment of the pre-Shakespearean play to which Nash and others made allusion: herein lies the chief merit of this soulless and coarse production.

DATE OF COMPOSITION

This question has been indirectly touched upon in the previous paragraphs, and it follows from what has been said that the date of revision, as represented by the Second Quarto, may be fixed at about 1603, while the First Quarto, judging by the entry in the Stationers' Books, belongs to about 1601; at all events a version of *Hamlet*, recognized as Shakespeare's, was in existence before 1602. It is significant that the play is not mentioned in Meres' *Palladis Tamia,* 1598. In the matter of the date of the play "the traveling of the players" (Act II, sc. ii, 353, *etc.*) is of interest. It must be noted that we have three different forms of the passage in question:—(i) the reason for the "traveling" in Q. 1 is the popularity of a Company of Children; (ii) in Q. 2 *"their inhibition comes by the means of the late innovation";* (iii) in the Folio (the reading in the text) both causes (i) and (ii) are combined.

Now it is known that (i) in 1601 Shakespeare's Company was in disgrace, perhaps because of its share in the Essex Conspiracy; (ii) that during this year the Children of the Chapel Royal were acting at Blackfriars; (iii) that towards the end of the year the Globe Company were "traveling." Two views are possible, either that *"inhibition"* is used technically for "a prohibition of theatrical performances by authority"; and *"innovation"* = "the political innovation," or that *inhibition* = "non-residence," and *"innovation"* refers to the Company of Children (*vide* Halliwell-Phillips' *Outlines of the Life of Shakespeare;* Fleay's *Chronicle History of the London Stage*).

Over and above these points of evidence in fixing the date there is the intimate connection of *Hamlet* and *Julius Cæsar.*

THE SOURCE OF THE STORY

The ultimate source of the plot of *Hamlet* is the *Historia Danica* of Saxo Grammaticus (*i. e.* "the Lettered"), Denmark's first writer of importance, who lived at the close of the twelfth century.[1] Saxo's Latinity was much admired, and even Erasmus wondered "how a Dane at that day could have such a force of eloquence." Epitomes in Latin and Low-German were made during the fifteenth century, and Saxo's materials were utilized in various ways, until at length the first printed edition appeared in the year 1514; a second was issued in 1534, and a third in 1576. The tale of Hamlet, contained in the third and fourth books, is certainly the most striking of all Saxo's mythical hero-stories, quite apart from its Shakespearean interest, and Goethe, recognizing its dramatic possibilities, thought of treating the subject dramatically on the basis of Saxo's narrative. It is noteworthy that already in the fifteenth century the story was well known throughout the North, "trolled far and wide in popular song"; but its connection with the English drama was due to the French version given in Belleforest's *Histoires Tragiques;* the Hamlet story first appeared in the fifth volume, published in 1570, and again in 1581, 1582, 1591, *etc.* A black-letter English rendering is extant, but the date of the

---

[1] There is an allusion to Hamlet in Icelandic literature some two hundred years before Saxo; and to this day *"Amlothe"* (*i. e. Hamlet*) is synonymous with *"fool"* among the folk there. The history of *Hamlet in Iceland* is of great interest (*vide* the *Ambales-saga,* edited by the present writer, published in 1898 by David Nutt). According to Zinzow and others the Saga is originally a nature-myth (*vide Die Hamletsage*).

unique copy is 1608, and in certain points shows the influence of the play. There is no evidence that an earlier English version existed. The author of the pre-Shakespearean *Hamlet*, and Shakespeare too, may well have read the story in Belleforest's *Histoires*.[1] Few studies in literary origins are more instructive than to examine how the "rich barbarous tale" of the Danish historian has become transformed into the great soul-tragedy of modern literature. In Saxo's *Amleth* we have at least the frame-work of Shakespeare's *Hamlet:*—the murder of the father by a jealous uncle; the mother's incestuous marriage with the murderer; the son's feigned madness in order to execute revenge; there are the vague originals of Ophelia and Polonius; the meeting of mother and son; the voyage to England; all these familiar elements are found in the old tale. But the ghost, the play-scene, and the culmination of the play in the death of the hero as well as of the objects of his revenge, these are elements which belong essentially to the machinery of the Elizabethan Drama of vengeance. It is of course unnecessary to dwell on the subtler distinction between the easily understood *Amleth* and "the eternal problem" of *Hamlet*.[2] Taine has said that the Elizabethan Renaissance was a Renaissance of the Saxon genius; from the point of view it is significant that its crowning glory should be the presentment of a typical Northern hero,—an embodiment of the Northern character;

'dark and true and tender is the North."

[1] To Mr. Oliver Elton, Prof. York Powell, and the Folk-Lore Society, we owe the first English rendering of the mythical portion of Saxo's work, and a valuable study of Saxo's sources (published by David Nutt, 1894).

[2] A *résumé* of Hamlet criticism is given in Vol. II. of Furness' noble edition of the play (London and Philadelphia, 1877).

INTRODUCTION

By HENRY NORMAN HUDSON, A.M.

The story on which Shakespeare founded *The Tragedy of Hamlet, Prince of Denmark*, was told by Saxo Grammaticus, the Danish historian, whose work was first printed in 1514, though written as early as 1204. The incidents as related by him were borrowed by Belleforest, and set forth in his *Histoires Tragiques*, 1564. It was probably through the French version of Belleforest that the tale first found its way to the English stage. The only English translation that has come down to us was printed in 1608; and of this only a single copy is known to have survived. The edition of 1608 was most likely a reprint; but, if so, we have no means of ascertaining when it was first printed: Mr. Collier thinks there can be no doubt that it originally came from the press considerably before 1600. The only known copy is preserved among Capell's books in the library of Trinity College, Cambridge, and has been lately republished by Collier in his *Shakespeare's Library*. It is entitled *The History of Hamblet*.

As there told, the story is, both in matter and style, uncouth and barbarous in the last degree; a savage, shocking tale of lust and murder, unredeemed by a single touch of art or fancy in the narrator. Perhaps there is nothing of the Poet's achieving more wonderful than that he should have reared so superb a dramatic structure out of materials so scanty and so revolting. The scene of the incidents is laid before the introduction of Christianity into Denmark, and when the Danish power held sway in England: further than this, the time is not specified. So much of the story as was made use of for the drama is soon told.

Roderick, king of Denmark, divided his kingdom into provinces, and placed governors in them. Among these were two valiant and warlike brothers, Horvendile and Fengon. The greatest honor that men of noble birth could at that time win, was by exercising the art of piracy on the seas; wherein Horvendile surpassed all others. Collere, king of Norway, was so wrought upon by his fame, that he challenged him to fight body to body; and the challenge was accepted on condition that the vanquished should lose all the riches he had in his ship, and the vanquisher should cause his body to be honorably buried. Collere was slain; and Horvendile, after making great havoc in Norway, returned home with a mass of treasure, most of which he sent to King Roderick, who thereupon gave him his daughter Geruth in marriage. Of this marriage proceeded Hamblet, the hero of the tale.

All this so provoked the envy of Fengon, that he determined to kill his brother. So, having secretly assembled certain men, when Horvendile was at a banquet with his friends, he suddenly set upon him and slew him; but managed his treachery with so much cunning that no man suspected him. Before doing this, he had corrupted his brother's wife, and was afterwards married to her. Young Hamblet, thinking that he was likely to fare no better than his father had done, went to feigning himself mad, and made as if he had utterly lost his wits; wherein he used such craft that he became an object of ridicule to the satellites of the court. Many of his actions, however, were so shrewd, and his answers were often so fit, that men of a deeper reach began to suspect somewhat, thinking that beneath his folly there lay hid a sharp and pregnant spirit. So they counselled the king to try measures for discovering his meaning. The plan hit upon for entrapping him was, to leave him with some beautiful woman in a secret place, where she could use her art upon him. To this end they led him out into the woods, and arranged that the woman should there meet with him. One of the men, however, who was a friend of the Prince, warned him, by certain signs, of the danger that was threatening him: so he escaped that treachery.

Among the king's friends there was one who more than all the rest suspected Hamblet's madness to be feigned; and he counselled the king to use some more subtle and crafty means for discovering his purpose. His device was, that the king should make as though he were going out on a long hunting excursion; and that, meanwhile, Hamblet should be shut up alone in a chamber with his mother, some one being hidden behind the hangings to hear their speeches. It was thought that, if there were any craft in the Prince, he would easily discover it to his mother, not fearing that she would make known his secret intent. So, the plot being duly arranged, the counsellor went into the chamber secretly and hid himself behind the arras, not long before the queen and Hamblet came thither. But the Prince, suspecting some treacherous practice, kept up his counterfeit of madness, and went to beating with his arms, as cocks use to strike with their wings, upon the hangings: feeling something stir under them, he cried, "A rat, a rat!" and thrust his sword into them; which done, he pulled the counseller out half dead, and made an end of him.

Hamblet then has a long interview with his mother, who weeps and torments herself, being sore grieved to see her only child made a mere mockery. He lays before her the wickedness of her life and the crimes of her husband, and also lets her into the secret of his madness being feigned. "Behold," says he, "into what distress I am fallen, and to what mischief your over-great lightness and want of wisdom have induced me, that I am constrained to play the madman to save my life, instead of practising arms, following adventures, and seeking to make myself known as the true heir of the valiant and virtuous Horvendile. The gestures of a fool are fit for me, to the end that, guiding myself wisely therein, I may preserve my life for the

Danes, and the memory of my deceased father; for the desire of revenging his death is sc engraven in my heart, that, if I die not shortly, I hope to take so great vengeance that these countries shall forever speak thereof. Nevertheless, I must stay my time and occasion, lest by making over-great haste I be the cause of mine own ruin and overthrow. To conclude, weep not, madam, to see my folly, but rather sigh and lament your own offence; for we are not to sorrow and grieve at other men's vices, but for our own misdeeds and great follies."

The interview ends in an agreement of mutual confidence between Hamblet and his mother; all her anger at his sharp reproofs being forgotten in the joy she conceives, to behold the gallant spirit of her son, and to think what she might hope from his policy and wisdom. She promises to keep his secret faithfully, and to aid him all she can in his purpose of revenge; swearing to him that she had often hindered the shortening of his life, and that she had never consented to the murder of his father.

Fengon's next device was, to send Hamblet into England, with secret letters to have him there put to death. Hamblet, again suspecting mischief, comes to some speech with his mother, and desires her not to make any show of grief at his departure, but rather to counterfeit gladness at being rid of his presence. He also counsels her to celebrate his funeral at the end of a year, and assures her that she shall then see him return from his voyage. Two of Fengon's ministers being sent along with him with secret letters to the king of England, when they were at sea, the Prince, his companions being asleep, read their commission, and substituted for it one requiring the messengers to be hung. After this was done, he returned to Denmark, and arrived the very day when the Danes were celebrating his funeral, supposing him to be dead. Fengon and his courtiers were then at their banquet, and Hamblet's arrival provoked them the more to drink and carouse; wherein Hamblet encouraged them, himself acting as butler, and keeping them supplied with liquor, until they were all laid drunk on the floor. When they were all fast asleep, he caused the hangings of the room to fall down and cover them; then, having nailed the edges fast to the floor so that none could escape, he set fire to the hall, and all were burned to death. Fengon having previously withdrawn to his chamber, Hamblet then went to him, and, after telling him what he had done, cut off his head with a sword.

The next day, Hamblet makes an oration to the Danes, laying open to them his uncle's treachery, and what himself has done in revenge of his father's death; whereupon he is unanimously elected king. After his coronation, he goes to England again. Finding that the king of England has a plot for putting him to death, he manages to kill him, and returns to Denmark with two wives. He is afterwards assailed by his uncle Wiglerus, and finally betrayed to death by one of his English wives named Hermetrude, who then marries Wiglerus.

There is, besides, an episodical passage in the tale, from which the Poet probably took some hints towards the part of his hero, especially his melancholy mood, and his suspicion that "the spirit he has seen may be a devil": "In those days, the north parts of the world, living then under Satan's laws, were full of enchanters, so that there was not any young gentleman that knew not something therein sufficient to serve his turn, if need required; and so Hamblet, while his father lived, had been instructed in that devlish art, whereby the wicked spirit abuseth mankind, and advertiseth them, as he can, of things past. It toucheth not the matter herein to discover the parts of divination in man, and whether this Prince, by reason of his overgreat melancholy, had received those impressions, divining that which never any had before declared; like such as are saturnists by complexion, who oftentimes speak of things which, their fury ceasing, they can hardly understand." It is hardly needful to add, that Shakespeare makes his persons Christians, giving them the sentiments and manners of a much later period than they have in the tale; though he still places the scene at a time when England paid some sort of homage to the Danish crown, which was before the Norman conquest.

The earliest edition of the tragedy, in its finished state, was a quarto pamphlet of fifty-one leaves, the title-page reading thus: *"The Tragical History of Hamlet, Prince of Denmark: By William Shakespeare. Newly imprinted and enlarged to almost as much again as it was, according to the true and perfect copy. At London: Printed by J. R. for N. L., and are to be sold at his shop under St. Dunstan's Church, in Fleet-street. 1604."* The same text was reissued in the same form in 1605, and again in 1611; besides an undated edition, which is commonly referred to 1607, as it was entered at the Stationers' in the fall of that year. In the folio of 1623, it stands the eighth of the tragedies, and is without any marking of the Acts and scenes save in the first two Acts. The folio also omits several passages that are among the best in the play, and some of them highly important to the right understanding of the hero's character. On the other hand, the folio has a few short passages, and here and there a line or two, that are not in the quartos. On the whole, the quartos give the play considerably longer than the folio; the latter having been most likely printed from a play-house copy, which had been shortened, in some cases not very judiciously, for the greater convenience of representation.

From the words, "enlarged to almost as much again as it was," in the title-page of 1604, it was for a long time conjectured that the play had been printed before. At length, in 1825, a single copy of an earlier edition was discovered, and the text accurately reprinted, with the following title-page: *"The Tragical History of Hamlet, Prince of Denmark: By William Shakespeare. As it hath been divers times acted by his Highness' Servants, in the city of London; as also in the two Universities of Cambridge and Oxford, and elsewhere. At London: Printed for N. L. and John Trundell. 1603."* There is no doubt that this edition was piratical: it gives the play but about half as long as the later quartos; and carries in its face abundant evidence of having been greatly marred and disfigured in the making-up.

As to the methods used in getting up the edition of 1603, a careful examination of the text has satisfied us that they were much the same as appear to have been made use of in the quarto issues of *King Henry V*, and *The Merry Wives of Windsor*. From divers minute particulars which cannot be specified without over much of detail, it seems very evident that the printing was done, for the most part, from rude reports taken at the theater during representation, with, perhaps, some subsequent eking out and patching up from memory. There are indeed a few passages that seem to be given with much purity and completeness; they have an integrity of sense and language, that argues a faithful transcript; as, for instance, the speech of Voltimand in Act II, sc. ii, which scarcely differs at all from the speech as we have it: but there is barely enough of this to serve as an exception to the rule. As to the other parts, the garbled and dislocated state of the text, where we often have the first of a sentence without the last, or the last without the first, or the first and last without the middle; the constant lameness of the verse where verse was meant, and the bungling attempts to print prose so as to look like verse;—all this proves beyond question, that the quarto of 1603 was by no means a faithful transcript of the play as it then stood; and the imperfectness is of just that kind and degree which would naturally adhere to the work of a slovenly or incompetent reporter.

On the other hand, it is equally clear, that at the time that copy was taken the play must have been very different from what it afterwards became. Polonius is there called Corambis, and his servant, Montano. Divers scenes and passages, some of them such as a reporter would have been least likely to omit, are there wanting altogether. The Queen is there represented as concerting and actively cooperating with Hamlet against the King's life; and she has an interview of considerable length with Horatio, who informs her of Hamlet's escape from the ship bound for England, and of his safe arrival in Denmark; of which scene the later issues have no traces whatsoever. All this fully ascertains that the play must have undergone a thorough revisal after the making up of the copy from which the first quarto was printed. But, what is not a little remarkable, some of the passages met with in the folio, but not in the enlarged quartos, are found in the quarto of 1603; which shows that they were omitted in the later quartos, and not added afterwards.

With such and so many copies before us, it may well be asked, where the true text of *Hamlet* is to be found. The quarto of 1603, though furnishing valuable aid in divers cases, is not of any real authority: this is clear enough from what has already been said about it. On the other hand, it can hardly be questioned that the issue of 1604 was as authentic and as well authorized, as any that were made of Shakespeare's plays while he was living. We therefore take this as our main standard of the text, retaining, however, all the additional passages found in the folio of 1623. Moreover, the folio has many important changes and corrections which no reasonable editor would make any question of adopting. Mr. Knight indeed, who, after the true style of Knight-errantry, everywhere gives himself up to an almost unreserved championship of the folio, takes that as the supreme authority. But in this case, as usual, his zeal betrays him into something of unfairness: for wherever he prefers a folio reading (and some of his preferences are odd enough), he carefully notes it; but in divers cases, where the quarto readings are so clearly preferable that he dare not reject them, we have caught him adopting them without making any note of them.

The next question to be considered is, at what time was the *Tragedy of Hamlet* originally written? On this point we find it extremely difficult to form a clear judgment. Thus much, however, is quite certain, that either this play was one of the Poet's very earliest productions, or else there was another play on the same subject. This certainty rests on a passage in an *Epistle* by Thomas Nash, prefixed to Greene's *Arcadia:* "It is a common practice now-a-days, among a sort of shifting companions that run through every art and thrive by none, to leave the trade of *Noverint* whereto they were born, and busy themselves with the endeavors of art, that could scarcely latinize their neck-verse, if they should have need; yet English *Seneca*, read by candle-light, yields many good sentences, as 'Blood is a beggar,' and so forth; and, if you entreat him fair in a frosty morning, he will afford you whole *Hamlets*, I should say handfuls, of tragical speeches." The words, "trade of *Noverint*," show that this squib was pointed at some writer of *Hamlet*, who had been known as an apprentice in the law; and Shakespeare's remarkable fondness for legal terms and allusions naturally suggests him as the person referred to. On the other hand, Nash's *Epistle* was written certainly as early as 1589, probably two years earlier, though this has been disputed. In 1589 Shakespeare was in his twenty-sixth year, and his name stood the twelfth in a list of sixteen, as a sharer in the Blackfriars play-house. The chief difficulty lies in believing that he could have been known so early as the author of a tragedy having Hamlet for its hero; but this difficulty is much reduced by the circumstance, that we have no knowledge how often or how much he may have improved a piece of that kind even before the copy of 1603 was made up.

Again: It appears from Henslowe's accounts that a play of *Hamlet* was performed in the theater at Newington Butts on June 9, 1594. At this time, "my lord admirell men and my lord chamberlen men" were playing together at that theater; the latter of whom was the company to which Shakespeare belonged. At the performance of *Hamlet*, Henslowe sets down nine shillings as his share of the receipts; whereas in case of new plays he commonly received a much larger sum. Besides, the item in question is without the mark which the manager usually prefixed in case of a new play; so that we may conclude the *Hamlet* of 1594 had at that time lost the feature of novelty. The question is, whether the *Hamlet* thus performed was Shakespeare's? That it was so, might naturally be inferred from the fact that the Lord Chamberlain's men were then playing there; besides, it has at least some probability, in that on the 11th of the same month Henslowe notes *The Taming of a Shrew* as having been performed at the same place. Whether this latter were Shakespeare's play, is sufficiently considered in our Introduction to *The Taming of the Shrew*.

The next particular, bearing upon the subject, is from a tract by Thomas Lodge, printed in 1596, and entitled *Wit's Misery, or The World's Madness, discovering the incarnate Devils of the Age;* where one of the devils is said to be "a foul lubber, and looks as pale as the vizard of the *Ghost*, who cried so miserably at the theatre, *Hamlet, revenge.*" All these three notices are regarded by Malone and some others as referring to another play of *Hamlet*, which they suppose to have been written by Thomas Kyd; though their only reason for thinking there was such another play, is the alleged improbability of the Poet's having so early written on that subject.

It is to be observed, further, that a copy of Speight's *Chaucer* once owned by Gabriel Harvey, and having his name written in it, together with the date of 1598, has, among others, the following manuscript note: "The younger sort take much delight in Shakespeare's *Venus and Adonis;* but his *Lucrece,* and his *Tragedy of Hamlet, Prince of Denmark,* have it in them to please the wiser sort." This, however, does not seem to infer any thing with certainty as to time; since the name and date may have been written when Harvey purchased the book, and the note at some later period.

The only other contemporary notice to be quoted of the play, is an entry at the Stationers' by James Roberts, on July 26, 1602: "*A Book,—The Revenge of Hamlet, Prince of Denmark, as it was lately acted by the Lord*

Chamberlain his Servants." As the quarto of 1604 was printed by James Roberts, we may reasonably conclude that this entry refers to the "enlarged" form of the play. Why the publication was not made till two years later, is beyond our reach: perhaps it was because no copy could be obtained for the press, until the maimed and stolen issue of 1603 had rendered it necessary to put forth an edition in self-defense, "according to the true and perfect copy." In the spring of 1603 "the Lord Chamberlain's Servants" became "His Majesty's Servants"; or, as they are called in the title-page of 1603, "His Highness' Servants."

A piece of internal evidence fixes the date of the enlarged *Hamlet* soon after June 22, 1600. It is the reason assigned by Rosencrantz, in Act II, sc. ii, why the players have left the city and gone to traveling: "I think their inhibition comes by means of the late innovation." The passage just quoted is not in the copy of 1603: a different reason is there assigned why the players travel: "*Novelty* carries it away; for the principal public audience that came to them are turned to *private* plays, and the humour of children."

Plays were acted in private by the choir-boys of the Chapel Royal and of St. Paul's before 1590, several of Lyly's pieces being used in that way. It appears that in 1591 these juvenile performances had been suppressed; as in the printer's address prefixed to Lyly's *Endymion*, which was published that year, we are told that, "since the plays in Paul's were dissolved, there are certain comedies come to my hand." Nash, in his *Have with You to Saffron Waldon*, published in 1596, expresses a wish to see the "plays at Paul's up again"; which infers that at that time the interdict was still in force. In 1600, however, we find that the interdict had been taken off, a play attributed to Lyly being that year "acted by the children of Paul's." From this time forward these juvenile performances appear to have been kept up, both in private and in public, until 1612, when, on account of the abuses attending them, they were again suppressed.

It would seem, then, that the reason assigned in the text of 1603 refers to a period when the acting of children was only in *private*, and was regarded as a *novelty;* whereas at the time of the later text the qualities of novelty and privacy had been removed. And it appears not improbable, that the taking-off of the interdict before 1600, and the consequent revival of plays by children, was "the late innovation" by means of which the "inhibition" had been brought about. Howbeit, so far as regards the date of the older text, the argument is by no means conclusive, and we are not for laying any very marked stress upon it; but it seems, at all events, worth considering. Its bearing as to the time of the later text is obvious enough, and will hardly be questioned.

Knight justly remarks, that the mention of Termagant and Herod, which occurs in the quarto of 1603, refers to a time when those personages trod the stage in pageants and mysteries; and that the directions to the players, as given in the older text, point to the customs and conduct of the stage, as it was before Shakespeare had, by his example and influence, raised and reformed it. The following passage from the first copy will show what we mean: "And then you have some again, that keeps one suit of jests, as a man is known by one suit of apparel; and gentlemen quote his jests down in their tables before they come to the play, as thus: 'Cannot you stay till I eat my porridge?' and, 'You owe me a quarter's wages'; and, 'My coat wants a cullison'; and, 'Your beer is sour'; and, blabbering with his lips, and thus keeping in his cinque-a-pace of jests, when, God knows, the warm clown cannot make a jest unless by chance, as the blind man catcheth a hare." From the absence of all this in the enlarged copy, we should naturally conclude that the evil referred to had at that time been done away, or at least much diminished. And indeed a comparison of the two texts in this part of the play will satisfy any one, we think, that, during the interval between them, the stage had been greatly elevated and improved: divers bad customs, no doubt, had been "reformed indifferently"; so that the point still remaining was, to "reform them altogether."

As to the general character of the additions in the enlarged *Hamlet*, it is to be noted that these are mostly in the contemplative and imaginative parts; very little being added in the way of action and incident. And in respect of the former there is indeed no comparison between the two copies: the difference is literally immense, and of such a kind as evinces a most astonishing growth of intellectual power and resource. In the earlier text, we have little more than a naked, though, in the main, well-ordered and firm-knit skeleton, which, in the later, is everywhere replenished and glorified with large, rich volumes of thought and poetry; where all that is incidental or circumstantial is made subordinate to the living energies of mind and soul. The difference is like that of a lusty grove of hickory or maple brethren in December with the winds whistling through them, and in June with the birds singing in them.

So that the enlarged *Hamlet* probably marks the germination of that "thoughtful philosophy," as Hallam calls it, which never afterwards deserted the Poet; though time did indeed abate its excess, and reduce it under his control; whereas it here overflows all bounds, and sweeps onward unchecked, so as to form the very character of the piece. Moreover, this play, in common with several others, though in a greater degree, bears symptoms of a much saddened and aggrieved, not to say embittered temper of mind: it is fraught, more than any other, with a spirit of profound and melancholy cogitation; as if written under the influence of some stroke that had shaken the Poet's disposition with thoughts beyond the reaches of his soul; or as if he were casting about in the darker and sterner regions of meditation in quest of an antidote for some deep distress that had touched him. For there can be little doubt, that the birth and first stages of "the philosophic mind" were in his case, for some cause unknown to us, hung about with clouds and gloom, which, however, were afterwards blown off, and replaced by an atmosphere of unblemished clearness and serenity.

From all which may be gathered how appropriately this play has been described as a tragedy of thought. Such is indeed its character. And in this character it stands alone, and that, not only of Shakespeare's dramas, but of all the dramas in being. As for action, the play has little that can be properly so called. The scenes are indeed richly diversified with incident; but the incidents, for the most part, engage our attention only as serving to start and shape the hero's far-reaching trains of reflection; themselves being lost sight of in the wealth of thought and sentiment which they call forth. In no other of Shakespeare's plays does the interest turn so entirely on the hero; and that, not because he overrides the other persons and crushes their individuality under, as *Richard III* does; but because his life is all centered in the mind, and the effluence of his mind and character is around all the others and within them; so that they are little interesting to us, but for his sake, for the effects they have upon him, and the thoughts he has of them. Observe, too, that of all dramatic personages, "out of sight, out of mind," can least be said of him: on the contrary, he is never more in mind, than when out of sight; and whenever others come in sight, the effect still is, to remind us of him, and deepen our interest in him.

The character of Hamlet has caused more of perplexity and discussion than any other in the whole range of art. He has a wonderful interest for all, yet none can explain him; and perhaps he is therefore the more interesting because inexplicable. We have found by experience, that one seems to understand him better after a little study than after a great deal, and that the less one sees *into* him, the more apt one is to think he sees *through* him; in which respect he is indeed like nature herself. We shall not presume to make clear what so many better eyes have found and left dark. The most we can hope to do is, to start a few thoughts, not towards explaining him, but towards showing why he cannot be explained; nor to reduce the variety of opinions touching him, but rather to suggest whence that variety proceeds, and why.

One man considers Hamlet great, but wicked; another, good, but weak; a third, that he lacks courage, and dare not act; a fourth, that he has too much intellect for his will, and so thinks away the time of action: some conclude him honestly mad; others, that his madness is wholly feigned. Yet, notwithstanding this diversity of conclusions, all agree in thinking and speaking of him as an actual person. It is easy to invest with plausibility almost any theory regarding him, but very hard to make any theory comprehend the whole subject; and, while all are impressed with the truth of the character, no one is satisfied with another's view of it. The question is, why such unanimity as to his being a man, and at the same time such diversity as to what sort of a man he is?

Now, in reasoning about facts, we are apt to forget what complex and many-sided things they are. We often speak of them as very simple and intelligible; and in some respects they are so; but, in others, they are inscrutably mysterious. For they present manifold elements and qualities in unity and consistency, and so carry a manifoldness of meaning which cannot be gathered up into logical expression. Even if we seize and draw out severally all the properties of a fact, still we are as far as ever from producing the effect of their combination. Thus there is somewhat in facts that still eludes the cunningest analysis; like the vital principle, which no subtlety of dissection can grasp or overtake. It is this mysteriousness of facts that begets our respect for them: could we master them, we should naturally lose our regard for them. For, to see round and through a thing, implies a sort of conquest over it; and when we seem to have conquered a thing, we are apt to put off that humility towards it, which is both the better part of wisdom, and also our key to the remainder.

This complexity of facts supposes the material of innumerable theories: for, in such a multitude of properties belonging to one and the same thing, every man's mind may take hold of some special consideration above the rest; and when we look at facts through a given theory they naturally seem to prove but that one, though they would really afford equal proof of fifty others. Hence, there come to be divers opinions respecting the same thing; and men arrive at opposite conclusions, forgetting, that of a given fact many things may be true in their place and degree, yet none of them true in such sort as to impair the truth of others.

Now, Hamlet is all varieties of character in one; he is continually turning up a new side, appearing under a new phase, undergoing some new development; so that he touches us at all points, and, as it were, surrounds us. This complexity and versatility of character are often mistaken for inconsistency: hence the contradictory opinions respecting him, different minds taking very different impressions of him, and even the same mind, at different times. In short, like other facts, he is many-sided, so that many men of many minds may see themselves in different sides of him; but, when they compare notes, and find him agreeing with them all, they are perplexed, and are apt to think him inconsistent: in so great a diversity of elements, they lose the perception of identity, and cannot see how he can be so many, and still be but one. Doubtless he seems the more real for this very cause; our inability to see through him, or to discern the source and manner of his impression upon us, brings him closer to nature, makes him appear the more like a fact, and so strengthens his hold on our thoughts. For, where there is life, there must needs be more or less of change, the very law of life being identity in mutability; and in Hamlet the variety and rapidity of changes are so managed as only to infer the more intense, active, and prolific vitality; though, in so great a multitude of changes, it is extremely difficult to seize the constant principle.

Coleridge's view of Hamlet is much celebrated, and the

currency it has attained shows there must be something of truth in it. "In the healthy processes of the mind," says he, "a balance is constantly maintained between the impressions from outward objects and the inward operations of the intellect: for, if there be an overbalance in the contemplative faculty, man thereby becomes the creature of mere meditation, and loses his natural power of action. Now, one of Shakespeare's modes of creating characters is, to conceive any one intellectual or moral faculty in morbid excess, and then to place himself, Shakespeare, thus mutilated or diseased, under given circumstances. In Hamlet he seems to have wished to exemplify the moral necessity of a due balance between our attention to the objects of our senses, and our meditation on the workings of our minds,—an *equilibrium* between the real and the imaginary worlds. In Hamlet this balance is disturbed: his thoughts and the images of his fancy are far more vivid than his actual perceptions; and his very perceptions, instantly passing through the *medium* of his contemplations, acquire, as they pass, a form and color not naturally their own. Hence we see a great, an almost enormous, intellectual activity, and a proportionate aversion to real action, consequent upon it, with all its symptoms and accompanying qualities. This character Shakespeare places in circumstances, under which it is obliged to act on the spur of the moment:—Hamlet is brave and careless of death; but he vacillates from sensibility, and procrastinates from thought, and loses the power of action in the energy of resolve.

"The effect of this overbalance of the imaginative power is beautifully illustrated in the everlasting broodings and superfluous activities of Hamlet's mind, which, unseated from its healthy relation, is constantly occupied with the world within, and abstracted from the world without; giving substance to shadows, and throwing a mist over all common-place actualities. It is the nature of thought to be indefinite;—definiteness belongs to external imagery alone. Hence it is that the sense of sublimity arises, not from the sight of an outward object, but from the beholder's reflection upon it; not from the sensuous impression, but from the imaginative reflex. Few have seen a celebrated waterfall without feeling something akin to disappointment: it is only subsequently that the image comes back full into the mind, and brings with it a train of grand or beautiful associations. Hamlet feels this; his senses are in a trance, and he looks upon external things as hieroglyphics."

This is certainly very noble criticism; and our main ground of doubt as to the view thus given is, that Hamlet seems bold, energetic, and prompt enough in action, when his course is free of moral impediments; as, for instance, in his conduct on shipboard, touching the commission, where his powers of thought all range themselves under the leading of a most vigorous and steady will. Our own belief is, though we are far from absolute in it, that the Poet's design was, to conceive a man great, perhaps equally so, in all the elements of character, mental, moral, and practical; and then to place him in such circumstances, bring such motives to bear upon him, and open to him such sources of influence and reflection, that all his greatness should be morally forced to display itself in the form of thought, even his strength of will having no practicable outlet but through the energies of the intellect. A brief review of the delineation will, if we mistake not, discover some reason for this belief.

Up to the time of his father's death, Hamlet's mind, busied in developing its innate riches, had found room for no sentiments towards others but generous trust and confidence. Delighted with the appearances of good, and shielded by his rank from the naked approaches of evil, he had no motive to pry through the semblance into the reality of surrounding characters. The ideas of princely elevation and moral rectitude, springing up simultaneously in his mind, had intertwisted their fibers closely together. While the chaste forms of young imagination had kept his own heart pure, he had framed his conceptions of others according to the model within himself. To the feelings of the son, the prince, the gentleman, the friend, the scholar, had lately been joined those of the lover; and his heart, oppressed with its own hopes and joys, had breathed forth its fulness in "almost all the holy vows of heaven." In his father he had realized the ideal of character which he aspired to exemplify. Whatsoever noble images and ideas he had gathered from the fields of poetry and philosophy, he had learned to associate with that venerated name. To the throne he looked forward with hope and fear, as an elevation for diffusing the blessings of a wise sovereignty, and receiving the homage of a grateful submission. As the crown was elective, he regarded his prospects of attaining it as suspended on the continuance of his father's life, till he could discover in himself such virtues as would secure him the succession. In his father's death, therefore, he lost the mainstay of both his affections and his pretensions.

Notwithstanding, the foundations of his peace and happiness were yet unshaken. The prospects of the man were perhaps all the brighter, that those of the prince had faded. The fireside and the student's bower were still open to him; truth and beauty, thought and affection, had not hidden their faces from him: with a mind saddened, but not diseased, his bereavement served to deepen and chasten his sensibilities, without untuning their music. Cunning and quick of heart to discover and appropriate the remunerations of life, he could compensate the loss of some objects with a more free and tranquil enjoyment of such as remained. In the absence of his father, he could concentrate upon his mother the feelings hitherto shared between them; and, in cases like this, religion towards the dead comes in to heighten and sanctify an affection for the living. Even if his mother too had died, the loss, however bitter, would not have been baleful to him; for, though separated from the chief objects of love and trust and reverence, he would still have retained those sentiments themselves unimpaired. It is not his mother, however, but his faith in her, that he has to part with. To his prophetic soul, the hasty and incestuous marriage brings at once conviction of his mother's infidelity, and suspicion of his uncle's treachery, to his father. Where he has most loved and trusted, there he has been most deceived. The sadness of bereavement now settles into the deep gloom of a wounded spirit, and life seems rather a burden to be borne than a blessing to be cherished. In this condition, the appearance of the Ghost, its awful disclosures, and more awful injunctions, confirming the suspicion of his uncle's treachery, and implicating his mother in the crime, complete his desolation of mind.

Nevertheless, he still retains all his integrity and uprightness of soul. In the depths of his being, even below the reach of consciousness, there lives the instinct and impulse of a moral law with which the injunction of the Ghost stands in direct conflict. What is the quality of the act required of him? Nothing less, indeed, than to kill at once his uncle, his mother's husband, and his king; and this, not as an act of justice, and in a judicial manner, but as an act of revenge, and by assassination! How shall he justify such a deed to the world? How vindicate himself from the very crime thus revenged? For, as he cannot subpoena the Ghost, the evidence on which he must act is in its nature available only in the court of his own conscience. To serve any good end either for himself or for others, the deed must so stand in the public eye, as it does in his own; else he will, in effect, be setting an example and precedent of murder, not of justice.

Thus Hamlet's conscience is divided, not merely against his inclination, but against itself. However he multiplies to himself reasons and motives for the deed, there yet springs up, from a depth in his nature which reflection has not fathomed, and overruling impulse against it. So that we have the triumph of a pure moral nature over temptation in its most imposing form,—the form of a sacred call from heaven, or what is such to him. He thinks he ought to do the thing, resolves that he will do it, blames himself for not doing it; but there is a power within him which still outwrestles his purpose. In brief, the trouble lies not in himself, but in his situation; it arises from the impossibility of translating the outward call of duty into a free moral impulse; and until so translated he cannot perform it; for in such an undertaking he must act from himself, not from another.

This strife of incompatible duties seems the true source of Hamlet's practical indecision. His moral sensitiveness, shrinking from the dreadful mandate of revenge, throws him back upon his reflective powers, and sends him through the abysses of thought in quest of a reconciliation between his conflicting duties, that so he may shelter either the performance of the deed from the reproach of irreligion, or the non-performance from that of filial impiety. Moreover, on reflection he discerns something in the mandate that makes him question its source: even his filial reverence leads him first to regret, then to doubt, and finally to disbelieve, that his *father* has laid on him such an injunction. It seems more likely that the Ghost should be a counterfeit, than that his father should call him to such a deed. Thus his mind is set in quest of other proofs. But when, by the stratagem of the play, he has made the King's guilt unkennel itself, this demonstration again arrests his hand, because his own conscience is startled into motion by the revelations made from that of another. Seeking ground of action in the workings of remorse, the very proofs, which to his mind would justify the inflicting of death, themselves spring from something worse than death.

And it should be remarked, withal, that by the very process of the case he is put in immediate contact with supernatural influences. The same voice that calls him to the undertaking also unfolds to him the retributions of futurity. The thought of that eternal blazon, which must not be to ears of flesh and blood, entrances him in meditation on the awful realities of the invisible world; so that, while nerved by a sense of the duty, he is at the same time shaken by a dread of the responsibility. Thus the Ghost works in Hamlet a sort of preternatural development: its disclosures bring forth into clear apprehension some moral ideas which before were but dim presentiments in him. It is as if he were born into the other world before dying out of this. And what is thus developed in him is at strife with the injunction laid upon him.

Thus it appears, that Hamlet is distracted with a purpose which he is at once too good a son to dismiss, and too good a man to perform. Under an injunction with which he knows not what to do, he casts about, now for excuses, now for censures, of his nonperformance; and religion still prevents him from doing what filial piety reproves him for leaving undone. Not daring to abandon the design of killing the King, he is yet morally incapable of forming any plan for doing it: he can only go through the work, as indeed he does at last, under a sudden frenzy of excitement, caused by some immediate provocation; not so much acting, as being acted upon; rather as an instrument of Providence, than as a self-determining agent.

Properly speaking, then, Hamlet, we think, does not lack force of will. In him, will is strictly subject to reason and conscience; and it rather shows strength than otherwise in refusing to move in conflict with them. We are apt to measure men's force of will only by what they do, whereas the true measure thereof often lies rather in what they do *not* do. On this point, Mr. E. P. Whipple suggests, that "will is a relative term; and, even admitting that Hamlet possessed more will than many who act with decision, the fact that his other powers were larger in proportion justifies the common belief, that he was deficient in energy of purpose." But this, it strikes us, does not exactly meet the position; which is, that force of will is shown rather in holding still, than in moving, where the moral understanding is not satisfied; and that Hamlet seems to lack rather the power of seeing what he ought to do, than of doing what he sees to be right. The question is, whether the peculiarity of this representation is not meant to consist in

the hero being so placed, that strength of will has its
proper outcome rather in thinking than in acting; the
working of his whole mind being thus rendered as anoma-
lous as his situation; which is just what the subject requires. Will it be said, that Hamlet's moral scruples are
born of an innate reluctance to act? that from defect of
will he *wishes* to hold back, and so *hunts* after motives for
doing so? We should ourselves be much inclined to say so,
but that those scruples seem to be the native and legiti-
mate offspring of reason. There being, as we think, sufficient grounds for them out of him, we cannot refer them
to any infirmity of his as their source.

It is true, Hamlet takes to himself all the blame of his
indecision. This, we think, is one of the finest points in
the delineation. For true virtue does not publish itself:
radiating from the heart through the functions of life, its
transpirations are so free and smooth and deep as to be
scarce heard even by the subject of them. Moreover, in
his conflict of duties, Hamlet naturally thinks he is taking the wrong one; the calls of the claim he meets being
hushed by satisfaction, while those of the other are increased by disappointment. The current that we go with
is naturally unnoticed by us; but that which we go against
compels our notice by the struggle it puts us to. In this
way Hamlet comes to mistake his clearness of conscience
for moral insensibility. For even so a good man is apt
to think he has not conscience enough, because it is quiet;
a bad man, that he has too much, because it troubles him;
which accounts for the readiness of bad men to supply their
neighbors with conscience.

But perhaps the greatest perplexity of all in Hamlet's
character turns on the point of his "antic disposition."
Whether his madness be real or feigned, or sometimes the
one, sometimes the other, or partly real, partly feigned, are
questions which, like many that arise on similar points in
actual life, perhaps can never be finally settled either way.
Aside from the common impossibility of deciding precisely
where sanity ends and insanity begins, there are peculiar-

ities in Hamlet's conduct,—resulting from the minglings of the supernatural in his situation,—which, as they transcend the reach of our ordinary experience, can hardly be reduced to any thing more than probable conjecture. If sanity consists in a certain harmony between a man's actions and his circumstances, it must be hard indeed to say what would be insanity in a man so circumstanced as Hamlet.

That his mind is thrown from its propriety, shaken from its due forms and measures of working, excited into irregular, fevered action, is evident enough: from the deeply-agitating experiences he has undergone, the horrors of guilt preternaturally laid open to him, and the terrible ministry enjoined upon him, he could not be otherwise. His mind is indeed full of unhealthy perturbation, being necessarily made so by the overwhelming thoughts that press upon him from without; but it nowhere appears enthralled by illusions spun from itself; there are no symptoms of its being torn from its proper holdings, or paralyzed in its power of steady thought and coherent reasoning. Once only, at the grave of Ophelia, does he lose his self-possession; and the result in this case only goes to prove how firmly he retains it everywhere else.

It is matter of common observation, that extreme emotions naturally express themselves by their opposites; as extreme sorrow, in laughter, extreme joy, in tears; utter despair, in a voice of mirth; a wounded spirit, in gushes of humor. Hence Shakespeare heightens the effect of some of his awfulest scenes by making the persons indulge in flashes of merriment; for what so appalling as to see a person laughing and playing from excess of anguish or terror? Now, the expressions of mirth, in such cases are plainly neither the reality nor the affectation of mirth. People, when overwhelmed with distress, certainly are not in a condition either to *feel* merry or to *feign* mirth; yet they do sometimes *express* it. The truth is, such extremes naturally and spontaneously express themselves by their opposites. In like manner, Hamlet's madness, it seems to

xl

us, is neither real nor affected, but a sort of natural and spontaneous imitation of madness; the triumph of his reason over his passion naturally expressing itself in the tokens of insanity, just as the agonies of despair naturally vent themselves in flashes of mirth. Accordingly, Coleridge remarks, that "Hamlet's wildness is but half false; he plays that subtle trick of pretending to act, only when he is very near really being what he acts."

Again: It is not uncommon for men, in times of great depression, to fly off into prodigious humors and eccentricities. We have known people under such extreme pressure to throw their most intimate friends into consternation by their extravagant playings and frolickings. Such symptoms of wildness are sometimes the natural, though spasmodic, reaction of the mind against the weight that oppresses it. The mind thus spontaneously becomes eccentric in order to recover or preserve its center. Even so Hamlet's aberrations seem the conscious, half-voluntary bending of his faculties beneath an overload of thought, to keep them from breaking. His mind being deeply disturbed, agitated to its center, but not disorganized, those irregularities are rather a throwing-off of that disturbance than a giving-way to it.

On the whole, therefore, Goethe's celebrated criticism seems quite beside the mark: nevertheless, as it is the calm judgment of a great mind, besides being almost too beautiful in itself not to be true, we gladly subjoin it. "It is clear to me," says he, "that Shakespeare's intention was, to exhibit the effects of a great action imposed as a duty upon a mind too feeble for its accomplishment. In this sense I find the character consistent throughout. Here is an oak planted in a china vase, proper to receive only the most delicate flowers: the roots strike out, and the vessel flies to pieces. A pure, noble, highly moral disposition, but without that energy of soul which constitutes the hero, sinks under a load which it can neither support nor resolve to abandon altogether. All his obligations are sacred to him; but this alone is above his powers. An impossibility is required at his hands; not an impossibility in itself, but that which is so to him."

Still we have to confess, as stated before, that there is a mystery about Hamlet, which baffles all our resources of criticism; and our remarks should be taken as expressing rather what we have thought on the subject than any settled judgment. We will dismiss the theme by quoting what seems to us a very admirable passage from a paper in *Blackwood's Magazine*, vol. ii, signed "T. C." The writer is speaking of Hamlet: "In him, his character, and his situation, there is a concentration of all the interests that belong to humanity. There is scarcely a trait of frailty or of grandeur, which may have endeared to us our most beloved friends in real life, that is not found in Hamlet. Undoubtedly Shakespeare loved him beyond all his other creations. Soon as he appears on the stage, we are satisfied: when absent, we long for his return. This is the only play which exists almost altogether in the character of one single person. Who ever knew a Hamlet in real life? yet who, ideal as the character is, feels not its reality? This is the wonder. We love him not, we think of him not, because he was witty, because he was melancholy, because he was filial; but we love him because he existed, and was himself. This is the grand sum-total of the impression. I believe that of every other character, either in tragic or epic poetry, the story makes a part of the conception; but, of Hamlet, the deep and permanent interest is the conception of himself. This seems to belong, not to the character being more perfectly drawn, but to there being a more intense conception of individual human life than perhaps in any other human composition; that is, a being with springs of thought, and feeling, and action, deeper than we can search. These springs rise up from an unknown depth, and in that depth there seems to be a *oneness* of being which we cannot distinctly behold, but which we believe to be there; and thus irreconcilable circumstances, floating on the surface of his actions, have not the effect of making us doubt the truth of the general picture."

From the same eloquent paper we must make another extract touching the apparition of "that fair and war-like form, in which the majesty of buried Denmark did sometimes march": "With all the mighty power which this tragedy possesses over us, arising from qualities now very generally described; yet, without that kingly shadow, who throws over it such preternatural grandeur, it could never have gained so universal an ascendancy over the minds of men. Now, the reality of a ghost is measured to that state of imagination in which we ought to be held for the fullest powers of tragedy. The appearance of such a phantom at once throws open those recesses of the inner spirit over which flesh was closing. Magicians, thunder-storms, and demons produce upon me something of the same effect. I feel myself brought instantaneously back to the creed of childhood. Imagination then seems not a power which I exert, but an impulse which I obey. Thus does the Ghost in *Hamlet* carry us into the presence of eternity.

"Never was a more majestic spirit more majestically re-vealed. The shadow of his kingly grandeur and his war-like might, rests massily upon him. He passes before us sad, silent, and stately. He brings the whole weight of the tragedy in his disclosures. His speech is ghost-like, and blends with ghost conceptions. The popular memory of his words proves how profoundly they sink into our souls. The preparation for his first appearance is most solemn. The night-watch,—the more common effect on the two soldiers,—the deeper effect on the next party, and their speculations,—Horatio's communication with the shadow, that seems as it were half way between theirs and Hamlet's,—his adjurations,—the degree of impression which they produce on the Ghost's mind, who is about to speak but for the due ghost-like interruption of the bird of morning;—all these things lead our minds up to the last pitch of breathless expectation; and while yet the whole weight of mystery is left hanging over the play, we feel that some dread disclosure is reserved for Hamlet's ear, and that an apparition from the world unknown is still a partaker of the noblest of all earthly affections."

Horatio is a very noble character; but he moves so quietly in the drama, that his modest worth and solid manliness have not had justice done them. Should we undertake to go through the play without him, we should then feel how much of the best spirit and impression of the scenes is owing to his presence and character. For he is the medium through which many of the hero's finest and noblest traits are conveyed to us; yet himself so clear and transparent that he scarcely catches the attention. Mr. Verplanck, we believe, was the first to give him his due. "While," says he, "every other character in this play, Ophelia, Polonius, and even Osrick, has been analyzed and discussed, it is remarkable that no critic has stepped forward to notice the great beauty of Horatio's character, and its exquisite adaptation to the effect of the piece. His is a character of great excellence and accomplishment; but while this is distinctly shown, it is but sketched, not elaborately painted. His qualities are brought out only by single and seemingly-accidental touches; the whole being toned down to a quiet and unobtrusive beauty that does not tempt the mind to wander from the main interest, which rests alone upon Hamlet; while it is yet distinct enough to increase that interest, by showing him worthy to be Hamlet's trusted friend in life, and the chosen defender of his honor after death. Such a character, in the hands of another author, would have been made the center of some secondary plot. But here, while he commands our respect and esteem, he never for a moment divides a passing interest with the Prince. He does not break in upon the main current of our feelings. He contributes only to the general effect; so that it requires an effort of the mind to separate him for critical admiration."

The main features of Polonius have been seized and set

forth by Dr. Johnson with the hand of a master. It is one of the best pieces of personal criticism ever penned. "Polonius," says he, "is a man bred in courts, exercised in business, stored with observation, confident in his knowledge, proud of his eloquence, and declining into dotage. His mode of oratory is designed to ridicule the practice of those times, of prefaces that made no introduction, and of method that embarrassed rather than explained. This part of his character is accidental, the rest natural. Such a man is positive and confident, because he knows that his mind was once strong, and knows not that it has become weak. Such a man excels in general principles, but fails in particular application. He is knowing in retrospect, and ignorant in foresight. While he depends upon his memory, and can draw from his depositaries of knowledge, he utters weighty sentences, and gives useful counsel; but, as the mind in its enfeebled state cannot be kept long busy and intent, the old man is subject to the dereliction of his faculties; he loses the order of his ideas, and entangles himself in his own thoughts, till he recover the leading principle, and fall into his former train. The idea of dotage encroaching upon wisdom will solve all the phenomena of the character of Polonius."

In all this Polonius is the exact antithesis of Hamlet, though Hamlet doubtless includes him, as the heavens do the earth. A man of but one method, that of intrigue; with his fingers ever itching to pull the wires of some intricate plot; and without any sense or perception of times and occasions; he is called to act in a matter where such arts and methods are peculiarly unfitting, and therefore only succeeds in over-reaching himself. Thus in him we have the type of a superannuated politician, and all his follies and blunders spring from undertaking to act the politician where he is most especially required to be a man. From books, too, he has gleaned maxims, but not gained development; sought to equip, not feed, his mind out of them: he has therefore made books his idols, and books have made him pedantic.

To such a mind, or rather half-mind, the character of Hamlet must needs be a profound enigma. It takes a whole man to know such a being as Hamlet; and Polonius is but the attic story of a man! As in his mind the calculative faculties have eaten out the perceptive, of course his inferences are seldom wrong, his premises seldom right. Assuming Hamlet to be thus and so, he reasons and acts most admirably in regard to him; but the fact is, he cannot *see* Hamlet; has no eye for the true premises of the case; and, being wrong in these, his very correctness of logic makes him but the more ridiculous. His method of coming at the meaning of men, is by reading them backwards; and this method, used upon such a character as Hamlet, can but betray the user's infirmity.

Shakespeare's skill in revealing a character through its most characteristic transpirations is finely displayed in the directions Polonius gives his servant, for detecting the habits and practices of his absent son. Here the old politician is perfectly at home; his mind seems to revel in the mysteries of wire-pulling and trap-setting. In the Prince, however, he finds an impracticable subject; here all his strategy is nonplussed, and himself caught in the trap he sets to catch the truth. The mere torch of policy, nature, or Hamlet, who is an embodiment of nature, blows him out; so that, in attempting to throw light on the Prince, he just rays out nothing but smoke. The sport of circumstances, it was only by a change of circumstances that Hamlet came to know him. Once the honored minister of his royal father, now the despised tool of that father's murderer, Hamlet sees in him only the crooked, supple time-server; and the ease with which he baffles and plagues the old fox shows how much craftier one *can* be who scorns craft, than one who courts it.

Habits of intrigue having extinguished in Polonius the powers of honest insight and special discernment, he therefore perceives not the unfitness of his old methods to the new exigency; while at the same time his faith in the craft, hitherto found so successful, stuffs him with overweening assurance. Hence, also, that singular but most characteristic specimen of grannyism, namely, his pedantic and impertinent dallying with artful turns of thought and speech amidst serious business; where he appears not unlike a certain person who "could speak no sense in several languages." Superannuated politicians, indeed, like him, seldom have any strength but as they fall back upon the resources of memory: out of these, the ashes, so to speak, of extinct faculties, they may seem wise after the fountains of wisdom are dried up within them; as a man who *has lost his sight* may seem to distinguish colors, so long as he refrains from speaking of the colors that are before him.

Of all Shakespeare's heroines, the impression of Ophelia is perhaps the most difficult of analysis, partly because she is so real, partly because so undeveloped. Like Cordelia, she is brought forward but little in the play, yet the whole play seems full of her. Her very silence utters her: unseen, she is missed, and so thought of the more: when absent in person, she is still present in effect, by what others bring from her. Whatsoever grace comes from Polonius and the Queen is of her inspiring: Laertes is scarce regarded but as he loves his sister: of Hamlet's soul, too, she is the sunrise and morning hymn. The soul of innocence and gentleness, wisdom seems to radiate from her insensibly, as fragrance is exhaled from flowers. It is in such forms that heaven most frequently visits us!

Ophelia's situation much resembles Imogen's; their characters are in marked contrast. Both appear amid the corruptions of a wicked court; Ophelia escapes them by insensibility of their presence, Imogen, by determined resistance: The former is unassailable in her innocence; the latter, unconquerable in her strength: Ignorance protects Ophelia, knowledge, Imogen: The conception of vice has scarce found its way into Ophelia's mind; in Imogen the daily perception of vice has called for a power to repel it. In Ophelia, again, as in Desdemona, the comparative want of intelligence, or rather intellectuality, is never felt as a defect. She fills up the idea of excellence just as completely as if she had the intellect of Shakespeare himself. In the rounded equipoise of her character we miss not the absent element, because there is no vacancy to be supplied; and high intellect would strike us rather as a superfluity than a supplement; its voice would rather drown than complete the harmony of the other tones.

Ophelia is exhibited in the utmost ripeness and mellowness, both of soul and sense, to impressions from without. With her susceptibilities just opening to external objects, her thoughts are so engaged on these as to leave no room for self-contemplation. This exceeding impressibility is the source at once of her beauty and her danger. From the lips and eyes of Hamlet she has drunk in pledges of his love, but has never heard the voice of her own; and knows not how full her heart is of Hamlet, because she has not a single thought or feeling there at strife with him. Mrs. Jameson rightly says, "she is far more conscious of being loved than of loving; and yet loving in the silent depths of her young heart far more than she is loved." For it is a singular fact that, though from Hamlet we have many disclosures, and from Ophelia only concealments, there has been much doubt of his love, but never any of hers. Ophelia's silence as to her own passion has been sometimes misderived from a wish to hide it from others; but, in truth, she seems not to be aware of it herself; and she unconsciously betrays it in the modest reluctance with which she yields up the secret of Hamlet's courtship. The extorted confession of what she has received reveals how much she has given; the soft tremblings of her bosom being made the plainer by the delicate lawn of silence thrown over it. Even when despair is wringing her innocent young soul into an utter wreck, she seems not to know the source of her affliction; and the truth comes out only when her sweet mind, which once breathed such enchanting music, lies broken in fragments before us, and the secrets of her maiden heart are hovering on her demented tongue.

One of the bitterest ingredients in poor Ophelia's cup is

the belief that by her repulse of Hamlet she has dismantled his fair and stately house of reason; and when, forgetting the wounds with which her own pure spirit is bleeding, over the spectacle of that "unmatch'd form and feature of blown youth blasted with ecstacy," she meets his, "I loved you not," with the despairing sigh, "I was the more deceived," we see that she feels not the sundering of the ties that bind her sweetly-tempered faculties in harmony. Yet we blame not Hamlet, for he is himself but a victim of an inexorable power which is spreading its ravages through him over another life as pure and heavenly as his own. Standing on the verge of an abyss which is yawning to engulf himself, his very effort to frighten her back from it only hurries her in before him. To snatch another jewel from Mrs. Jameson's casket,—"He has no thought to link his terrible destiny with hers: he cannot marry her: he cannot reveal to her, young, gentle, innocent as she is, the terrific influences which have changed the whole current of his life and purposes. In his distraction he overacts the painful part to which he has tasked himself; like that judge of the Areopagus who, being occupied with graver matters, flung from him the little bird which had sought refuge in his bosom, and with such angry violence, that he unwittingly killed it."

Ophelia's insanity exhausts the fountains of human pity. It is one of those mysterious visitings over which we can only brood in silent sympathy and awe; which Heaven alone has a heart adequately to pity, and a hand effectually to heal. Its pathos were too much to be borne, but for the sweet incense that rises from her crushed spirit, as "she turns thought and affliction, passion, hell itself, to favor and to prettiness." Of her death what shall be said? The victim of crimes in which she has no share but as a sufferer, we hail with joy the event that snatches her from the rack of this world. The "snatches of old lauds," with which she chaunts, as it were, her own burial service, are like smiles gushing from the very heart of woe. We must leave her, with the words of Hazlitt: "O, rose of May!

O, flower too soon faded! Her love, her madness, her death, are described with the truest touches of tenderness and pathos. It is a character which nobody but Shakespeare could have drawn in the way that he has done; and to the conception of which there is not the smallest approach, except in some of the old romantic ballads."

The Queen's affection for this lovely being is one of those unexpected strokes, so frequent in Shakespeare, which surprise us into reflection by their naturalness. That Ophelia should disclose a vein of goodness in the Queen, was necessary perhaps to keep us both from underrating the influence of the one, and from exaggerating the wickedness of the other. The love which she thus awakens tells us that her helplessness springs from innocence, not from weakness; and so serves to prevent the pity which her condition moves from lessening the respect due to her character.

Almost any other author would have depicted Gertrude without a single alleviating trait in her character. Beaumont and Fletcher would probably have made her simply frightful or loathsome, and capable only of exciting abhorrence or disgust; if, indeed, in her monstrous depravity she had not rather failed to excite any feeling. Shakespeare, with far more effect as well as far more truth, exhibits her with such a mixture of good and bad, as neither disarms censure nor precludes pity. Herself dragged along in the terrible train of consequences which her own guilt had a hand in starting, she is hurried away into the same dreadful abyss along with those whom she loves, and against whom she has sinned. In her tenderness towards Hamlet and Ophelia, we recognize the virtues of the mother without in the least palliating the guilt of the wife; while the crimes in which she is an accomplice almost disappear in those of which she is the victim.

The plan of this drama seems to consist in the persons being represented as without plans; for, as Goethe happily remarks, "the hero is without any plan, but the play itself is full of plan." As the action, so far as there is any, is shaped and determined rather *for* the characters than *from* them, all their energies could the better be translated into thought. Hence of all the Poet's dramas this probably combines the greatest strength and diversity of faculties. Sweeping round the whole circle of human thought and passion, its alternations of amazement and terror; of lust, ambition, and remorse; of hope, love, friendship, anguish, madness, and despair; of wit, humor, pathos, poetry, and philosophy; now congealing the blood with horror, now melting the heart with pity, now launching the mind into eternity, now startling conscience from her lonely seat with supernatural visitings;—it unfolds indeed a world of truth, and beauty, and sublimity.

Of its varied excellences, only a few of the less obvious need be specified. The platform scenes are singularly charged with picturesque effect. The chills of a northern winter midnight seem creeping on us, as the heart-sick sentinels pass in view, and, steeped in moonlight and drowsiness, exchange their meeting and parting salutations. The thoughts and images that rise in their minds are just such as the anticipation of preternatural visions would be likely to inspire. As the bitter cold stupefies their senses, an indescribable feeling of dread and awe steals over them, preparing the mind to realize its own superstitious imaginings. And the feeling one has in reading these scenes is not unlike that of a child passing a graveyard by moonlight. Out of the dim and drowsy moonbeams apprehension creates its own objects; his fancies embody themselves in surrounding facts; his fears give shape to outward things, while those things give outwardness to his fears.—The heterogeneous elements that are brought together in the grave-digging scene, with its strange mixture of songs and witticisms and dead men's bones, and its still stranger transitions of the grave, the sprightly, the meditative, the solemn, the playful, and the grotesque, make it one of the most wonderful yet most natural scenes in the drama.—In view of the terrible catastrophe, Goethe has the following weighty sentence: "It is the tendency of crime to spread its evils over innocence, as it is of virtue to diffuse its blessings over many who deserve them not; while, frequently, the author of the one or of the other is not, so far as we can see, punished or rewarded."

COMMENTS

By Shakespearean Scholars

THE CHARACTER OF HAMLET

The character of Hamlet stands quite by itself. It is not a character marked by strength of will or even of passion, but by refinement of thought and sentiment. Hamlet is as little of the hero as a man can well be: but he is a young and princely novice, full of high enthusiasm and quick sensibility—the sport of circumstances, questioning with fortune and refining on his own feelings, and forced from the natural bias of his disposition by the strangeness of his situation. He seems incapable of deliberate action, and is only hurried into extremities on the spur of the occasion, when he has no time to reflect, as in the scene where he kills Polonius, and again, where he alters the letters which Rosencrantz and Guildenstern are taking with them to England, purporting his death. At other times, when he is most bound to act, he remains puzzled, undecided, and sceptical, dallies with his purposes, till the occasion is lost, and finds out some pretense to relapse into indolence and thoughtfulness again. For this reason he refuses to kill the King when he is at his prayers, and by a refinement in malice, which is in truth only an excuse for his own want of resolution, defers his revenge to a more fatal opportunity, when he shall be engaged in some act "that has no relish of salvation in it."

He is the prince of philosophical speculators; and because he cannot have his revenge perfect, according to the most refined idea his wish can form, he declines it altogether. So he scruples to trust the suggestions of the ghost, contrives the scene of the play to have surer proof of his uncle's guilt, and then rests satisfied with this confirmation of his suspicions, and the success of his experiment, instead of acting upon it. Yet he is sensible of his own weakness, taxes himself with it, and tries to reason himself out of it.

Still he does nothing; and this very speculation on his own infirmity only affords him another occasion for indulging it. It is not from any want of attachment to his father or of abhorrence of his murder that Hamlet is thus dilatory, but it is more to his taste to indulge his imagination in reflecting upon the enormity of the crime and refining on his schemes of vengeance, than to put them into immediate practice. His ruling passion is to think, not to act: and any vague pretext that flatters this propensity instantly diverts him from his previous purposes.—HAZLITT, *Characters of Shakespear's Plays.*

THE MOOD OF HAMLET

The mood of Hamlet is necessarily an extraordinary and an unaccountable mood. In him exceptional influences agitate an exceptional temperament. He is wayward, fitful, excited, horror-stricken. The foundations of his being are unseated. His intellect and his will are ajar and unbalanced. He has become an exception to the common forms of humanity. The poet, in his turn, struck with this strange figure, seems to have resolved on bringing its special peculiarities into special prominence, and the story which he dramatized afforded him the most ample opportunity of accomplishing this design. Hamlet is not only in reality agitated and bewildered, but he is led to adopt a disguise of feigned madness, and he is thus perpetually intensifying and distorting the peculiarities of an already over-excited imagination. It was, we think, inevitable that a composition which attempted to follow the workings of so unusual an individuality should itself seem abrupt and capricious; and this natural effect of the scene is still further deepened not only by the exceptionally large genius, but by the exceptionally negligent workmanship, of the poet.—KENNY, *The Life and Genius of Shakespeare*.

THE PRINCIPLE OF HAMLET'S ACTION

The mind of Hamlet, violently agitated and filled with displeasing and painful images, loses all sense of felicity. He even wishes for a change of being. The appearance is wonderful, and leads us to inquire into affections and opinions that could render him despondent. The death of his father was a natural evil, and as such he endures it. That he is excluded from succeeding immediately to the royalty seems to affect him slightly; for to vehement and vain ambition he appears superior. He is moved by finer principles, by an exquisite sense of virtue, of moral beauty and turpitude. The impropriety of Gertrude's behavior, her ingratitude to the memory of her former husband and the depravity she discovers in the choice of a successor, afflict his soul, and cast him into utter agony. Here, then, is the principle and spring of all his actions.—RICHARDSON, *Essays on Some of Shakespeare's Dramatic Characters*.

THE INSANITY OF HAMLET

But let it be remembered that in those days mental phenomena were by no means accurately examined or generally known. There was but little attention paid to the peculiar forms of monomania, or to its treatment, beyond restraint and often cruelty. The poor idiot was allowed, if harmless, to wander about the village or the country to drivel or gibber amidst the teasing or ill-treatment of boys or rustics. The poor maniac was chained or tied in some wretched outhouse, at the mercy of some heartless guardian, with no protector but the constable. Shakespeare could not be supposed, in the little town of Statford, nor indeed in London itself, to have had opportunities of studying the influence and the appearance of mental derangement of a high-minded and finely-cultivated prince. How

then did Shakespeare contrive to point so highly-finished
and yet so complex an image? Simply by the exercise of
that strong sympathetic will which enabled him to trans-
port, or rather to transmute, himself into another person-
ality. While this character was strongly before him, he
changed himself into a maniac; he felt intuitively what
would be his own thought, what his feelings, were he in that
situation; he played with himself the part of a madman,
with his own grand mind as the basis of its action; he
grasped on every side the imagery which he felt would
have come into his mind, beautiful even when dislorded, sub-
lime even when it was grovelling, brilliant even when
dulled, and clothed it in words of fire and tenderness, with
a varied rapidity which partakes of wildness and of sense,
He needed not to look for a model out of himself, for it
cost him no more effort to change the angle of his mirror,
and sketch his own countenance awry. It was but little
for him to pluck away the crown from reason and con-
template it dethroned.—WISEMAN, *William Shakespeare.*

The very exhortations to secrecy, shown to be so important in Hamlet's imagination, are but illustrations of
one part of his character, and must be recognizable as such
by all physicians intimately acquainted with the begin-
nings of insanity. It is by no means unfrequent that when
the disease is only incipient, and especially in men of exercised minds, that the patient has an uneasy consciousness
of his own departure from a perfectly sound understanding. He becomes aware that, however he may refuse to acknowledge it, his command over his thoughts or his words
is not steadily maintained, whilst at the same time he has
not wholly lost control over either. He suspects that he
is suspected, and anxiously and ingeniously accounts for
his oddities. Sometimes he challenges inquiry, and courts
various tests of his sanity, and sometimes he declares that
in doing extravagant things he has only been pretending
to be eccentric, in order to astonish the fools about him

and who he knew were watching him. The young Hamlet
has suddenly become a changed man. The curse of madness,—ever fatal to beauty, to order, to happiness,—has
fallen upon him; deep vexation has undermined his reason,
and thoughts beyond the reaches of his soul have agitated
him beyond a cure. His affections are in disorder, and the
disorder will increase; so that he will become by turns suspicious and malicious, impulsive and reflective, pensive and
facetious, and undergo all the transformations of the most
afflicting of human maladies.—CONOLLY, *A Study of Hamlet.*

Shakespeare . . . . . recognized what none of his critics, not conversant with medical psychology in its present
advanced state, seem to have any conception of; namely,
that there are cases of melancholic madness of a delicate
shade, in which the reasoning faculties, the intellect proper,
so far from being overcome, or even disordered, may, on
the other hand, be rendered more active and vigorous, while
the will, the moral feelings, the sentiments and affections,
are the faculties which seem alone to suffer from the stroke
of disease. Such a case he has given us in the character
of Hamlet, with a fidelity to nature which continues more
and more to excite our wonder and astonishment as our
knowledge of this intricate subject advances.—KELLOGG,
*Shakespeare's Delineations of Insanity, Imbecility and
Suicide.*

The majority of readers at the present day believe that
Hamlet's madness was real. . . . . . A madness so skilfully feigned, and in so moderate and exact a degree as
to deceive not only those whom it was intended to deceive,
but also to deceive alike spectators and readers, who are
always privileged to know more of the action and the real
characters in a play than do the personages themselves,—
such a feigned madness serves to make a plot more ingenious and interesting than it would be if the hero's men-

tal aberration had been made to appear unmistakably real.
—STEARNS, *The Shakespeare Treasury of Wit and Knowledge.*

One of the probable causes of Hamlet's feigning of madness has never yet been indicated by the critics. Hamlet,
it is said, played the madman to hide his thought, like
Brutus. In fact, it is easy to cover a great purpose under
apparent imbecility; the supposed idiot carries out his de-
signs at his leisure. But the case of Brutus is not that
of Hamlet. Hamlet plays the madman for his safety.
Brutus cloaks his project; Hamlet, his person. The manners of these tragic courts being understood, from the
moment that Hamlet learns from the ghost of the crime of
Claudius, Hamlet is in danger. The superior historian
that is in the poet is here manifest, and we perceive in
Shakespeare the profound penetration into the dark shades
of ancient royalty. In the Middle Ages and in the latter
empire, and even more anciently, woe to him who discovered a murder or a poisoning committed by a king.
Ovid, Voltaire conjectured, was exiled from Rome for having seen something shameful in the house of Augustus.
To know that the king was an assassin was treason. When
it pleased the prince to have no witness, one must be shrewd
enough to know nothing. It was bad policy to have good
eyes. A man suspected of suspicion was lost. He had
only one refuge, insanity. Passing for an "innocent" he
was despised, and all was said.—VICTOR HUGO, *William
Shakespeare.*

The question of Hamlet's madness has been much discussed and variously decided. High medical authority has
pronounced, as usual, on both sides of the question. But
the induction has been drawn from too narrow premises,
being based on a mere diagnosis of the case, and not on
an appreciation of the character in its completeness. We
have a case of pretended madness in the Edgar of *King
Lear;* and it is certainly true that that is a charcoal sketch,

coarsely outlined, compared with the delicate drawing, the
lights, shades, and half-tints of the portraiture in Hamlet. But does this tend to prove that the madness of the
latter, because truer to the recorded observation of experts,
is real, and meant to be real, as the other to be fictitious?
Not in the least, as it appears to me. Hamlet, among all
the characters of Shakespeare, is the most eminently a
metaphysician and psychologist. He is a close observer,
continually analyzing his own nature and that of others,
letting fall his little drops of acid irony on all who come
near him, to make them show what they are made of. Even
Ophelia is not too sacred, Osric not too contemptible, for
experiment. If such a man assumed madness, he would
play his part perfectly. If Shakespeare himself, without
going mad, could so observe and remember all the abnormal
symptoms as to be able to reproduce them in Hamlet, why
should it be beyond the power of Hamlet to reproduce
them in himself? If you deprive Hamlet of reason, there
is no truly magic motive left. He would be a fit subject
for Bedlam, but not for the stage. We might have
pathology enough, but no pathos—Ajax first becomes
tragic when he recovers his wits. If Hamlet is irrespon-
sible, the whole play is chaos. That he is not might be
proven by evidence enough were it not labor thrown away.
—LOWELL, *Among My Books.*

But how this has ever come to be a matter of dispute
we are at a loss to understand. Had Hamlet kept his intention to play the madman to himself, there would have
been room for doubt; but after having taken Horatio and
Marcellus into his confidence, by stating plainly his resolve
to behave himself like a madman, it is inconceivable how
any misconception of the proper reading should exist. It
is no proof that his madness is real to say that the King,
Queen, Polonius, and others, think and say he is mad; this
only proves he imitated madness well when he succeeded in
creating this belief. When David scrabbled on the doors
of the gate at Gath, and let his spittle fall upon his beard,

was he mad? Surely not. But Achish and others thought
him mad. So it is in the present case; such proof is no
proof, and is not entitled to a moment's consideration.
There is not a whisper of Hamlet's madness up to the time
when he warns his friends, in future, to take no heed of his
acts,—not even from Polonius. The impression of his
madness is created by his acts subsequent to this warning.
In all his soliloquies, in his conversation with Horatio, in
his instruction to the Players, in his interview with his
mother, in his letter to Horatio, there is not the slightest
trace of unreason, while his interviews with the King,
Polonius, Ophelia, Rosencrantz and Guildenstern, are in-
variably and unmistakably associated with speech or actions resembling madness. Now, if Hamlet was really
mad he never could have preserved such an entire consistency throughout his behavior to so many people, only acting like a madman to those whom he wished to deceive.—
MEADOWS, *Hamlet: An Essay.*

IF

Hamlet, Prince of Denmark, was speculative and irresolute, and we have a great tragedy in consequence. But if
his father had lived to a good old age, and his uncle had
died an early death, we can conceive Hamlet's having married Ophelia, and got through life with a reputation of sanity, notwithstanding many soliloquies, and moody sarcasms
towards the fair daughter of Polonius, to say nothing of
frankest incivility to his father-in-law.—GEORGE ELIOT,
The Mill on the Floss.

OPHELIA

Still waters are deep is true of Ophelia, and: no fire, no
coal, so hotly glows, as the secret love of which nobody
knows. Thoroughly German, old German, is she in her
household relations. Her obedience as a daughter is im-
plicit; only to her brother, who warns her, does she reply

with the dry coolness which belongs to true natures, and which is also apparent, in the first scenes, in Cordelia and Desdemona. We know not what it costs her when she promises obedience to her father's stricter and weightier authority, "I will obey, sir"; further she says nothing. What is passing within her a good actress must tell us by a tone that reveals to us that under this obedience her heart is breaking, when she says, "With almost all the holy vows of Heaven." In this patriarchal submission to her father, in this touching defencelessness, this inability of resistance, which characterizes natures that are boundlessly good and created only for love, she allows herself without demur to be used, when she is sent in Hamlet's way, that they may talk together, while her father and the King privily listen; Hamlet, under the mask of madness, treats her rudely; the pure nobleness of her true, unstained tenderness speaks in the sorrowful words with which the return of his gifts is accompanied; unsuspicious, she believes in his feigned madness; and then her pain breaks out into a lament that points to an abyss from which comes no speech. The deepest tone of the heart, of which a voice is capable, is demanded in this soliloquy; there are few tragic passages sadder or more moving than, "And I, of ladies most deject and wretched, that sucked the honey of his music vows." If it ever can be said of a poetical creation that it has fragrancy in it, it is this picture of the crazed Ophelia, and the inmost secret of this bewitching fragrancy is innocence. Nothing deforms her; not the lack of sense in her sense, not the rude naïveté of those snatches of song: a soft mist, a twilight is drawn around her, veiling the rough reality of insanity, and in this sweet veil, this dissolving melancholy, the story of her death is told.— VISCHER, *Kritische Gänge*.

Beyond every character that Shakspeare has drawn (Hamlet alone excepted), that of Ophelia makes us forget the poet in his own creation. Whenever we bring her to mind, it is with the same exclusive sense of her real existence, without reference to the wondrous power which called her into life. The effect (and what an effect!) is produced by means so simple, by strokes so few, and so unobtrusive, that we take no thought of them. It is so purely natural and unsophisticated, yet so profound in its pathos, that, as Hazlitt observes, it takes us back to the old ballads; we forget that, in its perfect artlessness, it is the supreme and consummate triumph of art.—JAMESON, *Shakespeare's Heroines*.

With what a small outlay of dramatic contrivance has Shakspeare drawn the pathos of Ophelia's fate! It begins to infect us as soon as we discover that she loves; for her lover receives the visits of a murdered father. We know, but she does not, the cause of the apparent unsettling of the Prince's wits. We can anticipate into what tragedies that ghost beckons her Lord Hamlet, while she walks unconsciously so close that her garments, perfumed with rare ladyhood, brush the greaves of the grisly visitant. Her helplessness is not cast in a faint outline against the background of these palace treacheries and lusts; but it appears in startling vividness, because she is so pure, so remote from all the wicked world, so slenderly fitted out to contend with it. Tears are summoned when we see how simple she is, and fashioned solely for dependence: a disposition, not a will; a wife for Hamlet's will, but poor to husband one of her own.

What will become of her? What becomes of the vine when lightning splits its oak? The clipping tendrils and soft green have lost their reason for existing when the wood which centuries have grained is blasted in an hour. She will shrink into herself, will sicken, grow sere, rustle to and fro. Her leaves will blab loose songs to every wanton wind. To wither is all that is left to do, since all that she could do was to love, to climb, to cling, to cloak ruggedness with grace, to make strength and stature serve to lift and develop all her beauteous quality.—WEISS, *Wit, Humor, and Shakespeare*.

THE QUEEN

The Queen is a weak thing; she is Hamlet's mother. Her share in the crime remains doubtful; she is a receiver of stolen goods, buys stolen things cheap, and never asks if a theft has been committed. The King's masculine art overpowers her; her son's lamp of conscience, not lighted until midnight, burns only until morning, and she awakes with the sins of the day before.—BOERNE, *Gesammelte Shriften, Dram. Blätter.*

The Queen was not a bad-hearted woman, not at all the woman to think little of murder. But she had a soft animal nature, and was very dull and very shallow. She loved to be happy, like a sheep in the sun; and, to do her justice, it pleased her to see others happy, like more sheep in the sun. She never saw that drunkenness is disgusting till Hamlet told her so; and, though she knew that he considered her marriage "o'er-hasty" (II, ii, 57), she was untroubled by any shame at the feelings which had led to it. It was pleasant to sit upon her throne and see smiling faces round her, and foolish and unkind in Hamlet to persist in grieving for his father instead of marrying Ophelia and making everything comfortable. She was fond of Ophelia and genuinely attached to her son (though willing to see her lover exclude him from the throne); and, no doubt, she considered equality of rank a mere trifle compared with the claims of love. The belief at the bottom of her heart was that the world is a place constructed simply that people may be happy in it in a good-humored sensual fashion.

Her only chance was to be made unhappy. When affliction comes to her, the good in her nature struggles to the surface through the heavy mass of sloth. Like other faulty characters in Shakespeare's tragedies, she dies a better woman than she had lived. When Hamlet shows her what she has done she feels genuine remorse. It is true, Hamlet fears it will not last, and so at the end of the interview (III, iv, 180 ff.) he adds a warning that if she be-trays him, she will ruin herself as well.[1] It is true too that there is no sign of her obeying Hamlet in breaking off her most intimate connection with the King. Still she does feel remorse; and she loves her son, and does not betray him. She gives her husband a false account of Polonius's death, and is silent about the appearance of the Ghost. She becomes miserable;

> To her sick soul, as sin's true nature is,
> Each toy seems prologue to some great amiss.

She shows spirit when Laertes raises the mob, and one re-spects her for standing up for her husband when she can do nothing to help her son. If she had sense to realize Hamlet's purpose, or the probability of the King's taking some desperate step to foil it, she must have suffered tor-ture in those days. But perhaps she was too dull.

The last we see of her, at the fencing-match, is most characteristic. She is perfectly serene. Things have slipped back into their groove, and she has no apprehen-sions. She is, however, disturbed and full of sympathy for her son, who is out of condition and pants and perspires. These are afflictions she can thoroughly feel for, though they are even more common than the death of a father. But then she meets her death because she cannot resist the wish to please her son by drinking to his success. And more: when she falls dying, and the King tries to make out that she is merely swooning at the sight of blood, she collects her energies to deny it and to warn Hamlet:

> No, no, the drink, the drink,—O my dear Hamlet,—
> The drink, the drink! I am poison'd.   [*Dies.*

Was ever any other writer at once so pitiless and so just as Shakespeare? Did ever any other mingle the grotesque and the pathetic with a realism so daring and yet so true to "the modesty of nature"?—BRADLEY, *Shakespearean Tragedy.*

[1] *I. e.* the King will kill *her* to make all sure.

POLONIUS

Polonius is the comic character of the play. As Shakespeare advanced in art he threw aside the rude merriment of the clown, and contrived to satisfy the pit's demand for humor by the introduction of a laughable character as one of the regular *dramatis personæ*, and in the earlier part of *Hamlet* this *rôle* is played by Polonius. Polonius is the true father of both Laertes and Ophelia. Greatness of mind is utterly absent from his system. He is fitted out with a stock of "old saws and modern instances," which serve as contrasts to the imbecility of his own behavior. As a young man he has had the same pleasant trick of lecturing his friends as Laertes has now, and it has grown upon him. His loquaciousness has increased with his years. In figure he is ungainly to the point of exciting merriment, and though Shakespeare never raises laughter at mere deformity, he makes the combination of self-satisfied imbecility with ludicrous incompetence both of mind and body sufficiently amusing.—Ransome, *Short Studies of Shakespeare's Plots.*

I see in Polonius a real statesman. Discreet, politic, keen-sighted, ready at the council board, cunning upon occasions, he had been valued by the deceased King, and is now indispensable to his successor. How much he suspected as to the death of the former King, or how sincerely he accepted that event, the poet does not tell us. When Polonius speaks to Ophelia of her relations to Hamlet, he pretends ignorance; he has only heard through others that his daughter talks with the prince, and often and confidentially. Here the cunning courtier shows himself, for the visits of the prince to his house could not have been unknown to him. But these visits were made in the time of the late King, and afterwards in the interregnum before the new ruler ascended the throne. The election was doubtful; Hamlet, as we know, had the first right, and the prospect of becoming father-in-law to the King was

tempting. But Hamlet, who had no faculty for availing
himself of circumstances, or even for maintaining his rights
allowed himself to be set aside, and Polonius saw, even
when the great assembly was held, that Hamlet's position at court was Hamlet's own fault. Consequently, for
double reasons, Polonius forbids his daughter to have any
intercourse with the prince; first, because the prince was
a cypher, and then again, because the King might become
suspicious if he learned that such intercourse existed.—
Tieck, *Dramaturgische Blätter*.

ROSENCRANTZ AND GUILDENSTERN

Rosencrantz and Guildenstern are favorable samples of
the thorough-paced, time-serving court knave—servants of
all-work, ticketed, and to be hired for any hard or dirty
job. Shakespeare has at once, and unequivocally, signified
his opinion of the race, by making Rosencrantz, the time-
server, the schoolfellow of Hamlet, and, under the color
of their early associations, professing a personal friendship—even an affection for him, at the very time that he
had accepted the office of spy upon his actions, and traitor
to his confidence. "Good, my lord, what is your cause of
distemper? You do surely but bar the door upon your
own liberty, if you deny your griefs to your friend." Immediately upon the heel of this protestation he accepts the
king's commission to convey his "friend" to England,
where measures had been taken for his assassination.
Rosencrantz and his fellow would designate themselves as
thoroughly *"loyal"* men"; they make no compromise of
their calling; the "broad R" is burnt into them; they are
for the king's service exclusively; and with the scavenger's
calling, they would scoop all into that reservoir. The poet
has sketched them in few and bold outlines; their subtleties
of character stare out like the bones of a starved beast.
They are time-servers by profession, and upon hire; and
"verily they have their reward." The great Hebrew legis-
lator has said, "Thou shalt not muzzle the ox that treadeth

out the corn"; but the corn that such oxen tread out no
noble beast would consider worthy of "protective duty"
at all.   No one works so hard as a time-server; and, under
the fairest auspices, his labor is well worthy of his pay.
The machinery he constructs to accomplish his little ends,
is always complicated and eccentric in movement—like the
Laputan's invention for cutting a cabbage, requiring a
horse-power to put it in action; or like the painstaking of
Bardolph, who stole the lute-case, carried it seven leagues,
and sold it for three-halfpence.   The same great master-
spirit—Shakespeare—has made another time-server say,
"How wretched is that poor man that hangs on princes'
favors!" but how much more wretched is that poor prince
who needs such hangers-on as Guildenstern and Rosencrantz!   What a hell on earth has the man who is the
suborner of meanness and villainy!—the constant sense of
subjection—the instinctive sense of insincerity and sham
respect—the rising of the gorge at the fawning and the
mouth-honor, the self-inspection, (which will come,) the
surmises, the fears, the trepidations, the heartaches:
"Verily, both parties have their reward," even here, "on this
bank and shoal of time." . . . . . In the spirit of just
retribution, these two worthies fall into the trap they had
set for their old friend and schoolfellow.—CLARKE, *Shake-
speare-Characters*.

HORATIO

It is commonly understood that Hamlet and Horatio
were friends in the higher sense of the word, but such is not
the idea of the poet.   Horatio is an honest, loyal subject,
very modest, contented in the humblest sphere, without any
great elevation of mind, without indeed any uncommon degree of intellect, yet using well all he has learned.   But
why has not Shakespeare made Horatio a person of high
intellectual ability?   Because it would have distorted the
whole piece.   Were Horatio a strong, able man, he would
either have had an undue influence over his friend, or he

would have acted for him, and all would have been dif ferent. But as it is, he does not help the prince to act; in many respects, in acuteness, wit, imagination, eloquence he stands below the prince, although he excels him in his way of thinking, morally considered. It is, moreover, very tragic that the poor prince, among all around him, finds no greater friend than this Horatio, and must cling to him, as no other is at hand. Horatio is, however, at least an honest man, which is certainly *very much;* but Hamlet has to console and content himself with Horatio's intellectual mediocrity. Perfect love and reverence he has had for one only, his father, whose loss can never be supplied.— HORN, *Shakespeare Erläutert.*

THE GHOST

The Ghost only makes that an absolute certainty which already existed as a strong suspicion. The Ghost can communicate only with Hamlet, because Hamlet alone is capable of believing in the certainty that a crime had been committed. The Ghost can appear also to those who have kept themselves free from moral blight, who deplore the condition of Denmark, and who have thus naturally become the adherents of the prince.—ROETSHER, *Cyclus Dramatischer Charaktere.*

HAMLET AS AN EXPRESSION OF SHAKE-SPEARE'S MENTAL ATTITUDE

If Shakespeare's master-passion then was, as we have seen it to be, the love of intellectual activity for its own sake, his continual satisfaction with the simple pleasure of existence must have made him more than commonly liable to the fear of death, or at least made that change the great point of interest in his hours of reflection. Often and often must he have thought, that to be or not to be forever was a question which must be settled; as it is the foundation, and the only foundation, upon which we feel that

there can rest one thought, one feeling, or one purpose
worthy of a human soul. Here lie the materials out of
which this remarkable tragedy was built up. From the
wrestling of his own soul with the great enemy, comes that
depth and mystery which startles us in Hamlet. It is to
this condition that Hamlet has been reduced. . . . . . He
fears nothing save the loss of existence. But this thought
thunders at the very base of the cliff on which, ship-
wrecked of every other hope, he had been thrown.—VERY,
Essays and Poems.

MATURITY OF THE PLAY

To any of the new school of Victorian Shakspereans,
to any one who has a grasp of Shakspere's development,
who can trace the progress of his Mind and Art from the
whimsy quip and quirk, the youthful passion, the florid
rhetoric, of his First-Period farces, tragedy, and histories,
from these to the pathos of Constance, the grace of Portia,
the humor of Falstaff, the wit of Benedick and Beatrice,
the romance of Viola, the steadfastness of Helena, the
wealth and brilliancy of Shakspere's delightful Second
Period, and thence to the deeper Tragedies of his Third,—
to any such man, no words of mine are needed to make
him sure that *Hamlet* was no creation of the "rough enthusiasm of Shakspere's youth at Stratford."—FURNI-
VALL, *Hamlet* in the *Quarto Facsimile* of *Shakespeare.*

SUPERIORITY OF HAMLET

Consider Hamlet in whatsoever light you will, it stands
quite alone, most peculiarly apart, from every other play
of Shakespeare's. A vast deal has been written upon the
subject, and by a great number of commentators, by men
borne in different countries, educated after different fash-
ions. . . . . . We might hope to see a second Shakespeare,
if the world had ever produced a commentator worthy of
Hamlet. The qualities and faculties such a man should

possess would be, indeed "rare in their separate excellence, wonderful in their combinations." Such a man as Shakespeare imagined in him to whom his hero bequeathed the task of: Reporting him and his cause aright to the satisfied."—MAGINN, *Shakespeare Papers*.

Not one single alteration in the whole play can possibly have been made with a view to stage effect or to present popularity and profit; or we must suppose that Shakespeare, however great as a man, was naturally even greater as a fool. There is a class of mortals to whom this inference is always grateful—to whom the fond belief that every great man must needs be a great fool would seem always to afford real comfort and support: happy, in Prior's phrase, could their inverted rule prove every great fool to be a great man. Every change in the text of *Hamlet* has impaired its fitness for the stage and increased its value for the closet in exact and perfect proportion. Now this is not a matter of opinion—of Mr. Pope's opinion or Mr. Carlyle's; it is a matter of fact and evidence. Even in Shakespeare's time the actors threw out his additions; they throw out these very same additions in our own. The one especial speech, if any one such especial speech there be, in which the personal genius of Shakespeare soars up to the very highest of its height and strikes down to very deepest of its depth, is passed over by modern actors; it was cut away by Hemings and Condell. We may almost assume it as certain that no boards have ever echoed—at least, more than once or twice—to the supreme soliloquy of Hamlet. Those words which combine the noblest pleading ever proffered for the rights of human reason with the loftiest vindication ever uttered of those rights, no mortal ear within our knowledge has ever heard spoken on the stage. A convocation even of all priests could not have been more unhesitatingly unanimous in its rejection than seems to have been the hereditary verdict of all actors. It could hardly have been found worthier of theological than it has been found of theatrical condemnation. Yet, beyond all question, magnificent as is that monologue on suicide and doubt which has passed from a proverb into a byword, it is actually eclipsed and distanced at once on philosophic and on poetical grounds by the later soliloquy on reason and resolution.—SWINBURNE, *A Study of Shakespeare*.

SYNOPSIS

By J. Ellis Burdick

ACT I

The ghost of Hamlet, King of Denmark, walks on the battlements of the castle of Kronberg at Elsinore and is seen by the sentinels, who decide to tell young Hamlet about it, believing that the ghost, though dumb to them, will speak to him. Hamlet resolves to see it and to speak to it "though hell itself should gape and bid" him "hold his peace." The ghost tells how the king's brother Claudius had murdered him that he might obtain the throne and marry the king's wife. Hamlet promises to avenge his father and the ghost vanishes. The sentinels, who are good friends to the prince, are pledged to silence.

ACT II

From this time on, Hamlet feigns madness, that no one may suspect him of serious plans. The king and queen, not believing the death of his father sufficient cause for such madness, search for another reason for it. He writes an incoherent, passionate letter to Ophelia, daughter of a courtier named Polonius, and this letter they believe proves that the cause of his madness is love. A company of strolling players come to the court and Hamlet asks them to present "The Murder of Gonzago," a play similar in incidents to the murder of his father.

ACT III

During the play, the prince closely watches the king and queen. As Hamlet expected, his uncle is much moved and hastily ‿eaves the room, followed by the queen. The latter sends for her son, in order that she may reason with him over his conduct. Polonius is hidden behind a curtain, and Hamlet, hearing him call out and believing it to be the king, slays him. Hamlet reproaches his mother with her past life and she is over-whelmed with shame and remorse. Their interview is interrupted by the dead king's ghost, who is invisible and inaudible to the queen.

ACT IV

The king and queen and their counselors agree that Hamlet must be banished. He is sent to England under guard of two schoolmates. Sealed orders for his death await his arrival in that country. But when they were two days at sea a pirate ship gives chase to their vessel and Hamlet is taken prisoner. The pirates deal gently with him, for they hope that he will get them some favor from the court if they do so. Hamlet returns home and a sad sight is the first thing to greet his eyes. This is the funeral of Ophelia. She had become insane from fretting over her father's sudden death at her lover's hands, over Hamlet's madness, and over her brother's prolonged absence from home. She had wandered about the court for days singing and strewing flowers, and at last, having strayed to the banks of a stream, had been drowned.

ACT V

Hamlet's grief is intense, and he leaps into the open grave and there contests with Laertes, Ophelia's brother, for the place of chief mourner. They are separated by attendants, and later at the king's instigation they engage in a supposedly friendly fencing match. But Laertes' rapier is sharp and poisoned. To make certain of the prince's death the king prepares a poisoned drink and places the cup where Hamlet will be likely to pick it up should he be thirsty. At first Hamlet gains some advantages, but suddenly he receives a mortal blow from his opponent's weapon. In the scuffle which follows, the weapons are exchanged. Hamlet wounds Laertes with the death-giving rapier. Meanwhile the queen, desirous of encouraging her son and knowing nothing of the poisoned drink, picks up the cup near her to drink to him, and immediately dies. As the queen passes away, Hamlet realizes that there is treachery somewhere, and the dying Laertes confesses his share in it, begging forgiveness of the prince, and accuses the king of planning it all. The prince turns on his uncle and stabs him to death with the poisoned weapon, and having thus avenged his father, he dies.

...

THE TRAGEDY OF
HAMLET, PRINCE OF DENMARK

ACT FIRST

Scene I

Elsinore. A platform before the castle.

Francisco at his post. Enter to him Bernardo.

Ber. Who's there?

Fran. Nay, answer me: stand, and unfold your-
     self.

Ber. Long live the king!

2. *"answer me"*; that is, answer *me,* as I have the right to challenge *you.* Bernardo then gives in answer the watch-word, "Long
live the king!"—"Compare," says Coleridge, "the easy language of
common life, in which this drama commences, with the direful music
and wild wayward rhythm and abrupt lyrics of the opening of
Macbeth. The tone is quite familiar: there is no poetic description of night, no elaborate information conveyed by one speaker
to another of what both had immediately before their senses; and
yet nothing bordering on the comic on the one hand, nor any
striving of the intellect on the other. It is precisely the language
of sensation among men who feared no charge of effeminacy for
feeling what they had no want of resolution to bear. Yet the ar-
mour, the dead silence, the watchfulness that first interrupts it, the
welcome relief of the guard, the cold, the broken expressions of
compelled attention to bodily feelings still under control,—all ex-
cellently accord with, and prepare for, the after gradual rise into
tragedy; but, above all, into a tragedy, the interest of which is as
eminently *ad et apud intra,* as that of Macbeth is directly *ad extra."*
—H. N. H.

Fran. Bernardo?

Ber. He.

Fran. You come most carefully upon your hour.

Ber. 'Tis now struck twelve; get thee to bed, Francisco.

Fran. For this relief much thanks: 'tis bitter cold,
And I am sick at heart.

Ber. Have you had quiet guard?

Fran.   Not a mouse stirring.   10

Ber. Well, good night.
If you do meet Horatio and Marcellus,
The rivals of my watch, bid them make haste.

Fran. I think I hear them. Stand, ho! Who is
there?

Enter Horatio and Marcellus.

Hor. Friends to this ground.

Mar.   And liegemen to the Dane.

Fran. Give you good night.

Mar.   O, farewell, honest soldier:
Who hath relieved you?

Fran.   Bernardo hath my place.
Give you good night.   [*Exit.*

Mar.   Holla! Bernardo!

Ber.   Say,
What, is Horatio there?

Hor.   A piece of him.   19

Ber. Welcome, Horatio; welcome, good Marcellus.

18. *"give you good night";* this salutation is an abbreviated form
of, "May God give you a good night"; which has been still further
abbreviated in the phrase, "Good night."—H. N. H.

Mar. What, has this thing appear'd again to-
    night?
Ber. I have seen nothing.
Mar. Horatio says 'tis but our fantasy,
    And will not let belief take hold of him
    Touching this dreaded sight, twice seen of us:
    Therefore I have entreated him along
    With us to watch the minutes of this night,
    That if again this apparition come,
    He may approve our eyes and speak to it.
Hor. Tush, tush, 'twill not appear.
Ber.   Sit down a while;   30
    And let us once again assail your ears,
    That are so fortified against our story,
    What we have two nights seen.
Hor.   Well, sit we down,
    And let us hear Bernardo speak of this.

21. *"has this thing appeared,* etc.; the folio assigns this speech to
Marcellus. The quartos are probably right, as Horatio comes on
purpose to try his own eyes on the Ghost.—We quote from Coleridge again: "Bernardo's inquiry after Horatio, and the repetition
of his name in his own presence indicate a respect or an eagerness
that implies him as one of the persons who are in the foreground;
and the scepticism attributed to him prepares us for Hamlet's after
eulogy on him as one whose blood and judgment were happily commingled. Now, observe the admirable indefiniteness of the first
opening out of the occasion of all this anxiety. The preparative
information of the audience is just as much as was precisely necessary, and no more;—it begins with the uncertainty appertaining to
a question: 'What! has *this thing* appear'd again to-night?' Even
the word *again* has its *credibilizing* effect. Then Horatio, the repre-
sentative of the ignorance of the audience, not himself, but by Marcellus to Bernardo, anticipates the common solution.—''Tis but our
fantasy'; upon which Marcellus rises into,—'This dreaded sight
twice seen of us'; which immediately afterwards becomes 'this
apparition,' and that, too, an intelligent spirit that is to be spoken
to!"—H. N. H.

Ber. Last night of all,
> When yond same star that 's westward from the
> pole
> Had made his course to illume that part of
> heaven
> Where now it burns, Marcellus and myself,
> The bell then beating one,—

Enter Ghost.

Mar. Peace, break thee off; look, where it comes
again!   40
Ber. In the same figure, like the king that 's dead.
Mar. Thou art a scholar; speak to it, Horatio.
Ber. Looks it not like the king? mark it, Horatio.
Hor. Most like: it harrows me with fear and won-
der.

40. *"Peace, break thee off";* "this passage seems to contradict the
critical law, that what is told makes a faint impression compared
with what is beholden; for it does indeed convey to the mind more
than the eye can see; whilst the interruption of the narrative at the
very moment when we are most intensely listening for the sequel,
and have our thoughts diverted from the dreaded sight in expectation of the desired, yet almost dreaded, tale,—this gives all the
suddenness and surprise of the original appearance: 'Peace! break
thee off: look, where it comes again!' Note the judgment displayed
in having the two persons present, who, as having seen the Ghost
before, are naturally eager in confirming their former opinions;
whilst the sceptic is silent, and, after having been twice addressed by
his friends, answers with two hasty syllables,—'Most like,'—and a
confession of horror: 'It harrows me with fear and wonder'" (Coleridge).—H. N. H.

42. *"speak to it";* it was believed that a supernatural being could
only be spoken to with effect by persons of learning; exorcisms
being usually practiced by the clergy in Latin. So in *The Night
Walker* of Beaumont and Fletcher:

> "Let's call the butler up, for *he speaks Latin,*
> And that will daunt the devil."—H. N. H.

44. *"it harrows me";* to *harrow* is to *distress,* to vex, to disturb.

10

Ber. It would be spoke to.

Mar.   Question it, Horatio.

Hor. What art thou, that usurp'st this time of
     night,
     Together with that fair and warlike form
     In which the majesty of buried Denmark
     Did sometimes march? by heaven I charge thee,
          speak!

Mar. It is offended.

Ber.   See, it stalks away!   50

Hor. Stay! speak, speak! I charge thee, speak!
                              [*Exit Ghost.*

Mar. 'Tis gone, and will not answer.

Ber. How now, Horatio! you tremble and look
          pale:
     Is not this something more than fantasy?
     What think you on 't?

Hor. Before my God, I might not this believe
     Without the sensible and true avouch
     Of mine own eyes.

Mar.   Is it not like the king?

Hor. As thou art to thyself:
     Such was the very armor he had on   60
     When he the ambitious Norway combated;
     So frown'd he once, when, in an angry parle,
     He smote the sledded Polacks on the ice.
     'Tis strange.

To *harry* and to *harass* have the same origin. Milton has the word
in *Comus:* "Amaz'd I stood, *harrow'd* with grief and fear."—
"*Question* it," in the next line, is the reading of the folio; other old
copies have "*Speak to* it."—H. N. H.

  63. "*He smote the sledded Polacks on the ice*"; Q. 1, Q. 2, F. 1,
"*pollax,*" variously interpreted as "*Polacks,*" "*poleaxe,*" &c.; there is

Mar. Thus twice before, and jump at this dea
　　hour,
　　With martial stalk hath he gone by our watcl
Hor. In what particular thought to work I knov
　　not;
　　But, in the gross and scope of my opinion,
　　This bodes some strange eruption to our state
Mar. Good now, sit down, and tell me, he tha
　　knows,　　　　　　　　　　　　　　　　7
　　Why this same strict and most observant watc'
　　So nightly toils the subject of the land,
　　And why such daily cast of brazen cannon,
　　And foreign mart for implements of war;
　　Why such impress of shipwrights, whose sor
　　　　task
　　Does not divide the Sunday from the week;
　　What might be toward, that this sweaty haste
　　Doth make the night joint-laborer with the day
　　Who is 't that can inform me?
Hor.　　　　　　　　　　　　　That can I;
　　At least the whisper goes so.　Our last king, 8(
　　Whose image even but now appear'd to us,
　　Was, as you know, by Fortinbras of Norway
　　Thereto prick'd on by a most emulate pride,
　　Dared to the combat; in which our valiant Ham
　　　　let—
　　For so this side of our known world esteem'(
　　　　him—

very little to be said against the former interpretation, unless i
be that "the ambitious Norway" in the previous sentence woul(
lead one to expect "the sledded Polack," a commendable readin,
originally proposed by Pope.—I. G.

Did slay this Fortinbras; who by a seal'd com-
    pact,
Well ratified by law and heraldry,
Did forfeit, with his life, all those his lands
Which he stood seized of, to the conqueror:
Against the which, a moiety competent   90
Was gaged by our king; which had return'd
To the inheritance of Fortinbras,
Had he been vanquisher; as, by the same cove-
    nant
And carriage of the article design'd,
His fell to Hamlet. Now, sir, young Fortin-
    bras,
Of unimproved metal hot and full,
Hath in the skirts of Norway here and there
Shark'd up a list of lawless resolutes,
For food and diet, to some enterprise
That hath a stomach in 't: which is no other— 100
As it doth well appear unto our state—
But to recover of us, by strong hand
And terms compulsatory, those foresaid lands
So by his father lost: and this, I take it,
Is the main motive of our preparations,
The source of this our watch and the chief head
Of this post-haste and romage in the land.
Ber. I think it be no other but e'en so:
Well may it sort, that this portentous figure
Comes armed through our watch, so like the
    king   110
That was and is the question of these wars.

108–125. These lines occur in the Qq., but are omitted in Ff.—
I. G.

Hor. A mote it is to trouble the mind's eye.
In the most high and palmy state of Rome,
A little ere the mightiest Julius fell,
The graves stood tenantless, and the sheeted
　　dead
Did squeak and gibber in the Roman streets:
·　　·　　·　　·　　·　　·　　·　　·　　·

As stars with trains of fire and dews of blood,
Disasters in the sun; and the moist star,
Upon whose influence Neptune's empire stands,
Was sick almost to doomsday with eclipse: 120
And even the like precurse of fierce events,
As harbingers preceding still the fates
And prologue to the omen coming on,
Have heaven and earth together demonstrated
Unto our climatures and countrymen.

heaven sending down message

Re-enter Ghost.

But soft, behold! lo, where it comes again!
I 'll cross it, though it blast me.　Stay, illusion!
If thou hast any sound, or use of voice,
Speak to me:
If there be any good thing to be done,　　130
That may to thee do ease and grace to me,
Speak to me:
If thou art privy to thy country's fate,
Which, happily, foreknowing may avoid,
O, speak!
Or if thou hast uphoarded in thy life

113. *"palmy state"*; that is, victorious; the *Palm* being the emblem
of victory.—H. N. H.
118. *"Disasters"*; ominous signs, probably an eclipse.—C. H. H.

14

Extorted treasure in the womb of earth,
For which, they say, you spirits oft walk in death,
Speak of it: stay, and speak! [*The cock crows.*]
    Stop it, Marcellus.

Mar. Shall I strike at it with my partisan?   140
Hor. Do, if it will not stand.
Ber.   'Tis here!
Hor.   'Tis here!
Mar. 'Tis gone!   [*Exit Ghost.*
We do it wrong, being so majestical,
To offer it the show of violence;
For it is, as the air, invulnerable,
And our vain blows malicious mockery.
Ber. It was about to speak, when the cock crew.
Hor. And then it started like a guilty thing
Upon a fearful summons. I have heard,
The cock, that is the trumpet to the morn, 150
Doth with his lofty and shrill-sounding throat
Awake the god of day, and at his warning,
Whether in sea or fire, in earth or air,
The extravagant and erring spirit hies
To his confine: and of the truth herein
This present object made probation.
Mar. It faded on the crowing of the cock.
Some say that ever 'gainst that season comes
Wherein our Saviour's birth is celebrated,
The bird of dawning singeth all night long: 160

---

157. *"crowing of the cock";* this is a very ancient superstition.
Philostratus, giving an account of the apparition of Achilles' shade
to Apollonius of Tyanna, says, "it vanished with a little gleam as
soon as the cock crowed." There is a *Hymn* of *Prudentius,* and another of St. Ambrose, in which it is mentioned; and there are some
lines in the latter very much resembling Horatio's speech.—H. N. H.

And then, they say, no spirit dare stir abroad,
The nights are wholesome, then no planets
    strike,
No fairy takes nor witch hath power to charm,
So hallow'd and so gracious is the time.
Hor. So have I heard and do in part believe it.
But look, the morn, in russet mantle clad,
Walks o'er the dew of yon high eastward hill:
Break we our watch up; and by my advice,
Let us impart what we have seen to-night
Unto young Hamlet; for, upon my life,　170
This spirit, dumb to us, will speak to him:
Do you consent we shall acquaint him with it,
As needful in our loves, fitting our duty?
Mar. Let's do't, I pray; and I this morning know
Where we shall find him most conveniently.

　　　　　　　　　　　　　　　　[Exeunt.

167. *"eastward,"* so Qq.; Ff., *"easterne";* the latter reading was
perhaps in Milton's mind, when he wrote:—

　　　*"Now morn her rosy steps in th' eastern clime
　　　Advancing, sowed the earth with orient pearls."*
　　　　　　　　　　　　　Par. Lost, v. 1.—I. G.

170. *"young Hamlet";* "note the inobtrusive and yet fully ade-
quate mode of introducing the main character, "young Hamlet,"
upon whom is transferred all the interest excited for the acts and
concerns of the king his father" (Coleridge).—H. N. H.

Scene II

A room of state in the castle.

*Flourish.   Enter the King, Queen, Hamlet,
Polonius, Laertes, Voltimand, Cornelius,
Lords, and Attendants.*

King. Though yet of Hamlet our dear brother's
    death
   The memory be green, and that it us befitted
   To bear our hearts in grief and our whole king-
    dom
   To be contracted in one brow of woe,
   Yet so far hath discretion fought with nature
   That we with wisest sorrow think on him,
   Together with remembrance of ourselves.
   Therefore our sometime sister, now our queen,
   The imperial jointress to this warlike state,
   Have we, as 'twere with a defeated joy,—   10
   With an auspicious and a dropping eye,
   With mirth in funeral and with dirge in mar-
    riage,
   In equal scale weighing delight and dole,—
   Taken to wife: nor have we herein barr'd
   Your better wisdoms, which have freely gone
   With this affair along.   For all, our thanks.
   Now follows, that you know, young Fortinbras,

9. *"to";* the reading of Qq.; Ff., *"of."*—I. G.

11. *"dropping eye";* the same thought occurs in *The Winter's Tale:*
"She had *one eye declin'd* for the loss of her husband, *another
elevated* that the oracle was fulfill'd." There is an old proverbial
phrase, "To laugh with one eye, and cry with the other."—H. N. H.

Holding a weak supposal of our worth,
Or thinking by our late dear brother's death
Our state to be disjoint and out of frame,   20
Colleagued with this dream of his advantage,
He hath not fail'd to pester us with message,
Importing the surrender of those lands
Lost by his father, with all bonds of law,
To our most valiant brother.   So much for him.
Now for ourself, and for this time of meeting:
Thus much the business is: we have here writ
To Norway, uncle of young Fortinbras,—
Who, impotent and bed-rid, scarcely hears
Of this his nephew's purpose,—to suppress   30
His further gait herein; in that the levies,
The lists and full proportions, are all made
Out of his subject: and we here dispatch
You, good Cornelius, and you, Voltimand,
For bearers of this greeting to old Norway,
Giving to you no further personal power
To business with the king more than the scope
Of these delated articles allow.
Farewell, and let your haste commend your
    duty.
Cor. ⎫   In that and all things will we show our
Vol. ⎭   duty.   40
King.   We doubt it nothing: heartily farewell.
                    [*Exeunt Voltimand and Cornelius.*
And now, Laertes, what 's the news with you?
You told us of some suit; what is 't, Laertes?
You cannot speak of reason to the Dane,
And lose your voice: what wouldst thou beg,
    Laertes,

18

That shall not be my offer, not thy asking? *KING TELL*
The head is not more native to the heart, *LAER THAT*
The hand more instrumental to the mouth, *HIS FATHER*
Than is the throne of Denmark to thy father. *IS SUCH A*
What wouldst thou have, Laertes? *GOOD FRIE*
WHAT EVER LAER
WANTS HES
GO IT

Laer.   My dread lord,   50
    Your leave and favor to return to France,
    From whence though willingly I came to Den-
      mark,
    To show my duty in your coronation,
    Yet now, I must confess, that duty done,
    My thoughts and wishes bend again toward
      France
    And bow them to your gracious leave and
      pardon.
King. Have you your father's leave? What says
      Polonius?
Pol. He hath, my lord, wrung from me my slow
      leave
    By laborsome petition, and at last
    Upon his will I seal'd my hard consent: 60
    I do beseech you, give him leave to go.
King. Take thy fair hour, Laertes; time be thine,
    And thy best graces spend it at thy will!
    But now, my cousin Hamlet, and my son,—
Ham. [*Aside*] A little more than kin, and less
      than kind. *HAM DOESNT WANT TO BE CEIATED*
      TO KING.

58-60. Omitted in Ff.—I. G.

62. *"Take thy fair hour"*; the king's speech may be thus explained: "Take an auspicious hour, Laertes; be your time your
own, and thy best virtues guide thee in spending of it at thy will."
Johnson thought that we should read, "And *my* best graces." The
editors had rendered this passage obscure by placing a colon at
graces.—H. N. H.

King. How is it that the clouds still hang on you?

Ham. Not so, my lord; I am too much i' the sun.

Queen. Good Hamlet, cast thy nighted color off,
And let thine eye look like a friend on Den-
    mark.
Do not for ever with thy vailed lids   70
Seek for thy noble father in the dust:
Thou know'st 'tis common; all that lives must
    die,
Passing through nature to eternity.

Ham. Aye, madam, it is common.

Queen.   If it be,
Why seems it so particular with thee?

Ham. Seems, madam! nay, it is; I know not 'seems.'
'Tis not alone my inky cloak, good mother,
Nor customary suits of solemn black,
Nor windy suspiration of forced breath,
No, nor the fruitful river in the eye,   80
Nor the dejected havior of the visage,
Together with all forms, moods, shapes of grief,
That can denote me truly: these indeed seem,
For they are actions that a man might play:
But I have that within which passeth show;
These but the trappings and the suits of woe.

74. *"Aye, madam, it is common";* "Here observe Hamlet's delicacy
to his mother, and how the suppression prepares him for the over-
flow in the next speech, in which his character is more developed by
bringing forward his aversion to externals, and which betrays his
habit of brooding over the world within him, coupled with a prod-
igality of beautiful words, which are the half-embodyings of
thought, and are more than thought, and have an outness, a reality
sui generis, and yet retain their correspondence and shadowy af-
finity to the images and movements within. Note, also, Hamlet's
silence to the long speech of the King, which follows, and his re-
spectful, but general, answer to his mother" (Coleridge).—H. N. H.

King. 'Tis sweet and commendable in your nature,
    Hamlet,
    To give these mourning duties to your father:
    But, you must know, your father lost a father,
    That father lost, lost his, and the survivor
        bound   90
    In filial obligation for some term
    To do obsequious sorrow: but to persevere
    In obstinate condolement is a course
    Of impious stubbornness; 'tis unmanly grief:
    It shows a will most incorrect to heaven,
    A heart unfortified, a mind impatient,
    An understanding simple and unschool'd:
    For what we know must be and is as common
    As any the most vulgar thing to sense,
    Why should we in our peevish opposition   100
    Take it to heart? Fie! 'tis a fault to heaven,
    A fault against the dead, a fault to nature,
    To reason most absurd, whose common theme
    Is death of fathers, and who still hath cried,
    From the first corse till he that died to-day,
    'This must be so.' We pray you, throw to earth
    This unprevailing woe, and think of us
    As of a father: for let the world take note,
    You are the most immediate to our throne,
    And with no less nobility of love   110
    Than that which dearest father bears his son
    Do I impart toward you. For your intent
    In going back to school in Wittenberg,
    It is most retrograde to our desire:
    And we beseech you, bend you to remain
    Here in the cheer and comfort of our eye,

Our chiefest courtier, cousin and our son.

Queen. Let not thy mother lose her prayers, Ham-
    let:

I pray thee, stay with us; go not to Wittenberg.

Ham. I shall in all my best obey you, madam. 120

King. Why, 'tis a loving and a fair reply:

Be as ourself in Denmark. Madam, come;

This gentle and unforced accord of Hamlet

Sits smiling to my heart: in grace whereof,

No jocund health that Denmark drinks to-day,

But the great cannon to the clouds shall tell,

And the king's rouse the heaven shall bruit
    again,

Re-speaking earthly thunder. Come away.

            [Flourish. Exeunt all but Hamlet.

Ham. O, that this too too solid flesh would melt,

Thaw and resolve itself into a dew!   130

Or that the Everlasting had not fix'd

His canon 'gainst self-slaughter! O God! God!

 How weary, stale, flat and unprofitable

Seem to me all the uses of this world!

Fie on't! ah fie! 'tis an unweeded garden,

That grows to seed; things rank and gross in
    nature

Possess it merely. That it should come to this!

But two months dead! nay, not so much, not
    two:

So excellent a king; that was, to this,

Hyperion to a satyr: so loving to my mother, 140

That he might not beteem the winds of heaven

Visit her face too roughly. Heaven and earth!

125. *"Denmark"; i. e.* the king.—C. H. H.

Must I remember? why, she would hang on him,
As if increase of appetite had grown
By what it fed on: and yet, within a month—
Let me not think on't—Frailty, thy name is
     woman!—
A little month, or ere those shoes were old
With which she follow'd my poor father's body,
Like Niobe, all tears:—why she, even she,—
O God! a beast that wants discourse of
     reason   150
Would have mourn'd longer,—married with my
     uncle,
My father's brother, but no more like my father
Than I to Hercules: within a month;
Ere yet the salt of most unrighteous tears
Had left the flushing in her galled eyes,
She married. O, most wicked speed, to post
With such dexterity to incestuous sheets!
It is not, nor it cannot come to good:
But break, my heart, for I must hold my
     tongue!

Enter Horatio, Marcellus, and Bernado.

159. *"I must hold my tongue";* "This *tædium vitæ* is a common
oppression on minds cast in the Hamlet mould, and is caused by
disproportionate mental exertion, which necessitates exhaustion of
bodily feeling. Where there is a just coincidence of external and
internal action, pleasure is always the result; but where the former
is deficient, and the mind's appetency of the ideal is unchecked,
realities will seem cold and unmoving. In such cases, passion combines itself with the indefinite alone. In this mood of his mind, the
relation of the appearance of his father's spirit in arms is made all at
once to Hamlet:—it is—Horatio's speech, in particular—a perfect
model of the true style of dramatic narrative; the purest poetry, and
yet in the most natural language, equally remote from the ink-horn
and the plough" (Coleridge).—H. N. H.

Hor. Hail to your lordship!

Ham.   I am glad to see you well: 160
 Horatio,—or I do forget myself.

Hor. The same, my lord, and your poor servant
 ever.

Ham. Sir, my good friend; I'll change that name
 with you:
 And what make you from Wittenberg, Horatio?
 Marcellus?

Mar. My good lord?

Ham. I am very glad to see you. [*To Ber.*]
 Good even, sir.
 But what, in faith, make you from Wittenberg?

Hor. A truant disposition, good my lord.

Ham. I would not hear your enemy say so, 170
 Nor shall you do my ear that violence,
 To make it truster of your own report
 Against yourself: I know you are no truant.
 But what is your affair in Elsinore?
 We'll teach you to drink deep ere you depart.

Hor. My lord, I came to see your father's funeral.

Ham. I pray thee, do not mock me, fellow-student;
 I think it was to see my mother's wedding.

Hor. Indeed, my lord, it follow'd hard upon.

167. The words, *"Good even, sir,"* are evidently addressed to Bernardo, whom Hamlet has not before known; but as he now meets
him in company with old acquaintances, like a true gentleman, as
he is, he gives him a salutation of kindness. Some editors have
changed *even* to *morning,* because Marcellus has said before of
Hamlet,—"I this *morning* know where we shall find him." It needs
but be remembered that *good even* was the common salutation after
noon.—"What *make* you?" in the preceding speech, is the old language for, "what *do* you?"—H. N. H.

24

Ham. Thrift, thrift, Horatio! the funeral baked-
          meats   180
      Did coldly furnish forth the marriage tables.
      Would I had met my dearest foe in heaven
      Or ever I had seen that day, Horatio!
      My father!—methinks I see my father.
Hor. O where, my lord?
Ham.   In my mind's eye, Horatio.
Hor. I saw him once; he was a goodly king.
Ham. He was a man, take him for all in all,
      I shall not look upon his like again.
Hor. My lord, I think I saw him yesternight.
Ham. Saw? who?   190
Hor. My lord, the king your father.
Ham.   The king my father!
Hor. Season your admiration for a while
      With an attent ear, till I may deliver,
      Upon the witness of these gentlemen,
      This marvel to you.
Ham.   For God's love, let me hear.
Hor. Two nights together had these gentlemen,
      Marcellus and Bernardo, on their watch,
      In the dead vast and middle of the night,

187. *"He was a man";* some would read this as if it were pointed
thus: "He was a man: take him for all in all," &c.; laying marked
stress on *man,* as if it were meant to intimate a correction of
Horatio's *"goodly king."* There is, we suspect, no likelihood that the
Poet had any such thought, as there is no reason why he should
have had.—H. N. H.

190. *"Saw? who?";* the original has no mark after "saw." In
colloquial language, it was common, as indeed it still is, thus to use
the nominative where strict grammar would require the objective.
Modern editions embellish the two words with various pointing; as
above: "Saw? who?" or thus: "Saw! who?"—H. N. H.

Been thus encounter'd. A figure like your
    father,
Armed at point exactly, cap-a-pe,   200
Appears before them, and with solemn march
Goes slow and stately by them: thrice he walk'd
By their oppress'd and fear-surprised eyes,
Within his truncheon's length; whilst they,
    distill'd
Almost to jelly with the act of fear,
Stand dumb, and speak not to him. This to me
In dreadful secrecy impart they did;
And I with them the third night kept the
    watch:
Where, as they had deliver'd, both in time,
Form of the thing, each word made true and
    good,   210
The apparition comes: I knew your father;
These hands are not more like.
Ham.   But where was this?
Mar. My lord, upon the platform where we
    watch'd.
Ham. Did you not speak to it?
Hor.   My lord, I did.
But answer made it none: yet once methought
It lifted up its head and did address
Itself to motion, like as it would speak:

217. *"like as it would speak";* "It is a most inimitable circumstance in Shakespeare so to have managed this popular idea, as to
make the Ghost, which has been so long obstinately silent, and of
course must be dismissed by the morning, begin or rather prepare
to speak, and to be interrupted at the very critical time of the
crowing of a cock. Another poet, according to custom, would have
suffered his ghost tamely to vanish, without contriving this start,
which is like a start of guilt: to say nothing of the aggravation of

But even then the morning cock crew loud,
And at the sound it shrunk in haste away
And vanish'd from our sight.
Ham.   'Tis very strange. 220
Hor. As I do live, my honor'd lord, 'tis true,
And we did think it writ down in our duty
To let you know of it.
Ham. Indeed, indeed, sirs, but this troubles me.
Hold you the watch to-night?
Mar.
Ber. }   We do, my lord.
Ham. Arm'd, say you?
Mar.
Ber. }   Arm'd, my lord.
Ham.   From top to toe?
Mar.
Ber. } My lord, from head to foot.
Ham. Then saw you not his face?
Hor. O, yes, my lord; he wore his beaver up. 230
Ham. What, look'd he frowningly?
Hor. A countenance more in sorrow than in anger.
Ham. Pale, or red?
Hor. Nay, very pale.
Ham.   And fix'd his eyes upon you?
Hor. Most constantly.
Ham.   I would I had been there.
Hor. It would have much amazed you.
Ham. Very like, very like. Stay'd it long?
Hor. While one with moderate haste might tell a
hundred.

the future suspense occasioned by this preparation to speak, and to
impart some mysterious secret. Less would have been expected if
nothing had been promised" (T. Warton).—H. N. H.

Mar. }
Ber. } Longer, longer.

Hor. Not when I saw't.

Ham.   His beard was grizzled? no? 240

Hor. It was, as I have seen it in his life,
     A sable silver'd.

Ham.   I will watch to-night;
     Perchance 'twill walk again.

Hor.   I warrant it will.

Ham. If it assume my noble father's person,
     I 'll speak to it, though hell itself should gape
     And bid me hold my peace. I pray you all,
     If you have hitherto conceal'd this sight,
     Let it be tenable in your silence still,
     And whatsoever else shall hap to-night,
     Give it an understanding, but no tongue: 250
     I will requite your loves.   So fare you well:
     Upon the platform, 'twixt eleven and twelve,
     I 'll visit you,

All.   Our duty to your honor.

Ham. Your loves, as mine to you: farewell.
                              [*Exeunt all but Hamlet.*
     My father's spirit in arms! all is not well;
     I doubt some foul play: would the night were
         come!
     Till then sit still, my soul: foul deeds will rise,
     Though all the earth o'erwhelm them, to men's
         eyes.   [*Exit.*

HAMLET: I'll speak to it, though hell itself should gape—
Act I, Scene 2.

Scene III

A room in Polonius's house.

Enter Laertes and Ophelia.

Laer. My necessaries are embark'd: farewell:
    And, sister, as the winds give benefit
    And convoy is assistant, do not sleep,
    But let me hear from you.
Oph.   Do you doubt that?
Laer. For Hamlet, and the trifling of his favor,
    Hold it a fashion, and a toy in blood,
    A violet in the youth of primy nature,
    Forward, not permanent, sweet, not lasting,
    The perfume and suppliance of a minute;
    No more.
Oph. No more but so?
Laer.   Think it no more: 10
    For nature crescent does not grow alone
    In thews and bulk; but, as this temple waxes,
    The inward service of the mind and soul
    Grows wide withal.   Perhaps he loves you now;
    And now no soil nor cautel doth besmirch
    The virtue of his will: but you must fear,
    His greatness weigh'd, his will is not his own;
    For he himself is subject to his birth:

11. *"crescent";* growing.—C. H. H.
12. *"this temple";* so Qq.; Ff., *"his temple."*—I. G.
16. *"will,"* so Qq.; Ff., *"fear."*—I. G.
18. Omitted in Qq.—I. G.
"he himself is subject to his birth"; this line is found only in the folio.—"This scene," says Coleridge, "must be regarded as one of Shakespeare's lyric movements in the play, and the skill with which

He may not, as unvalued persons do,
Carve for himself, for on his choice depends　20
The safety and health of this whole state,
And therefore must his choice be circumscribed
Unto the voice and yielding of that body
Whereof he is the head.　Then if he says he
　　loves you,
It fits your wisdom so far to believe it
As he in his particular act and place
May give his saying deed; which is no further
Than the main voice of Denmark goes withal.
Then weigh what loss your honor may sustain,
If with too credent ear you list his songs,　30
Or lose your heart, or your chaste treasure open
To his unmaster'd importunity.
Fear it, Ophelia, fear it, my dear sister,
And keep you in the rear of your affection,
Out of the shot and danger of desire.
The chariest maid is prodigal enough,
If she unmask her beauty to the moon:
Virtue itself 'scapes not calumnious strokes:
The canker galls the infants of the spring
Too oft before their buttons be disclosed,　40
And in the morn and liquid dew of youth
Contagious blastments are most imminent.
Be wary then; best safety lies in fear:

it is interwoven with the dramatic parts is peculiarly an excellence
with our Poet. *You experience the sensation of a pause, without the
sense of a stop.* You will observe, in Ophelia's short and general
answer to the long speech of Laertes, the natural carelessness of
innocence, which cannot think such a code of cautions and prudences
necessary to its own preservation."—H. N. H.

26. *"particular act and place,"* so Qq.; Ff., *"peculiar sect and
force."*—I. G.

Youth to itself rebels, though none else near.

Oph. I shall the effect of this good lesson keep,
    As watchman to my heart. But, good my
        brother,
    Do not, as some ungracious pastors do,
    Show me the steep and thorny way to heaven,
    Whilst, like a puff'd and reckless libertine,
    Himself the primrose path of dalliance treads 50
    And recks not his own rede.

Laer.   O, fear me not.
    I stay too long: but here my father comes.

Enter Polonius.

    A double blessing is a double grace;
    Occasion smiles upon a second leave.

Pol. Yet here, Laertes! Aboard, aboard, for
        shame!
    The wind sits in the shoulder of your sail,
    And you are stay'd for. There; my blessing
        with thee!
    And these few precepts in thy memory
    Look thou character. Give thy thoughts no
        tongue,
    Nor any unproportion'd thought his act.   60
    Be thou familiar, but by no means vulgar.

59. Polonius' precepts have been traced back to Euphues' advice
to Philautus; the similarity is certainly striking (*vide* Rushton's
Shakespeare's Euphuism); others see in the passage a reference to
Lord Burleigh's "ten precepts," enjoined upon Robert Cecil when
about to set out on his travels (French's *Shakespeareana Genealogica,*
v. Furness, Vol. II. p. 239).—I. G.

61. *"Vulgar"* is here used in its old sense of *common.*—In the
second line below, divers modern editions have *"hooks"* instead of
hoops, the reading of all the old copies. It is not easy to see what
is gained by the unauthorized change.—H. N. H.

Those friends thou hast, and their adoption
    tried,
Grapple them to thy soul with hoops of steel,
But do not dull thy palm with entertainment
Of each new-hatch'd unfledged comrade. Be-
    ware
Of entrance to a quarrel; but being in,
Bear 't, that the opposed may beware of thee.
Give every man thy ear, but few thy voice:
Take each man's censure, but reserve thy judg-
    ment.
Costly thy habit as thy purse can buy,   70
But not express'd in fancy; rich, not gaudy:
For the apparel oft proclaims the man;
And they in France of the best rank and station
Are of a most select and generous chief in that.
Neither a borrower nor a lender be:
For loan oft loses both itself and friend,
And borrowing dulls the edge of husbandry.
This above all: to thine own self be true,
And it must follow, as the night the day,
Thou canst not then be false to any man.   80
Farewell: my blessing season this in thee!

65. *"comrade"* (accented on the second syllable), so F. 1; Qq.
(also Q. 1), *"cowrage."*—I. G.

74. *"Are of a most select and generous chief in that"*; so F. 1;
Q. 1, *"are of a most select and general chiefe in that"*; Q. 2, *"Or of a
most select and generous chiefe in that"*; the line is obviously incorrect; the simplest emendation of the many proposed is the omission
of the words *"of a"* and *"chief,"* which were probably due to
marginal corrections of *"in"* and *"best"* in the previous line:—

      "Are most select and generous in that."

(Collier *"choice"* for *"chief"*; Staunton *"sheaf,"* i. e. set, clique,
suggested by the Euphuistic phrase "gentlemen of the best sheaf").
—I. G.

Laer. Most humbly do I take my leave, my lord.

Pol. The time invites you; go, your servants tend.

Laer. Farewell, Ophelia, and remember well
What I have said to you.

Oph.   'Tis in my memory lock'd,
And you yourself shall keep the key of it.

Laer. Farewell.   [*Exit.*

Pol. What is 't, Ophelia, he hath said to you?

Oph. So please you, something touching the Lord
Hamlet.

Pol. Marry, well bethought: 90
'Tis told me, he hath very oft of late
Given private time to you, and you yourself
Have of your audience been most free and
bounteous:
If it be so—as so 'tis put on me,
And that in way of caution—I must tell you,
You do not understand yourself so clearly
As it behoves my daughter and your honor.
What is between you? give me up the truth.

Oph. He hath, my lord, of late made many tenders
Of his affection to me.   100

Pol. Affection! pooh! you speak like a green girl,
Unsifted in such perilous circumstance.
Do you believe his tenders, as you call them?

Oph. I do not know, my lord, what I should think.

Pol. Marry, I 'll teach you: think yourself a baby,
That you have ta'en these tenders for true pay,
Which are not sterling.   Tender yourself more
dearly;
Or—not to crack the wind of the poor phrase,

Running it thus—you 'll tender me a fool.

Oph. My lord, he hath importuned me with
    love   110
In honorable fashion.

Pol. Aye, fashion you may call it; go to, go to.

Oph. And hath given countenance to his speech,
    my lord,
With almos all the holy vows of heaven.

Pol. Aye, springes to catch woodcocks. I do
    know,
When the blood burns, how prodigal the soul
Lends the tongue vows: these blazes, daughter,
Giving more light than heat, extinct in both,
Even in their promise, as it is a-making,
You must not take for fire.   From this time 120
Be something scanter of your maiden presence;
Set your entreatments at a higher rate
Than a command to parley.   For Lord Ham-
    let,
Believe so much in him, that he is young,
And with a larger tether may he walk
Than may be given you: in few, Ophelia,
Do not believe his vows; for they are brokers,
Not of that dye which their investments show,
But mere implorators of unholy suits,

109. *"Running,"* Collier's conj.; Qq., *"Wrong"*; F. 1, *"Roaming"*;
Pope, *"Wronging"*; Warburton, *"Wronging"*; Theobald, *"Ranging,"*
&c.—I. G.

123. *"Than a command to parley";* "be more difficult of access, and
let the *suits to you* for that purpose be of higher respect, than a
command to parley."—H. N. H.

125. *"larger tether";* that is, with a *longer line;* a horse, fastened
by a string to a stake, is *tethered.*—H. N. H.

Breathing like sanctified and pious bawds, 130
The better to beguile. This is for all:
I would not, in plain terms, from this time
     forth,
Have you so slander any moment leisure,
As to give words or talk with the Lord Ham-
     let.
Look to 't, I charge you: come your ways.
Oph. I shall obey, my lord.   [*Exeunt.*

SCENE IV

The platform.

Enter Hamlet, Horatio, and Marcellus.

Ham.   The air bites shrewdly; it is very cold.
Hor. It is a nipping and an eager air.

130. *"bawds";* Theobald's emendation of *"bonds,"* the reading of
Qq. and F. 1.—I. G.

135. *"come your ways";* I do not believe that in this or any other
of the foregoing speeches of Polonius, Shakespeare meant to bring
out the senility or weakness of that personage's mind. In the great
ever-recurring dangers and duties of life, where to distinguish the
fit objects for the application of the maxims collected by the experience of a long life, requires no fineness of tact, as in the admoni-
tions to his son and daughter, Polonius is uniformly made re-
spectable. It is to Hamlet that Polonius is, and is meant to be,
contemptible, because, in inwardness and uncontrollable activity of
movement, Hamlet's mind is the logical contrary to that of Polonius;
and besides, Hamlet dislikes the man as false to his true allegiance
in the matter of the succession to the crown (Coleridge).—H. N. H.

2. "The unimportant conversation," says Coleridge, "with which
this scene opens, is a proof of Shakespeare's minute knowledge
of human nature. It is a well-established fact, that on the brink
of any serious enterprise, or event of moment, men almost in-
variably endeavour to elude the pressure of their own thoughts by
turning aside to trivial objects and familiar circumstances. Thus

Ham. What hour now?

Hor.   I think it lacks of twelve.

Mar. No, it is struck.

Hor. Indeed? I heard it not: it then draws near the season

Wherein the spirit held his wont to walk.

[*A flourish of trumpets, and ordnance shot off within.*

What doth this mean, my lord?

Ham. The king doth wake to-night and takes his rouse,

Keeps wassail, and the swaggering up-spring reels;

And as he drains his draughts of Rhenish down,   10

The kettle-drum and trumpet thus bray out

The triumph of his pledge.

Hor.   Is it a custom?

the dialogue on the platform begins with remarks on the coldness of the air, and inquiries, obliquely connected indeed with the expected hour of visitation, but thrown out in a seeming vacuity of topics, as to the striking of the clock and so forth. The same desire to escape from the impending thought is carried on in Hamlet's account of, and moralizing on, the Danish custom of wassailing: he runs off from the particular to the universal, and, in his repugnance to personal and individual concerns, escapes, as it were, from himself in generalizations, and smothers the impatience and uneasy feelings of the moment in abstract reasoning. Besides this, another purpose is answered;—for, by thus entangling the attention of the audience in the nice distinctions and parenthetical sentences of this speech of Hamlet, Shakespeare takes them completely by surprise on the appearance of the Ghost, which comes upon them in all the suddenness of its visionary character. Indeed, no modern writer would have dared, like Shakespeare, to have preceded this last visitation by two distinct appearances; or could have contrived that the third should rise upon the former two in impressiveness and solemnity of interest."—H. N. H.

Ham. Aye, marry, is 't:
 But to my mind, though I am native here
 And to the manner born, it is a custom
 More honor'd in the breach than the observance.
 This heavy-headed revel east and west
 Makes us traduced and tax'd of other nations:
 They clepe us drunkards, and with swinish
   phrase
 Soil our addition; and indeed it takes   20
 From our achievements, though perform'd at
   height,
 The pith and marrow of our attribute.
 So, oft it chances in particular men,
 That for some vicious mole of nature in them,
 As, in their birth,—wherein they are not guilty,
 Since nature cannot choose his origin,—
 By the o'ergrowth of some complexion,
 Oft breaking down the pales and forts of
   reason,
 Or by some habit that too much o'er-leavens
 The form of plausive manners, that these
   men,—   30
 Carrying, I say, the stamp of one defect,
 Being nature's livery, or fortune's star,—
 Their virtues else—be they as pure as grace,
 As infinite as man may undergo—
 Shall in the general censure take corruption
 From that particular fault: the dram of eale

16. *"More honor'd in the breach than the observance"; better* **to**
break than observe.—C. H. H.
17–38, omitted in F. 1 (also Q. 1).—I. G.
36–38.
         "the dram of eale
   Doth all the noble substance of a doubt
   To his own scandal";

Doth all the noble substance of a doubt
To his own scandal.

Enter Ghost.

Hor.   Look, my lord. it comes!
Ham. Angels and ministers of grace defend us!

this famous crux has taxed the ingenuity of generations of
scholars, and some fifty various readings and interpretations have
been proposed. The general meaning of the words is clear, em-
phasizing as they do the previous statement that as a man's virtues,
be they as pure as grace, shall in the general censure take corruption from one particular fault, even so "the dram of eale" reduces
all the noble substance to its own low level.

The difficulty of the passage lies in (i.) *"eale"* and (ii.) *"doth
. . . of a doubt";* a simple explanation of (1) is that *"eale"=
"e'il," i. e. "evil"* (similarly in Q. 2, II. ii. 627, *"deale"="de'ile"=
"devil").* The chief objection to this plausible conjecture is that
one would expect something rather more definite than "dram of
evil"; it is said, however, that *"eale"* is still used in the sense of
"reproach" in the western counties. Theobald proposed "base," probably having in mind the lines in Cymbeline (III. v. 88):—

> *"From whose so many weights of baseness cannot
> A dram of worth be drawn."*

As regards (ii.), no very plausible emendation has been proposed;
"of a doubt" has been taken to be a printer's error for *"often dout,"*
"oft endoubt," "offer doubt," "oft work out," &c. To the many
questions which these words have called forth, the present writer is
rash enough to add one more:—Could, perhaps, "doth of a doubt"=
deprives of the benefit of a doubt? Is there any instance of "do"
in XVIth century English ="deprive"; the usage is common in
modern English slang.—I. G.

38. "In addition to all the other excellences of Hamlet's speech
concerning the wassel-music,—so finely revealing the predominant
idealism, the ratiocinative meditativeness of his character,— it has
the advantage of giving nature and probability to the impassioned
continuity of the speech instantly directed to the Ghost. The *mo-
mentum* had been given to his mental activity; the full current of
the thoughts and words had set in; and the very forgetfulness, in
the fervour of his argumentation, of the purpose of which he was
there, aided in preventing the appearance from benumbing the
mind. Consequently, it acted as a new impulse,— a sudden stroke
which increased the velocity of the body already in motion, whilst

Be thou a spirit of health or goblin damn'd, 40
Bring with thee airs from heaven or blasts from
    hell,
Be thy intents wicked or charitable,
Thou comest in such a questionable shape
That I will speak to thee: I 'll call thee Hamlet,
King, father, royal Dane: O, answer me!
Let me not burst in ignorance; but tell
Why thy canonized bones, hearsed in death,
Have burst their cerements; why the sepulcher,
Wherein we saw thee quietly inurn'd,
Hath oped his ponderous and marble jaws, 50
To cast thee up again.   What may this mean,
That thou, dead corse, again, in complete steel,
Revisit'st thus the glimpses of the moon,
Making night hideous; and we fools of nature
So horridly to shake our disposition
With thoughts beyond the reaches of our souls?
Say, why is this? wherefore? what should we
    do?   [*Ghost beckons Hamlet.*
Hor. It beckons you to go away with it,
    As if it some impartment did desire
    To you alone.

it altered the direction. The co-presence of Horatio and Marcellus
is most judiciously contrived; for it renders the courage of Hamlet,
and his impetuous eloquence, perfectly intelligible. The knowledge
—the sensation—of human auditors acts as a support and a stimula-
tion *a tergo,* while the front of the mind, the whole consciousness of
the speaker, is filled, yea, absorbed, by the apparition. Add, too,
that the apparition itself has, by its previous appearances, been
brought nearer to a thing of this world. This accrescence of objec-
tivity in a ghost that yet retains all its ghostly attributes and fearful
subjectivity, is truly wonderful" (Coleridge).—H. N. H.

  52. *"in complete steel";* it appears from Olaus Wormius that it
was the custom to bury the Danish kings in their armor.—H. N. H.

Mar.   Look, with what courteous action 60
   It waves you to a more removed ground:
   But do not go with it.
Hor.   No, by no means.
Ham. It will not speak; then I will follow it.
Hor. Do not, my lord.
Ham.   Why, what should be the fear?
   I do not set my life at a pin's fee;
   And for my soul, what can it do to that,
   Being a thing immortal as itself?
   It waves me forth again: I 'll follow it.
Hor. What if it tempt you toward the flood, my
     lord,
   Or to the dreadful summit of the cliff   70
   That beetles o'er his base into the sea,
   And there assume some other horrible form,
   Which might deprive your sovereignty of
     reason
   And draw you into madness? think of it:
   The very place puts toys of desperation,
   Without more motive, into every brain
   That looks so many fathoms to the sea
   And hears it roar beneath.
Ham.   It waves me still.
   Go on; I 'll follow thee.
Mar. You shall not go, my lord.
Ham.   Hold off your hands. 80
Hor. Be ruled; you shall not go.
Ham.   My fate cries out,
   And makes each petty artery in this body
   As hardy as the Nemean lion's nerve.

75–78, omitted in F. 1.—I. G.
40

Still am I call'd, unhand me, gentlemen;
By heaven, I 'll make a ghost of him that lets
    me:
I say, away!   Go on; I 'll follow thee.

                [Exeunt Ghost and Hamlet.

Hor. He waxes desperate with imagination.
Mar. Let 's follow; 'tis not fit thus to obey him.
Hor. Have after.   To what issue will this come?
Mar. Something is rotten in the state of Den-
    mark.   90
Hor. Heaven will direct it.
Mar.   Nay, let 's follow him.
                           [Exeunt.

SCENE V

Another part of the platform.

Enter Ghost and Hamlet.

Ham. Whither wilt thou lead me? speak; I 'll go
    no further.
Ghost. Mark me.
Ham.   I will.
Ghost.   My hour is almost come,
When I to sulphurous and tormenting flames
Must render up myself.
Ham.   Alas, poor ghost!
Ghost. Pity me not, but lend thy serious hearing
To what I shall unfold.

91. *"Heaven will direct it";* Marcellus answers Horatio's question,
"To what issue will this come?" and Horatio also answers it himself with pious resignation, "Heaven will direct it."—H. N. H.

Ham.   Speak; I am bound to hear.

Ghost. So art thou to revenge, when thou shalt hear.

Ham. What?

Ghost. I am thy father's spirit;

Doom'd for a certain term to walk the night, 10
And for the day confined to fast in fires,
Till the foul crimes done in my days of nature
Are burnt and purged away. But that I am forbid
To tell the secrets of my prison-house,
I could a tale unfold whose lightest word
Would harrow up thy soul, freeze thy young blood,
Make thy two eyes, like stars, start from their spheres,
Thy knotted and combined locks to part
And each particular hair to stand an end,
Like quills upon the fretful porpentine: 20
But this eternal blazon must not be
To ears of flesh and blood. List, list, O, list!
If thou didst ever thy dear father love—

11. *"fast in fires";* the spirit being supposed to feel the same desires and appetites as when clothed in the flesh, the pains and punishments promised by the ancient moral teachers are often of a sensual nature. Chaucer in the *Persones Tale* says, "The misese of hell shall be *in defaute of mete and drinke.*" So, too, in *The Wyll of the Devyll:* "Thou shalt lye in frost and fire, with sicknes and hunger."—Heath proposed *"lasting* fires," and such is the change in Collier's second folio.—H. N. H.

13. *"burnt and purged";* Gawin Douglas really changes the Platonic hell into "the punytion of the saulis in purgatory." "It is a nedeful thyng to suffer paines and torment;—sum in the wyndis, sum under the watter, and in the fire uther sum: thus the mony vices contrakkit in the corpis *be done away and purgit.*"—H. N. H.

22. *"List, list, O, list!"* so Qqs.; F. 1, *"list, Hamlet, oh list.*'—I. G.

Ham. O God!

Ghost. Revenge his foul and most unnatural
    murder.

Ham. Murder!

Ghost. Murder most foul, as in the best it is,
    But this most foul, strange, and unnatural.

Ham. Haste me to know 't, that I, with wings as
    swift
    As meditation or the thoughts of love,   30
    May sweep to my revenge.

Ghost.   I find thee apt;
    And duller shouldst thou be than the fat weed
    That roots itself in ease on Lethe wharf,
    Wouldst thou not stir in this. Now, Hamlet,
    hear:
    'Tis given out that, sleeping in my orchard,
    A serpent stung me; so the whole ear of Den-
    mark
    Is by a forged process of my death
    Rankly abused: but know, thou noble youth,
    The serpent that did sting thy father's life
    Now wears his crown.

Ham.   O my prophetic soul! 40
    My uncle!

Ghost. Aye, that incestuous, that adulterate beast,
    With witchcraft of his wit, with traitorous
    gifts,—
    O wicked wit and gifts, that have the power
    So to seduce!—won to his shameful lust

37. *"process of my death";* narrative of my death.—C. H. H.

40. *"my prophetic soul";* cf. i. 2. 255, "I doubt some foul play."—
C. H. H.

The will of my most seeming-virtuous queen:
O Hamlet, what a falling-off was there!
From me, whose love was of that dignity
That it went hand in hand even with the vow
I made to her in marriage; and to decline   50
Upon a wretch, whose natural gifts were poor
To those of mine!
But virtue, as it never will be moved,
Though lewdness court it in a shape of heaven,
So lust, though to a radiant angel link'd,
Will sate itself in a celestial bed
And prey on garbage.
But, soft! methinks I scent the morning air;
Brief let me be.   Sleeping within my orchard,
My custom always of the afternoon,   60
Upon my secure hour thy uncle stole,
With juice of cursed hebenon in a vial,
And in the porches of my ears did pour
The leperous distilment; whose effect
Holds such an enmity with blood of man
That swift as quicksilver it courses through
The natural gates and alleys of the body;
And with a sudden vigor it doth posset
And curd, like eager droppings into milk,
The thin and wholesome blood: so did it
     mine;   70
And a most instant tetter bark'd about,
Most lazar-like, with vile and loathsome crust,
All my smooth body.
Thus was I, sleeping, by a brother's hand
Of life, of crown, of queen, at once dispatch'd:
Cut off even in the blossoms of my sin,

Unhousel'd, disappointed, unaneled;
No reckoning made, but sent to my account
With all my imperfections on my head:
O, horrible! O, horrible! most horrible!   80
If thou hast nature in thee, bear it not;
Let not the royal bed of Denmark be
A couch for luxury and damned incest.
But, howsoever thou pursuest this act,
Taint not thy mind, nor let thy soul contrive
Against thy mother aught: leave her to heaven,
And to those thorns that in her bosom lodge,
To prick and sting her.   Fare thee well at once!
The glow-worm shows the matin to be near,
And 'gins to pale his uneffectual fire: 90
Adieu, adieu, adieu! remember me.   [*Exit.*

Ham. O all you host of heaven! O earth! what
      else?
And shall I couple hell?   O, fie!   Hold, hold,
      my heart;
And you, my sinews, grow not instant old,
But bear me stiffly up.   Remember thee!
Aye, thou poor ghost, while memory holds a
      seat
In this distracted globe.   Remember thee!
Yea, from the table of my memory
I 'll wipe away all trivial fond records,
All saws of books, all forms, all pressures
      past,   100
That youth and observation copied there;
And thy commandment all alone shall live
Within the book and volume of my brain,
Unmix'd with baser matter: yes, by heaven!

O most pernicious woman!
O villain, villain, smiling, damned villain!
My tables,—meet it is I set it down,
That one may smile, and smile, and be a
    villain;
At least I'm sure it may be so in Denmark.
                       [Writing.
So, uncle, there you are. Now to my word; 110
It is 'Adieu, adieu! remember me.'
I have sworn 't.

Hor.
Mar. } *[Within]* My lord, my lord!

      Enter Horatio and Marcellus.

Mar.   Lord Hamlet!
Hor.   Heaven secure him!
Ham. So be it!
Mar. Illo, ho, ho, my lord!
Ham. Hillo, ho, ho, boy! come, bird, come.
Mar. How is 't, my noble lord?
Hor.   What news, my lord?
Ham. O, wonderful!
Hor. Good my lord, tell it.
Ham.   No; you will reveal it.
Hor. Not I, my lord, by heaven.

108. *"and be a villain";* "I remember nothing equal to this burst,
unless it be the first speech of Prometheus, in the Greek drama,
after the *exit* of Vulcan and the two Afrites. But Shakespeare
alone could have produced the vow of Hamlet to make his memory
a blank of all maxims and generalized truths that 'observation had
copied there,'—followed immediately by the speaker noting down
the generalized fact, 'That one may smile, and smile, and be a
villain" (Coleridge).—H. N. H.

116. *"Hillo, ho, ho";* Hamlet imitates the falconer's call to his
hawk.—C. H. H.

46

Mar.   Nor I, my lord.   120

Ham. How say you, then; would heart of man
         once think it?

     But you' ll be secret?

Hor. ⎫
Mar. ⎭   Aye, by heaven, my lord.

Ham. There 's ne'er a villain dwelling in all Den-
         mark

     But he 's an arrant knave.

Hor. There needs no ghost, my lord, come from the
         grave

     To tell us this.

Ham.   Why, right; you are i' the right;

     And so, without more circumstance at all,

     I hold it fit that we shake hands and part:

     You, as your business and desire shall point you;

     For every man hath business and desire,   130

     Such as it is; and for my own poor part,

     Look you, I 'll go pray.

Hor. These are but wild and whirling words, my
         lord.

Ham. I 'm sorry they offend you, heartily;

     Yes, faith, heartily.

Hor.   There 's no offense, my lord.

Ham. Yes, by Saint Patrick, but there is, Horatio,

     And much offense too. Touching this vision
         here,

     It is an honest ghost, that let me tell you:

     For your desire to know what is between us,

     O'ermaster 't as you may.   And now, good
         friends,   140

     As you are friends, scholars and soldiers,

47

Give me one poor request.

Hor. What is 't, my lord? we will.

Ham. Never make known what you have seen to-
night.

Mar.}
Hor.} My lord, we will not.

Ham. 　　　　　　　　　　　Nay, but swear 't.

Hor. 　　　　　　　　　　　　　　　　In faith,
My lord, not I.

Mar. 　　　　　　　Nor I, my lord, in faith.

Ham. Upon my sword.

Mar. 　　　　　We have sworn, my lord, already.

Ham. Indeed, upon my sword, indeed.

Ghost. [*Beneath*] Swear.

Ham. Ah, ha, boy! say'st thou so? art thou there,
truepenny?　　　　　　　　　　　　　　　150
Come on: you hear this fellow in the cellarage:
Consent to swear.

Hor. 　　　　　　Propose the oath, my lord.

Ham. Never to speak of this that you have seen,
Swear by my sword.

Ghost. [*Beneath*] Swear.

Ham. Hic et ubique? then we 'll shift our ground.
Come hither, gentlemen,

148. *"upon my sword";* the custom of swearing by the sword, or
rather by the cross at the upper end of it, is very ancient. The
name of Jesus was not unfrequently inscribed on the handle. The
allusions to this custom are very numerous in our old writers.—
H. N. H.

149. *"swear";* here again we follow the folio, with which the first
quarto agrees. In the other quartos, this speech reads, "Swear *by
his sword";* and the last two lines of the preceding speech are
transposed. In the next line, the folio has *ground* instead of *earth.*
—H. N. H.

And lay your hands again upon my sword:
Never to speak of this that you have heard,
Swear by my sword.   160

Ghost. [*Beneath*] Swear.

Ham. Well said, old mole! canst work i' the earth
    so fast?
A worthy pioner! Once more remove, good
    friends.

Hor. O day and night, but this is wondrous
    strange!

Ham. And therefore as a stranger give it welcome.
There are more things in heaven and earth,
    Horatio,
Than are dreamt of in your philosophy.
But come;
Here, as before, never, so help you mercy,
How strange or odd soe'er I bear myself,   170
As I perchance hereafter shall think meet
To put an antic disposition on,
That you, at such times seeing me, never shall,
With arms encumber'd thus, or this head-shake,
Or by pronouncing of some doubtful phrase,
As 'Well, well, we know,' or 'We could, an if
    we would,'
Or 'If we list to speak,' or 'There be, an if they
    might,'
Or such ambiguous giving out, to note

167. *"your philosophy"*; so read all the quartos; the folio, *"our*
philosophy." The passage has had so long a lease of familiarity,
as it stands in the text, that it seems best not to change it. Besides,
your gives a nice characteristic shade of meaning that is lost in *our*.
Of course it is not *Horatio's* philosophy, but your *philosophy,* that
Hamlet is speaking of.—H. N. H.

That you know aught of me: this not to do,

So grace and mercy at your most need help
you,   180

Swear.

Ghost. [*Beneath*] Swear.

Ham. Rest, rest, perturbed spirit! [*They swear.*]
So, gentlemen,

With all my love I do commend me to you:

And what so poor a man as Hamlet is

May do, to express his love and friending to
you,

God willing, shall not lack. Let us go in together;

And still your fingers on your lips, I pray.

The time is out of joint: O cursed spite,

That ever I was born to set it right!   190

Nay, come, let's go together.   [*Exeunt.*

187. *"Let us go in together";* "This part of the scene after Hamlet's interview with the Ghost has been charged with an improbable
eccentricity. But the truth is, that after the mind has been
stretched beyond its usual pitch and tone, it must either sink into
exhaustion and inanity, or seek relief by change. It is thus well
known, that persons conversant in deeds of cruelty contrive to escape
from conscience by connecting something of the ludicrous with them,
and by inventing grotesque terms and a certain technical phraseology
to disguise the horror of their practices. Indeed, paradoxical as it
may appear, the terrible by a law of the human mind always
touches on the verge of the ludicrous. Both arise from the perception of something out of the common order of things,—something,
in fact, out of its place; and if from this we can abstract the
danger, the uncommonness alone will remain, and the sense of the
ridiculous be excited. The close alliance of these opposites—they
are not contraries—appears from the circumstance, that laughter
is equally the expression of extreme anguish and horror as of joy:
as there are tears of sorrow and tears of joy, so there is a laugh
of terror and a laugh of merriment. These complex causes will
naturally have produced in Hamlet the disposition to escape from
his own feelings of the overwhelming and supernatural by a wild
transition to the ludicrous,—a sort of cunning bravado, bordering on the flights of delirium" (Coleridge).—H. N. H.

ACT SECOND

SCENE I

A room in Polonius's house.

Enter Polonius and Reynaldo.

Pol. Give him this money and these notes, Reynaldo.

Rey. I will, my lord.

Pol. You shall do marvelous wisely, good Reynaldo,

    Before you visit him, to make inquire

    Of his behavior.

Rey.   My lord, I did intend it.

Pol. Marry, well said, very well said. Look you, sir,

    Inquire me first what Danskers are in Paris,

    And how, and who, what means, and where they keep,

    What company, at what expense, and finding

    By this encompassment and drift of question 10

    That they do know my son, come you more nearer

    Than your particular demands will touch it:

The stage direction in Qq.:—*Enter old Polonius, with his man or two;* Ff., *Polonius and Reynaldo;* in Q. 1, *Reynaldo* is called *Montano,* hence perhaps the reading of later Qq.—I. G.

4. *"to make inquire";* so Qq.; Ff. read, *"you make inquiry."*—I. G.

Take you, as 'twere, some distant knowledge of
    him,
As thus, 'I know his father and his friends,
And in part him:' do you mark this, Reynaldo?
Rey. Aye, very well, my lord.
Pol. 'And in part him; but' you may say, 'not well:
But if 't be he I mean, he 's very wild,
Addicted so and so;' and there put on him
What forgeries you please; marry, none so
    rank   20
As may dishonor him; take heed of that;
But, sir, such wanton, wild and usual slips
As are companions noted and most known
To youth and liberty.
Rey.   As gaming, my lord.
Pol. Aye, or drinking, fencing, swearing, quarrel-
    ing,
Drabbing: you may go so far.
Rey. My lord, that would dishonor him.
Pol. Faith, no; as you may season it in the charge.
You must not put another scandal on him,
That he is open to incontinency;   30
That 's not my meaning: but breathe his faults
    so quaintly
That they may seem the taints of liberty,
The flash and outbreak of a fiery mind,
A savageness in unreclaimed blood,
Of general assault.

27. *"fencing, swearing, quarreling";* "the cunning of *fencers* is
now applied to *quarrelling;* they thinke themselves no men, if, for
stirring of a straw, they prove not their valure uppon some bodies
fleshe." (Gosson's *Schole of Abuse,* 1579).—H. N. H.

Rey.   But, my good lord,—

Pol. Wherefore should you do this?

Rey.   Aye, my lord,
    I would know that.

Pol.   Marry, sir, here 's my drift,
    And I believe it is a fetch of warrant:
    You laying these slight sullies on my son,
    As 'twere a thing a little soil'd i' the working, 40
    Mark you,
    Your party in converse, him you would sound,
    Having ever seen in the prenominate crimes
    The youth you breathe of guilty, be assured
    He closes with you in this consequence;
    'Good sir,' or so, or 'friend,' or 'gentleman,'
    According to the phrase or the addition
    Of man and country.

Rey.   Very good, my lord.

Pol. And then, sir, does he this—he does—what
    was I about to say? By the mass, I was 50
    about to say something: where did I leave?

Rey. At 'closes in the consequence,' at 'friend
    or so,' and 'gentleman.'

Pol. At 'closes in the consequence,' aye, marry;
    He closes with you thus: 'I know the gentleman;
    I saw him yesterday, or t' other day,
    Or then, or then, with such, or such, and, as you
      say,
    There was a' gaming, there o'ertook in 's rouse,
    There falling out at tennis:' or perchance,
    'I saw him enter such a house of sale,'   60
    Videlicet, a brothel, or so forth.
    See you now;

Your bait of falsehood takes this carp of truth:
And thus do we of wisdom and of reach,
With windlasses and with assays of bias,
By indirections find directions out:
So, by my former lecture and advice,
Shall you my son.　You have me, have you not?
Rey. My lord, I have.
Pol.　　　　　　　　God be wi' ye; fare ye well.
Rey. Good, my lord!　　　　　　　　　　70
Pol. Observe his inclination in yourself.
Rey. I shall, my lord.
Pol. And let him ply his music.
Rey.　　　　　　　　　Well, my lord.
Pol. Farewell!　　　　　　　　[*Exit Reynaldo.*

Enter Ophelia.

　　　　How now, Ophelia! what's the matter?
Oph. O, my lord, my lord, I have been so affrighed!
Pol. With what, i' the name of God?
Oph. My lord, as I was sewing in my closet,
Lord Hamlet, with his doublet all unbraced,
No hat upon his head, his stockings foul'd,
Ungarter'd and down-gyved to his ankle;　80
Pale as his shirt, his knees knocking each other,
And with a look so pitious in purport
As if he had been loosed out of hell
To speak of horrors, he comes before me.
Pol. Mad for thy love?
Oph.　　　　　　　　My lord, I do not know,
But truly I do fear it.

71. *"observe his inclination in you"*; that is, in your own person;
add your own observations of his conduct to these inquiries respecting him.—H. N. H.

Pol.   What said he?

Oph. He took me by the wrist and held me hard;
    Then goes he to the length of all his arm,   .
    And with his other hand thus o'er his brow,
    He falls to such perusal of my face   90
    As he would draw it.   Long stay'd he so;
    At last, a little shaking of mine arm,
    And thrice his head thus waving up and down,
    He raised a sigh so piteous and profound
    As it did seem to shatter all his bulk
    And end his being: that done, he lets me go:
    And with his head over his shoulder turn'd,
    He seem'd to find his way without his eyes;
    For out o' doors he went without their helps,
    And to the last bended their light on me.   100

Pol. Come, go with me: I will go seek the king.
    This is the very ecstasy of love;
    Whose violent property fordoes itself
    And leads the will to desperate undertakings
    As oft as any passion under heaven
    That does afflict our natures.   I am sorry.
    What, have you given him any hard words of
        late?

Oph. No, my good lord, but, as you did command,
    I did repel his letters and denied
    His access to me.

Pol.   That hath made him mad.   110
    I am sorry that with better heed and judgment
    I had not quoted him: I fear'd he did but trifle
    And meant to wreck thee; but beshrew my jeal-
        ousy!
    By heaven, it is as proper to our age

To cast beyond ourselves in our opinions
As it is common for the younger sort
To lack discretion.   Come, go we to the king:
This must be known; which, being kept close,
    might move
More grief to hide than hate to utter love.
Come.   [*Exeunt.*

SCENE II

A room in the castle.

*Flourish.   Enter King, Queen, Rosencrantz,
Guildenstern, and Attendants.*

King. Welcome, dear Rosencrantz and Guilden-
    stern!
Moreover that we much did long to see you,
The need we have to use you did provoke
Our hasty sending.   Something have you heard
Of Hamlet's transformation; so call it,
Sith nor the exterior nor the inward man
Resembles that it was.   What it should be,
More than his father's death, that thus hath put
    him

118. *"being kept close";* "this must be made known to the king, for
the hiding Hamlet's love might occasion more mischief to us from
him and the queen, than the uttering or revealing it will occasion
hate and resentment from Hamlet." Johnson, whose explanation
this is, attributes the obscurity to the Poet's *"affectation"* of conclud-
ing the scene with a couplet." There would surely have been more
affectation in deviating from the universally established custom.—
The quartos add *Come,* after the closing couplet.—H. N. H.

2. *"Moreover that";* we do not recollect another instance of *moreover that* used in this way. Of course, the sense is the same as
besides that, or "over and above the fact that," &c.—H. N. H.

So much from the understanding of himself,
I cannot dream of: I entreat you both,   10
That, being of so young days brought up with
    him
And sith so neighbor'd to his youth and havior,
That you vouchsafe your rest here in our court
Some little time: so by your companies
To draw him on to pleasures, and to gather
So much as from occasion you may glean,
Whether aught to us unknown afflicts him thus,
That open'd lies within our remedy.

Queen. Good gentlemen, he hath much talk'd of
    you,
And sure I am two men there are not living 20
To whom he more adheres. If it will please
    you
To show us so much gentry and good will
As to expend your time with us awhile
For the supply and profit of our hope,
Your visitation shall receive such thanks
As fits a king's remembrance.

Ros.   Both your majesties
Might, by the sovereign power you have of us,
Put your dread pleasures more into command
Than to entreaty.

Guil.   But we both obey,
And here give up ourselves, in the full bent   30
To lay our service freely at your feet,
To be commanded.

10. *"dream of";* so the quartos; the folio, *"deem* of."—H. N. H.
17. Omitted in Ff.—I. G.

King. Thanks, Rosencrantz and gentle Guilden-
    stern.

Queen. Thanks, Guildenstern and gentle Rosen-
    crantz:

    And I beseech you instantly to visit

    My too much changed son.   Go, some of you,

    And bring these gentlemen where Hamlet is.

Guil. Heavens make our presence and our practices

    Pleasant and helpful to him!

Queen.   Aye, amen!

    [*Exeunt Rosencrantz, Guildenstern, and some
    Attendants.*

Enter Polonius.

Pol. The ambassadors from Norway, my good

    lord,   40

    Are joyfully return'd.

King. Thou still hast been the father of good news.

Pol. Have I, my lord?   I assure my good liege,

    I hold my duty as I hold my soul,

    Both to my God and to my gracious king:

    And I do think, or else this brain of mine

    Hunts not the trail of policy so sure

    As it hath used to do, that I have found

    The very cause of Hamlet's lunacy.

King. O, speak of that; that do I long to hear. 50

Pol. Give first admittance to the ambassadors;

    My news shall be the fruit to that great feast.

King. Thyself do grace to them, and bring them in.

                          [*Exit Polonius.*

    He tells me, my dear Gertrude, he hath found

    The head and source of all your son's distemper.

Queen. I doubt it is no other but the main;
    His father's death and our o'erhasty marriage.
King. Well, we shall sift him.

Re-enter Polonius, with Voltimand and Cornelius.

            Welcome, my good friends!
    Say, Voltimand, what from our brother Nor-
        way?
Volt. Most fair return of greetings and desires. 60
    Upon our first, he sent out to suppress
    His nephew's levies, which to him appear'd
    To be a preparation 'gainst the Polack,
    But better look'd into, he truly found
    It was against your highness: whereat grieved,
    That so his sickness, age and impotence
    Was falsely borne in hand, sends out arrests
    On Fortinbras; which he, in brief, obeys,
    Receives rebuke from Norway, and in fine
    Makes vow before his uncle never more   70
    To give the assay of arms against your majesty.
    Whereon old Norway, overcome with joy,
    Gives him three thousand crowns in annual fee
    And his commission to employ those soldiers,
    So levied as before, against the Polack:
    With an entreaty, herein further shown,
                  [Giving a paper.
    That it might please you to give quiet pass
    Through your dominions for this enterprise,
    On such regards of safety and allowance
    As therein are set down.

61. *"Upon our first";* on our first application.—C. H. H.
73. *"three";* so Q. 1 and Ff.; Qq. read *"threescore."*—I. G.

King.   It likes us well,   8

And at our more consider'd time we 'll read,

Answer, and think upon this business.

Meantime we thank you for your well-took

   labor:

Go to your rest; at night we 'll feast together

Most welcome home!

                    [*Exeunt Voltimand and Cornelius*

Pol.   This business is well ended.

My liege, and madam, to expostulate

What majesty should be, what duty is,

Why day is day, night night, and time is time

Were nothing but to waste night, day and time

Therefore, since brevity is the soul of wit   9

And tediousness the limbs and outward flour-

   ishes,

I will be brief.   Your noble son is mad:

Mad call I it; for, to define true madness,

What is 't but to be nothing else but mad?

But let that go.

Queen.   More matter, with less art.

Pol. Madam, I swear I use no art at all.

That he is mad, 'tis true: 'tis true 'tis pity,

And pity 'tis 'tis true: a foolish figure;

But farewell it, for I will use no art.

Mad let us grant him then: and now remains 10

That we find out the cause of this effect,

Or rather say, the cause of this defect,

For this effect defective comes by cause:

Thus it remains and the remainder thus.

Perpend.

I have a daughter,—have while she is mine,—

Who in her duty and obedience, mark,
Hath given me this: now gather and surmise.

[*Reads.*

'To the celestial, and my soul's idol, the
most beautified Ophelia,'—   110
That's an ill phrase, a vile phrase; 'beauti-
fied' is a vile phrase; but you shall hear.
Thus: [*Reads.*
'In her excellent white bosom, these,' &c.

Queen. Came this from Hamlet to her?
Pol. Good madam, stay awhile; I will be faith-
    ful.   [*Reads.*

'Doubt thou the stars are fire;
    Doubt that the sun doth move;
    Doubt truth to be a liar;   120
    But never doubt I love.

'O dear Ophelia, I am ill at these numbers;
I have not art to reckon my groans: but that
I love thee best, O most best, believe it.
Adieu.   'Thine evermore, most dear lady,
whilst this machine is to him,   HAMLET.'

This in obedience hath my daughter shown me;

108. *"Hath given me this."* We must suppose Hamlet's letter
to have been one of those received by Ophelia before she was required to "repel" them (i. 3. 122); written, therefore, before the
opening of the play, and unaffected by Hamlet's feigned eccentricity.
—C. H. H.
110. *"beautified"* is not uncommon in dedications and encomiastic
verses of the Poet's age.—H. N. H.
113. The word *"these"* was usually added at the end of the super-
scription of letters.—H. N. H.
114. Elizabethan ladies wore a pocket in the fore-part of their
stays, to which they consigned their more confidential correspondence.
—C. H. H.

61

And more above, hath his solicitings,
As they fell out by time, by means and place
All given to mine ear.　　　　　　　13

King.　　　　　　　But how hath she
Received his love?

Pol.　　　　　　　What do you think of me?

King. As of a man faithful and honorable.

Pol. I would fain prove so.　But what might you
　think,
When I had seen this hot love on the wing,—
As I perceived it, I must tell you that,
Before my daughter told me,—what might you
Or my dear majesty your queen here, think,
If I had play'd the desk or table-book,
Or given my heart a winking, mute and dumb
Or look'd upon this love with idle sight;　　14
What might you think?　No, I went round t
　work,
And my young mistress thus I did bespeak:
'Lord Hamlet is a prince, out of thy star;
This must not be:' and then I prescripts gav
　her,
That she should lock herself from his resort,
Admit no messengers, receive no tokens.
Which done, she took the fruits of my advice;
And he repulsed, a short tale to make,
Fell into a sadness, then into a fast,
Thence to a watch, thence into a weakness,　15
Thence to a lightness, and by this declension
Into the madness wherein now he raves
And all we mourn for.

King. Do you think this?

Queen.   It may be, very like.

Pol. Hath there been such a time, I 'ld fain know
    that,
    That I have positively said ''tis so,'
    When it proved otherwise?

King.   Not that I know.

Pol. [*Pointing to his head and shoulder*] Take this
    from this, if this be otherwise:
    If circumstances lead me, I will find
    Where truth is hid, though it were hid indeed 160
    Within the center.

King.   How may we try it further?

Pol. You know, sometimes he walks four hours to-
    gether
    Here in the lobby.

Queen.   So he does, indeed.

Pol. At such a time I 'll loose my daughter to him:
    Be you and I behind an arras then;
    Mark the encounter: if he love her not,
    And be not from his reason fall'n thereon,
    Let me be no assistant for a state,
    But keep a farm and carters.

King.   We will try it.

Queen. But look where sadly the poor wretch
    comes reading.   170

Pol. Away, I do beseech you, both away:
    I 'll board him presently.

        [*Exeunt King, Queen, and Attendants.*

      Enter Hamlet, reading.

O, give me leave: how does my good Lord
Hamlet?

Ham. Well, God-a-mercy.

Pol. Do you know me, my lord?

Ham. Excellent well; you are a fishmonger.

Pol. Not I, my lord.

Ham. Then I would you were so honest a man.

Pol. Honest, my lord.

Ham. Aye, sir; to be honest, as this world goes, 180
is to be one man picked out of ten thousand.

Pol. That's very true, my lord.

Ham. For if the sun breed maggots in a dead
dog, being a god kissing carrion—Have you
a daughter?

Pol. I have, my lord.

Ham. Let her not walk i' the sun: conception is
a blessing; but as your daughter may conceive,—friend, look to 't.

Pol. [*Aside*] How say you by that? Still 190
harping on my daughter: yet he knew me
not at first; he said I was a fishmonger: he
is far gone: and truly in my youth I suffered much extremity for love; very near
this. I'll speak to him again.—What do
you read, my lord?

Ham. Words, words, words.

Pol. What is the matter, my lord?

Ham. Between who?

Pol. I mean, the matter that you read, my lord. 200

Ham. Slanders, sir: for the satirical rogue says
here that old men have gray beards, that
their faces are wrinkled, their eyes purging
thick amber and plum-tree gum, and that
they have a plentiful lack of wit, together

with most weak hams: all which, sir, though
I most powerfully and potently believe, yet
I hold it not honesty to have it thus set
down; for yourself, sir, shall grow old as I
am, if like a crab you could go backward.   210

Pol. [*Aside*] Though this be madness, yet there
is method in 't.—Will you walk out of the
air, my lord?

Ham. Into my grave.

Pol. Indeed, that's out of the air.   [*Aside*]
How pregnant sometimes his replies are! a
happiness that often madness hits on, which
reason and sanity could not so prosperously
be delivered of. I will leave him, and suddenly contrive the means of meeting between 220
him and my daughter.—My honorable lord,
I will most humbly take my leave of you.

Ham. You cannot, sir, take from me any thing
that I will more willingly part withal: except my life, except my life, except my life.

Pol. Fare you well, my lord.

Ham. These tedious old fools.

Re-enter Rosencrantz and Guildenstern.

Pol. You go to seek the Lord Hamlet; there he is.

Ros. [*To Polonius*] God save you, sir!
                                    [*Exit Polonius.*

219–220, 249–281. The reading of Ff.; omitted in Qq.—I. G.
222. *"take my leave of you";* such is the folio reading; the quartos
give the latter part of the speech thus: "I will leave him and my
daughter.—My lord, I will take my leave of you."—In the next
speech, the folio has, "except my life, my life." Coleridge says of
the quarto reading,—"This repetition strikes me as most admirable."
—H. N. H.

Guil. My honored lord!   230

Ros. My most dear lord!

Ham. My excellent good friends! How dost
thou, Guildenstern? Ah, Rosencrantz!
Good lads, how do you both?

Ros. As the indifferent children of the earth.

Guil. Happy, in that we are not over-happy;
On Fortune's cap we are not the very button.

Ham. Nor the soles of her shoe?

Ros. Neither, my lord.

Ham. Then you live about her waist, or in the 240
middle of her favors?

Guil. Faith, her privates we.

Ham. In the secret parts of Fortune? O,
most true; she is a strumpet. What's the
news?

Ros. None, my lord, but that the world's
grown honest.

Ham. Then is doomsday near: but your news
is not true. Let me question more in particular: what have you, my good friends, de- 250
served at the hands of Fortune, that she
sends you to prison hither?

Guil. Prison, my lord!

Ham. Denmark's a prison.

Ros. Then is the world one.

Ham. A goodly one; in which there are many
confines, wards and dungeons, Denmark being one o' the worst.

Ros. We think not so, my lord.

Ham. Why, then, 'tis none to you; for there is 260

nothing either good or bad, but thinking
makes it so: to me it is a prison.

Ros. Why, then your ambition makes it one;
'tis too narrow for your mind.

Ham. O God, I could be bounded in a nut-shell
and count myself a king of infinite space,
were it not that I have bad dreams.

Guil. Which dreams indeed are ambition; for
the very substance of the ambitious is merely
the shadow of a dream.   270

Ham. A dream itself is but a shadow.

Ros. Truly, and I hold ambition of so airy and
light a quality that it is but a shadow's
shadow.

Ham. Then are our beggars bodies, and our
monarchs and outstretched heroes the beggars' shadows.   Shall we to the court? for,
by my fay, I cannot reason.

Ros. ⎰
Guil. ⎱ We 'll wait upon you.

Ham. No such matter: I will not sort you with 280
the rest of my servants; for, to speak to you
like an honest man, I am most dreadfully
attended.   But, in the beaten way of friendship, what make you at Elsinore?

Ros. To visit you, my lord; no other occasion.

275. *"Then are our beggars bodies,"* etc. If the ambitions are
shadows, "beggars"—the "antitypes of ambition"—are substance, and
as such throw shadow; it is Hamlet's caprice to identify the shadowy ambitious "monarchs and outstretch'd heroes" with the "beggars'
shadows,"—a caprice which he impatiently dismisses the next moment: "for, by my fay, I cannot reason."—C. H. H.

282. *"dreadfully attended"*; by his "bad dreams."—C. H. H.

284. *"what make you"*; what do you.

Ham. Beggar that I am, I am even poor in
    thanks; but I thank you: and sure, dear
    friends, my thanks are too dear a halfpenny.
    Were you not sent for? Is it your own in-
    clining? Is it a free visitation? Come, deal 290
    justly with me: come, come; nay, speak.

Guil. What should we say, my lord?

Ham. Why, any thing, but to the purpose.
    You were sent for; and there is a kind of
    confession in your looks, which your modes-
    ties have not craft enough to color: I know
    the good king and queen have sent for you.

Ros. To what end, my lord?

Ham. That you must teach me. But let me
    conjure you, by the rights of our fellowship, 300
    by the consonancy of our youth, by the obli-
    gation of our ever-preserved love, and by
    what more dear a better proposer could
    charge you withal, be even and direct with
    me, whether you were sent for, or no.

Ros. [*Aside to Guil.*] What say you?

Ham. [*Aside*] Nay then, I have an eye of
    you.—
    If you love me, hold not off.

Guil. My lord, we were sent for.   310

Ham. I will tell you why; so shall my anticipa-
    tion prevent your discovery, and your se-
    crecy to the king and queen moult no
    feather. I have of late—but wherefore I

288. *"too dear a halfpenny"; i. e.* at a halfpenny.—C. H. H.
313. *"moult no feather";* that is, not *change* a feather; *moult* being
an old word for *change;* applied especially to birds when putting on

68

know not—lost all my mirth, forgone all
custom of exercises; and indeed it goes so
heavily with my disposition that this goodly
frame, the earth, seems to me a sterile prom-
ontory; this most excellent canopy, the air,
look you, this brave o'erhanging firmament, 320
this majestical roof fretted with golden fire,
why, it appears no other thing to me than a
foul and pestilent congregation of vapors.
What a piece of work is a man! how noble
in reason! how infinite in faculty! in form
and moving how express and admirable! in
action how like an angel! in apprehension
how like a god! the beauty of the world! the
paragon of animals! And yet, to me, what is
this quintessence of dust? man delights not 330
me; no, nor woman neither, though by your
smiling you seem to say so.

Ros. My lord, there was no such stuff in my
   thoughts.

Ham. Why did you laugh then, when I said
   'man delights not me'?

a new suit of clothes. So in Bacon's *Naturall Historie:* "Some
birds there be, that upon their *moulting* do turn colour; as robin-
redbreasts, after their *moulting,* grow red again by degrees."—
The whole passage seems to mean, "my anticipation shall prevent
your discovering to me the purpose of your visit, and so your promise
of secrecy will be perfectly kept."—H. N. H.

   320. *"o'erhanging firmament";* so the quartos; the folio omits *firmament,* and so of course turns *o'erhanging* into a substantive. It may
well be thought, that by the omission the language becomes more
Shakespearean, without any loss of eloquence. But the passage, as
it stands, is so much a household word, that it seems best not to
change it.—The folio also has, *"appears no other thing* to me *than,"*
instead of, *"appeareth nothing* to me *but."*—H. N. H.

Ros. To think, my lord, if you delight not in
man, what lenten entertainment the players
shall receive from you: we coted them on the
way; and hither are they coming, to offer 340
you service.

Ham. He that plays the king shall be welcome;
his majesty shall have tribute of me; the
adventurous knight shall use his foil and tar-
get; the lover shall not sigh gratis; the humorous man shall end his part in peace; the
clown shall make those laugh whose lungs
are tickle o' the sere, and the lady shall say
her mind freely, or the blank verse shall halt
for 't.   What players are they?   350

Ros. Even those you were wont to take such delight in, the tragedians of the city.

Ham. How chances it they travel? their residence, both in reputation and profit, was better both ways.

Ros. I think their inhibition comes by the means
of the late innovation.

Ham. Do they hold the same estimation they
did when I was in the city? are they so
followed?   360

Ros. No, indeed, are they not.

Ham. How comes it? do they grow rusty?

Ros. Nay, their endeavor keeps in the wonted

347–349. *"the clown . . . sere,"* omitted in Qq.; *vide* Glossary,
"Tickle o' the sere."—I. G.

356–357. *"I think their inhibition comes by the means of the late
innovation"; vide* Preface.—I. G.

62–389. Omitted in Qq.—I. G.

70

pace: but there is, sir, an eyrie of children,
little eyases, that cry out on the top of question and are most tyrannically clapped
for 't: these are now the fashion, and so berattle the common stages—so they call them
—that many wearing rapiers are afraid of
goose-quills, and dare scarce come thither. 370
Ham. What, are they children? who maintains
'em? how are they escorted? Will they pursue the quality no longer than they can sing?
will they not say afterwards, if they should
grow themselves to common players,—as it
is most like, if their means are no better,—
their writers do them wrong, to make them
exclaim against their own succession?
Ros. Faith, there has been much to do on both

364–378, *cp.*:—

> "I saw the children of Powles last night:
> And troth they pleas'd me pretty, pretty well,
> The apes, in time, will do it handsomely.
> —I like the audience that frequenteth there
> With much applause."
>   *Jack Drum's Entertainment* (1601).—I. G.

364. *"Aiery,"* from *eyren,* eggs, properly means a *brood,* but sometimes a *nest.*—*Eyas* is a name for an unfledged hawk.—"Top of
question" probably means, top of their *voice; question* being often
used for *speech.*—The allusion is to the children of St. Paul's and
of the Revels, whose performing of plays was much in fashion at
the time this play was written. From an early date, the choir-boys
of St. Paul's, Westminster, Windsor, and the Chapel Royal, were
engaged in such performances, and sometimes played at Court. The
complaint here is, that these juveniles so abuse "the common stages,"
that is, the theaters, as to deter many from visiting them.—H. N. H.
367. *"berattle";* abuse.—C. H. H.

sides, and the nation holds it no sin to tarre 380
them to controversy: there was for a while
no money bid for argument unless the poet
and the player went to cuffs in the question.

Ham. Is 't possible?

Guil. O, there has been much throwing about of
brains.

Ham. Do the boys carry it away?

Ros. Aye, that they do, my lord; Hercules and
his load too.

Ham. It is not very strange; for my uncle is 390
king of Denmark, and those that would
make mows at him while my father lived,
give twenty, forty, fifty, a hundred ducats
a-piece, for his picture in little. 'Sblood,
there is something in this more than natural,
if philosophy could find it out.

            [*Flourish of trumpets within.*

Guil. There are the players.

Ham. Gentlemen, you are welcome to Elsinore.
Your hands, come then: the appurtenance of
welcome is fashion and ceremony: let me 400
comply with you in this garb, lest my extent
to the players, which, I tell you, must show
fairly outwards, should more appear like entertainment than yours.   You are welcome:
but my uncle-father and aunt-mother are deceived.

Guil. In what, my dear lord?

Ham. I am but mad north-north-west: when

---

408. *"mad north-north-west";* just touched with madness.—C. H. H.

the wind is southerly I know a hawk from a
handsaw. 410

Re-enter Polonius.

Pol. Well be with you, gentlemen!

Ham. Hark you, Guildenstern; and you too:
at each ear a hearer: that great baby you see
there is not yet out of his swaddling clouts.

Ros. Happily he's the second time come to
them; for they say an old man is twice a
child.

Ham. I will prophesy he comes to tell me of the
players; mark it. You say right, sir: o'
Monday morning; 'twas so, indeed. 420

Pol. My lord, I have news to tell you.

Ham. My lord, I have news to tell you. When
Roscius was an actor in Rome,—

Pol. The actors are come hither, my lord.

Ham. Buz, buz!

Pol. Upon my honor,—

Ham. Then came each actor on his ass,—

Pol. The best actors in the world, either for
tragedy, comedy, history, pastoral, pasto-
ral-comical, historical-pastoral, tragical-his- 430
torical, tragical-comical-historical-pastoral,
scene individable, or poem unlimited: Seneca cannot be too heavy, nor Plautus too
light. For the law of writ and the liberty,
these are the only men.

Ham. O Jephthah, judge of Israel, what a
treasure hadst thou!

Pol. What a treasure had he, my lord?

73

Ham. Why,

> 'One fair daughter, and no more,　　44(
>> The which he loved passing well.'

Pol. [*Aside*] Still on my daughter.

Ham. Am I not i' the right, old Jephthah?

Pol. If you call me Jephthah, my lord, I have a daughter that I love passing well.

Ham. Nay, that follows not.

Pol. What follows, then, my lord?

Ham. Why,

> 'As by lot, God wot,'

and then you know,　　45(

> 'It came to pass, as most like it was,'—

the first row of the pious chanson will show you more; for look, where my abridgment comes.

Enter four or five Players.

You are welcome, masters; welcome, all. I am glad to see thee well. Welcome, good

---

440. These lines are from an old ballad, entitled *"Jephtha, Judge of Israel."* It was first printed in Percy's *Reliques,* having been "retrieved from utter oblivion by a lady, who wrote it down from memory, as she had formerly heard it sung by her father." A more correct copy has since been discovered, and reprinted in Evans' *Old Ballads,* 1810; where the first stanza runs thus:

> "I have read that many years agoe,
>> When Jephtha, judge of Israel,
> Had one fair daughter and no moe,
>> Whom he loved passing well;
>>> As by lot, God wot,
>>>> It came to passe, most like it was,
>>> Great warrs there should be,
> And who should be the chiefe but he, but he."
>
> --H. N. H.

friends. O, my old friend! Why thy face
is valanced since I saw thee last; comest thou
to beard me in Denmark? What, my young
lady and mistress! By'r lady, your ladyship 460
is nearer to heaven than when I saw you
last, by the altitude of a chopine. Pray
God, your voice, like a piece of uncurrent
gold, be not cracked within the ring. Masters, you are all welcome. We 'll e'en to 't
like French falconers, fly at any thing we
see: we 'll have a speech straight: come, give
us a taste of your quality; come, a passionate speech.

First Play. What speech, my good lord? 470

Ham. I heard thee speak me a speech once, but
it was never acted; or, if it was, not above
once; for the play, I remember, pleased not
the million; 'twas caviare to the general: but
it was—as I received it, and others, whose
judgments in such matters cried in the top of
mine—an excellent play, well digested in the
scenes, set down with as much modesty as
cunning. I remember, one said there were
no sallets in the lines to make the matter sav- 480
ory, nor no matter in the phrase that might
indict the author of affection; but called it
an honest method, as wholesome as sweet,
and by very much more handsome than fine.
One speech in it I chiefly loved: 'twas
Æneas' tale to Dido; and thereabout of it

466. *"French falconers";* so the folio and the first quarto; the other
quartos have *friendly* instead of *French.*—H. N. H.

486. *"Æneas' tale to Dido";* one cannot but believe that Hamlet's

especially, where he speaks of Priam's
slaughter: if it live in your memory, begin
at this line; let me see, let me see;
'The rugged Pyrrhus, like th' Hyrcanian
   beast,'—   490
It is not so: it begins with 'Pyrrhus.'
'The rugged Pyrrhus, he whose sable arms,
Black as his purpose, did the night resemble
When he lay couched in the ominous horse,

criticism of the play is throughout ironical, and that the speeches
quoted are burlesque. "The fancy that a burlesque was intended,"
wrote Coleridge, "sinks below criticism; the lines, as epic narrative,
are superb"; perhaps he would have changed his mind, and would
have recognized them as mere parody, if he had read *Dido, Queen
of Carthage,* a play left incomplete by Marlowe and finished by
Nash (*cp. e. g.* Act II. Sc. i., which seems to be the very passage
Shakespeare had in view).—I. G.

492. *"The rugged Pyrrhus";* Schlegel observes, that "this speech
must not be judged by itself, but in connexion with the place where
it is introduced. To distinguish it as dramatic poetry in the play
itself, it was necessary that it should rise above the dignified poetry
of that in the same proportion that the theatrical elevation does
above simple nature. Hence Shakespeare has composed the play
in Hamlet altogether in sententious rhymes, full of antithesis. But
this solemn and measured tone did not suit a speech in which violent emotion ought to prevail; and the Poet had no other expedient
than the one of which he made use, overcharging the pathos."—
H. N. H.

To the remarks of Schlegel on this speech should be added
those of Coleridge, as the two appear to have been a coincidence
of thought, and not a borrowing either way: "This admirable
substitution of the epic for the dramatic, giving such reality to the
dramatic diction of Shakespeare's own dialogue, and authorized,
too, by the actual style of the tragedies before his time, is well
worthy of notice. The fancy, that a burlesque was intended, sinks
below criticism: the lines, as epic narrative, are superb.—In the
thoughts, and even in the separate parts of the diction, this description is highly poetical: in truth, taken by itself, that is its fault,
that it is too poetical!—the language of lyric vehemence and epic
pomp, and not of the drama. But if Shakespeare had made the
diction truly dramatic, where would have been the contrast between
Hamlet and the play in Hamlet?"—H. N. H.

    Hath now this dread and black complexion
      smear'd
    With heraldry more dismal: head to foot
    Now is he total gules; horridly trick'd
    With the blood of fathers, mothers, daughters,
      sons,
    Baked and impasted with the parching streets
    That lend a tyrannous and a damned light 500
    To their lord's murder: roasted in wrath and
      fire,
    And thus o'er-sized with coagulate gore,
    With eyes like carbuncles, the hellish Pyrrhus
    Old grandsire Priam seeks.'
    So, proceed you.
Pol. 'Fore God, my lord, well spoken, with
    good accent and good discretion.
First Play.   'Anon he finds him
    Striking too short at Greeks; his antique sword,
    Rebellious to his arm, lies where it falls,
    Repugnant to command: unequal match'd, 510
    Pyrrhus at Priam drives; in rage strikes wide;
    But with the whiff and wind of his fell sword
    The unnerved father falls. Then senseless
      Ilium,
    Seeming to feel this blow, with flaming top
    Stoops to his base, and with a hideous crash
    Takes prisoner Pyrrhus' ear: for, lo! his sword,
    Which was declining on the milky head
    Of reverend Priam, seem'd i' the air to stick:

504. Omitted in Ff.—I. G.
  513. *"Then senseless Ilium"*; 545, *mobled* . . . *good"* omitted
in Qq.—I. G.

So, as a painted tyrant, Pyrrhus stood,
And like a neutral to his will and matter,   520
Did nothing.
But as we often see, against some storm,
A silence in the heavens, the rack stand still,
The bold winds speechless and the orb below
As hush as death, anon the dreadful thunder
Doth rend the region, so after Pyrrhus' pause
Aroused vengeance sets him new a-work;
And never did the Cyclops' hammers fall
On Mars's armor, forged for proof eterne,
With less remorse than Pyrrhus' bleeding sword
Now falls on Priam.   531
Out, out, thou strumpet, Fortune! All you
   gods,
In general synod take away her power,
Break all the spokes and fellies from her wheel,
And bowl the round nave down the hill of
   heaven
As low as to the fiends!'

Pol. This is too long.

Ham. It shall to the barber's, with your beard.
   Prithee, say on: he's for a jig or a tale of
   bawdry, or he sleeps: say on: come to 540
   Hecuba.

First Play. 'But who, O, who had seen the
   mobled queen—'

Ham. 'The mobled queen?'

Pol. That's good; 'mobled queen' is good.

First Play. 'Run barefoot up and down, threatening the flames
   With bisson rheum; a clout upon that head

Copy 1   78

Where late the diadem stood; and for a robe,
About her lank and all o'er-teemed loins,   550
A blanket, in the alarm of fear caught up:
Who this had seen, with tongue in venom steep'd
'Gainst Fortune's state would treason have pronounced:
But if the gods themselves did see her then,
When she saw Pyrrhus make malicious sport
In mincing with his sword her husband's limbs,
The instant burst of clamor that she made,
Unless things mortal move them not at all,
Would have made milch the burning eyes of heaven
And passion in the gods.'   560

Pol. Look, whether he has not turned his color and has tears in 's eyes. Prithee, no more.

Ham. 'Tis well; I 'll have thee speak out the rest of this soon. Good my lord, will you see the players well bestowed? Do you hear, let them be well used, for they are the abstract and brief chronicles of the time: after your death you were better have a bad epitaph than their ill report while you live.

Pol. My lord, I will use them according to their 570 desert.

559. *"burning eyes of heaven";* by a hardy poetical license this expression means, "Would have *filled with tears* the burning eye of heaven." We have "Lemosus, *milch*-hearted," in Huloet's and Lyttleton's *Dictionaries.* It is remarkable that, in old Italian, *lattuoso* is used for *luttuoso,* in the same metaphorical manner.—H. N. H.

561. *"whether";* Malone emendation; Qq., Ff., *"where"* (*i. e.* *"wh'ere* = *whether"*).—I. G.

Ham. God's bodykins, man, much better: use
every man after his desert, and who shall
'scape whipping? Use them after your own
honor and dignity: the less they deserve, the
more merit is in your bounty. Take them
in.

Pol. Come, sirs.

Ham. Follow him, friends: we'll hear a play
to-morrow. [*Exit Polonius with all the* 580
Players but the First.] Dost thou hear me,
old friend; can you play the Murder of
Gonzago?

First Play. Aye, my lord.

Ham. We'll ha't to-morrow night. You
could, for a need, study a speech of some
dozen or sixteen lines, which I would set
down and insert in't, could you not?

First Play. Aye, my lord.

Ham. Very well. Follow that lord; and look 590
you mock him not. [*Exit First Player.*]
My good friends, I'll leave you till night:
you are welcome to Elsinore.

Ros. Good my lord!

Ham. Aye, so, God be wi' ye! [*Exeunt Rosencrantz and Guildenstern.*] Now I am alone.

586. *"a speech of some dozen or sixteen lines";* there was much
throwing about of brains in the attempt to find these lines in the
play-scene in Act III. Sc. ii. "The discussion," as Furness aptly
puts it, "is a tribute to Shakespeare's consummate art," and the
view of this scholar commends itself—viz., that "in order to give
an air of probability to what everyone would feel [otherwise]
highly improbable, Shakespeare represents Hamlet as adapting an
old play to his present needs by inserting in it some pointed lines."
—I. G.

O, what a rogue and peasant slave am I!
Is it not monstrous that this player here,
But in a fiction, in a dream of passion,
Could force his soul so to his own conceit   600
That from her working all his visage wann'd;
Tears in his eyes, distraction in 's aspect,
A broken voice, and his whole function suiting
With forms to his conceit? and all for nothing!
For Hecuba!
What 's Hecuba to him, or he to Hecuba,
That he should weep for her?   What would he
    do,
Had he the motive and the cue for passion
That I have?   He would drown the stage with
    tears
And cleave the general air with horrid speech,
Make mad the guilty and appal the free,   611
Confound the ignorant, and amaze indeed
The very faculties of eyes and ears.
Yet I,
A dull and muddy-mettled rascal, peak,
Like John-a-dreams, unpregnant of my cause,
And can say nothing; no, not for a king,
Upon whose property and most dear life
A damn'd defeat was made. Am I a coward?
Who calls me villain? breaks my pate across? 620
Plucks off my beard, and blows it in my face?
Tweaks me by the nose? gives me the lie i' the
    throat,
As deep as to the lungs? who does me this?
Ha!
'Swounds, I should take it: for it cannot be

But I am pigeon-liver'd and lack gall
To make oppression bitter, or ere this
I should have fatted all the region kites
With this slave's offal: bloody, bawdy villain!
Remorseless, treacherous, lecherous, kindless vil-
    lain!   630
O, vengeance!
Why, what an ass am I!   This is most brave,
That I, the son of a dear father murder'd,
Prompted to my revenge by heaven and hell,
Must, like a whore, unpack my heart with words,
And fall a-cursing, like a very drab,
A scullion!
Fie upon 't! foh!   About, my brain!   Hum, I
    have heard
That guilty creatures, sitting at a play,

627. *"oppression bitter";* of course the meaning is, "lack gall to make me feel the bitterness of oppression." There were no need of saying this, but that Collier, on the strength of his second folio, would read *transgression,* and Singer, on the strength of nothing, *aggression.* Dyce justly pronounces the alteration "nothing less than villainous."—H. N. H.

632. *"dear father murdered";* thus the folio; some copies of the undated quarto, and the quarto of 1611, read, "the son of *a* dear father murder'd." The quartos of 1604 and 1605 are without father; and that of 1603 reads, "the son of my dear father." There can be no question that the reading we have adopted, besides having the most authority, is much the more beautiful and expressive, though modern editors commonly take the other.—The words, "O, vengeance!" are found only in the folio.—H. N. H.

638:—

> *"Hum, I have heard*
> *That guilty creatures, sitting at a play,"* &c.,

vide Heywood's *Apology for Actors,* where a number of these stories are collected; perhaps, however, Shakespeare had in mind the plot of *A Warning for Faire Women,* a play on this theme published in 1599, referring to a *cause célèbre* which befell at Lynn in Norfolk. —I. G.

Have by the very cunning of the scene   640
Been struck so to the soul that presently
They have proclaim'd their malefactions;
For murder, though it have no tongue, will
     speak
With most miraculous organ. I 'll have these
     players
Play something like the murder of my father
Before mine uncle: I 'll observe his looks;
I 'll tent him to the quick: if he but blench,
I know my course. The spirit that I have seen
May be the devil; and the devil hath power
To assume a pleasing shape; yea, and perhaps
Out of my weakness and my melancholy.   651
As he is very potent with such spirits,
Abuses me to damn me. I 'll have grounds
More relative than this. The play 's the thing
Wherein I 'll catch the conscience of the king.
                                        [*Exit.*

ACT THIRD

Scene I

A room in the castle.

*Enter King, Queen, Polonius, Ophelia, Rosen-
crantz, and Guildenstern.*

King. And can you, by no drift of circumstance,
　Get from him why he puts on this confusion,
　Grating so harshly all his days of quiet
　With turbulent and dangerous lunacy?
Ros. He does confess he feels himself distracted,
　But from what cause he will by no means speak.
Guil. Nor do we find him forward to be sounded;
　But, with a crafty madness, keeps aloof,
　When we would bring him on to some confes-
　　sion
　Of his true state.
Queen.　　　　　　Did he receive you well?　10
Ros. Most like a gentleman.
Guil. But with much forcing of his disposition.
Ros. Niggard of question, but of our demands
　Most free in his reply.

　13–14. *"Niggard of question, but of our own demands most free";*
Hanmer, *"Most free of our question, but to our demands most niggard";* Warburton, *"Most free of question, but of our demands most
niggard";* Collier MS., *"niggard of our question, but to our demands
most free."*—I. G.

84

Queen.   Did you assay him
    To any pastime?
Ros. Madam, it so fell out that certain players
    We o'er-raught on the way: of these we told
        him,
    And there did seem in him a kind of joy
    To hear of it: they are about the court,
    And, as I think, they have already order   20
    This night to play before him.
Pol.   'Tis most true:
    And he beseech'd me to entreat your majesties
    To hear and see the matter.
King. With all my heart; and it doth much content
        me
    To hear him so inclined.
    Good gentlemen, give him a further edge,
    And drive his purpose on to these delights.
Ros. We shall, my lord.
            [*Exeunt Rosencrantz and Guildenstern.*
King.   Sweet Gertrude, leave us too;
    For we have closely sent for Hamlet hither,
    That he, as 'twere by accident, may here   30
    Affront Ophelia:
    Her father and myself, lawful espials,
    Will so bestow ourselves that, seeing unseen,
    We may of their encounter frankly judge,
    And gather by him, as he is behaved,
    If 't be the affliction of his love or no
    That thus he suffers for.
Queen.   I shall obey you:
    And for your part, Ophelia, I do wish
    That your good beauties be the happy cause

Of Hamlet's wildness: so shall I hope your vir-
    tues   40
Will bring him to his wonted way again,
To both your honors.

Oph.   Madam, I wish it may.   [*Exit Queen.*
Pol. Ophelia, walk you here.   Gracious, so please
    you,
We will bestow ourselves.   [*To Ophelia.*] Read
    on this book;
That show of such an exercise may color
Your loneliness.   We are oft to blame in this,—
'Tis too much proved—that with devotion's
    visage
And pious action we do sugar o'er
The devil himself.

King.   [*Aside*]   O, 'tis too true!
How smart a lash that speech doth give my con-
    science!   50
The harlot's cheek, beautied with plastering art,
Is not more ugly to the thing that helps it
Than is my deed to my most painted word:
O heavy burthen!

Pol. I hear him coming: let's withdraw, my lord.
                    [*Exeunt King and Polonius.*

Enter Hamlet.

Ham. To be, or not to be: that is the question:
Whether 'tis nobler in the mind to suffer
The slings and arrows of outrageous fortune,
Or to take arms against a sea of troubles,

59. *"to take arms against a sea of troubles,"* &c.; the alleged con-

And by opposing end them.   To die: to sleep;
No more; and by a sleep to say we end   61
The heart-ache, and the thousand natural shocks
That flesh is heir to, 'tis a consummation
Devoutly to be wish'd.   To die, to sleep;
To sleep: perchance to dream: aye, there 's the
    rub;
For in that sleep of death what dreams may
    come,
When we have shuffled off this mortal coil,
Must give us pause: there 's the respect
That makes calamity of so long life;
For who would bear the whips and scorns of
    time,   70
The oppressor's wrong, the proud man's con-
    tumely,
The pangs of despised love, the law's delay,
The insolence of office, and the spurns
That patient merit of the unworthy takes,
When he himself might his quietus make
With a bare bodkin? who would fardels bear,
To grunt and sweat under a weary life,
But that the dread of something after death,
The undiscover'd country from whose bourn
No traveler returns, puzzles the will,   80

fusion of metaphors in this passage was due to the commentator's
ignorance, not to Shakespeare's; *vide* Glossary, "*take arms.*"—I. G.
    79, 80:—

> "*The undiscovered country from whose bourn*
>   *No traveler returns.*"

In Catullus' *Elegy on a Sparrow*, occur the words:—

> "*Qui nunc it per iter tenebricosum*
>   *Illuc unde negant redire quenquam.*"—I. G.

And makes us rather bear those ills we have,
Than fly to others that we know not of?
Thus conscience does make cowards of us all,
And thus the native hue of resolution
Is sicklied o'er with the pale cast of thought,
And enterprises of great pitch and moment,
With this regard their currents turn awry
And lose the name of action.   Soft you now!
The fair Ophelia!   Nymph, in thy orisons
Be all my sins remember'd.

Oph.   Good my lord,   90
How does your honor for this many a day?

Ham. I humbly thank you: well, well, well.

Oph. My lord, I have remembrances of yours,
That I have longed to re-deliver;
I pray you, now receive them.

Ham.   No, not I;
I never gave you aught.

Oph. My honor'd lord, you know right well you
      did;
And with them words of so sweet breath com-
      posed

---

83. *"conscience"*; speculative reflection.—C. H. H.

89. *"Be all my sins remembered"*; "This is a touch of nature. Hamlet, at the sight of Ophelia, does not immediately recollect that he is to personate madness, but makes an address grave and solemn, such as the foregoing meditation excited in his thoughts" (Johnson). —H. N. H.

92. *"well, well, well"*; thus the folio; the quartos have *well* but once. The repetition seems very apt and forcible, as suggesting the opposite of what the word means.—H. N. H.

97. *"you know"*; the quartos have *"you* know" instead of *"I* know." We scarce know which to prefer; but, on the whole, the folio reading seems to have more of delicacy, and at least equal feeling.—H. N. H.

As made the things more rich: their perfume
lost,
Take these again; for to the noble mind   10C
Rich gifts wax poor when givers prove unkind
There, my lord.

Ham. Ha, ha! are you honest?

Oph. My lord?

Ham. Are you fair?

Oph. What means your lordship?

Ham. That if you be honest and fair, your hon
esty should admit no discourse to your
beauty.

Oph. Could beauty, my lord, have better com- 110
merce than with honesty?

Ham. Aye, truly; for the power of beauty will
sooner transform honesty from what it is to a
bawd than the force of honesty can trans-

103. *"are you honest?";* "Here it is evident that the penetrating
Hamlet perceives, from the strange and forced manner of Ophelia,
that the sweet girl was not acting a part of her own, but was a
decoy; and his after speeches are not so much directed to her as
to the listeners and spies. Such a discovery in a mood so anxious
and irritable accounts for a certain harshness in him;—and yet a
wild up-working of love, sporting with opposites in a wilful self-
tormenting strain of irony, is perceptible throughout. "I did love
you once,"—"I loved you not":—and particularly in his enumeration
of the faults of the sex from which Ophelia is so free, that the mere
freedom therefrom constitutes her character. Note Shakespeare's
charm of composing the female character by absence of characters,
that is, marks and out-juttings" (Coleridge).—H. N. H.

108. *"your honesty should admit";* that is, "your honesty should
not admit your beauty to any discourse with it."—The quartos have
merely *you* instead of *your honesty.*—In the next speech, the folio
substitutes *your* for *with.*—It should be noted, that in these speeches
Hamlet refers, not to Ophelia personally, but to the sex in general.
So, especially, when he says, "I have heard of your paintings too,"
he does not mean that Ophelia paints, but that the use of paintings
is common with her sex.—H. N. H.

late beauty into his likeness: this was sometime a paradox, but now the time gives it
proof.   I did love you once.

Oph. Indeed, my lord, you made me believe so.

Ham. You should not have believed me; for
virtue cannot so inoculate our old stock, but 120
we shall relish of it: I loved you not.

Oph. I was the more deceived.

Ham. Get thee to a nunnery: why wouldst thou
be a breeder of sinners?   I am myself indifferent honest; but yet I could accuse me of
such things that it were better my mother
had not borne me: I am very proud, revenge-
ful, ambitious; with more offenses at my
beck than I have thoughts to put them in,
imagination to give them shape, or time to 130
act them in.   What should such fellows as
I do crawling between heaven and earth!
We are arrant knaves all; believe none of us.
Go thy ways to a nunnery.   Where's your
father?

Oph. At home, my lord.

Ham. Let the doors be shut upon him, that he
may play the fool no where but in's own
house.   Farewell.   *his*

Oph. O, help him, you sweet heavens!   140

Ham. If thou dost marry, I'll give thee this
plague for thy dowry: Be thou as chaste as
ice, as pure as snow, thou shalt not escape
calumny.   Get thee to a nunnery, go: farewell.   Or, if thou wilt needs marry, marry a
fool; for wise men know well enough what

monsters you make of them.   To a nunnery,
   go; and quickly too.   Farewell.
Oph. O heavenly powers, restore him!
Ham. I have heard of your paintings too, well 150
   enough; God hath given you one face, and
   you make yourselves another: you jig, you
   amble, and you lisp, and nick-name God's
   creatures, and make your wantonness your
   ignorance. Go to, I'll no more on't; it
   hath made me mad.   I say, we will have no
   more marriages: those that are married already, all but one, shall live; the rest shall
   keep as they are.   To a nunnery, go.   [*Exit.*
Oph. O, what a noble mind is here o'erthrown! 160
   The courtier's, soldier's, scholar's, eye, tongue,
      sword:
   The expectancy and rose of the fair state,
   The glass of fashion and the mould of form,
   The observed of all observers, quite, quite down!
   And I, of ladies most deject and wretched,
   That suck'd the honey of his music vows,
   Now see that noble and most sovereign reason,
   Like sweet bells jangled, out of tune and harsh;
   That unmatch'd form and feature of blown
      youth

150. *"paintings"*; so (Q. 1) Qq.; F. 1, *"pratlings"*; Ff. 2, 3, 4,
"pratling"; Pope, *"painting"*; Macdonald conj. *"prancings."*—I. G.

158. *"all but one"*; "Observe this dallying with the inward purpose,
characteristic of one who had not brought his mind to the steady
acting-point.   He would fain sting the uncle's mind;—but to stab
his body!—The soliloquy of Ophelia, which follows, is the perfection
of love,—so exquisitely unselfish!" (Coleridge).—H. N. H.

164. *"The observed of all observers"*; the object of all men's courtly
deference.—C. H. H.

Blasted with ecstasy: O, woe is me,   170
To have seen what I have seen, see what I see!

Re-enter King and Polonius.

King. Love! his affections do not that way tend;
  Nor what he spake, though it lack'd form a
    little,
  Was not like madness. There's something in
    his soul
  O'er which his melancholy sits on brood,
  And I do doubt the hatch and the disclose
  Will be some danger: which for to prevent,
  I have in quick determination
  Thus set it down:—he shall with speed to Eng-
    land,
  For the demand of our neglected tribute: 180
  Haply the seas and countries different
  With variable objects shall expel
  This something-settled matter in his heart,
  Whereon his brains still beating puts him thus
  From fashion of himself. What think you
    on 't?
Pol. It shall do well: but yet do I believe
  The origin and commencement of his grief
  Sprung from neglected love. How now,
    Ophelia!   189
  You need not tell us what Lord Hamlet said;
  We heard it all. My lord, do as you please;
  But, if you hold it fit, after the play,
  Let his queen mother all alone entreat him
  To show his grief: let her be round with him;
  And I'll be placed, so please you, in the ear

Of all their conference.   If she find him not,
To England send him, or confine him where
Your wisdom best shall think.

King.   It shall be so:
Madness in great ones must not unwatch'd go.

[*Exeunt.*

SCENE II

A hall in the castle.

Enter Hamlet and Players.

Ham. Speak the speech, I pray you, as I pronounced it to you, trippingly on the tongue:
but if you mouth it, as many of your players do, I had as lief the town-crier spoke my
lines.   Nor do not saw the air too much with
your hand, thus; but use all gently: for in
the very torrent, tempest, and, as I may say,
whirlwind of your passion, you must acquire
and beget a temperance that may give it
smoothness. O, it offends me to the soul to   10
hear a robustious periwig-pated fellow tear
a passion to tatters, to very rags, to split
the ears of the groundlings, who, for the
most part, are capable of nothing but inexplicable dumb-shows and noise: I would
have such a fellow whipped for o'erdoing

4. *"I had as lief the town-crier,"* etc.; "this dialogue of Hamlet
with the players," says Coleridge, "is one of the happiest instances
of Shakespeare's power of diversifying the scene while he is carrying on the plot."—H. N. H.

Termagant; it out-herods Herod: pray you,
avoid it.

First Play. I warrant your honor.

Ham. Be not too tame neither, but let your own   20
discretion be your tutor: suit the action to
the word, the word to the action; with this
special observance, that you o'erstep not the
modesty of nature: for anything so overdone
is from the purpose of playing, whose end,
both at the first and now, was and is, to hold,
as 'twere, the mirror up to nature; to show
virtue her own feature, scorn her own image,
and the very age and body of the time his
form and pressure. Now this overdone or   30
come tardy off, though it make the unskillful
laugh, cannot but make the judicious grieve;
the censure of the which one must in your allowance o'erweigh a whole theater of others.
O, there be players that I have seen play,
and heard others praise, and that highly, not
to speak it profanely, that neither having
the accent of Christians nor the gait of
Christian, pagan, nor man, have so strutted
and bellowed, that I have thought some of   40
nature's journeymen had made men, and
not made them well, they imitated humanity
so abominably.

First Play. I hope we have reformed that indifferently with us, sir.

33. *"allowance";* judgment.—C. H. H.

39. *"nor man";* so Qq.; Ff., *"or Norman."*—I. G.

43. *"abominably";* the word was currently derived from **"ab**
homine"; hence the point of its use here.—C. H. H.

Ham. O, reform it altogether.   And let those
　　that play your clowns speak no more than is
　　set down for them: for there be of them that
　　will themselves laugh, to set on some quan-
　　tity of barren spectators to laugh too, though   50
　　in the mean time some necessary question of
　　the play be then to be considered: that 's vil-
　　lainous, and shows a most pitiful ambition in
　　the fool that uses it.   Go, make you ready.
　　　　　　　　　　　　　　　[Exeunt Players.

Enter Polonius, Rosencrantz, and Guildenstern.

　　How now, my lord! will the king hear this
　　　piece of work?
Pol. And the queen too, and that presently.
Ham. Bid the players make haste.
　　　　　　　　　　　　　　　[Exit Polonius.]
　　Will you two help to hasten them?
Ros. ⎱
Guil. ⎰ We will, my lord.　　　　　　　　　60

　　　　　[Exeunt Rosencrantz and Guildenstern.
Ham. What ho! Horatio!

　　　　　　　　Enter Horatio.

Hor. Here, sweet lord, at your service.
Ham. Horatio, thou art e'en as just a man
　　As e'er my conversation coped withal.
Hor. O, my dear lord,—
Ham.　　　　　　Nay, do not think I flatter;

---

53. There is a striking passage in Q. 1, omitted in Q. 2 and Ff.,
concerning those "that keep one suit of jests, as a man is known
by one suit of apparell"; the lines have a Shakespearean note, and
are probably of great interest.—I. G.

For what advancement may I hope from thee,
That no revenue hast but thy good spirits,
To feed and clothe thee? Why should the poor
    be flatter'd?
No, let the candied tongue lick absurd pomp,
And crook the pregnant hinges of the knee   70
Where thrift may follow fawning. Dost thou
    hear?
Since my dear soul was mistress of her choice,
And could of men distinguish, her election
Hath seal'd thee for herself: for thou hast been
As one, in suffering all, that suffers nothing;
A man that fortune's buffets and rewards
Hast ta'en with equal thanks: and blest are
    those
Whose blood and judgment are so well com-
    mingled
That they are not a pipe for fortune's finger
To sound what stop she please. Give me that
    man   80
That is not passion's slave, and I will wear him
In my heart's core, aye, in my heart of heart,
As I do thee. Something too much of this.
There is a play to-night before the king;
One scene of it comes near the circumstance
Which I have told thee of my father's death:
I prithee, when thou seest that act a-foot,
Even with the very comment of thy soul
Observe my uncle: if his occulted guilt

73. *"her election hath sealed thee"*; thus the folio; the quartos make *election* the object of *distinguish,* and use *She* as the subject of *hath seal'd.*—In the fourth line after, the quartos have *co-meddled* instead of *commingled.*—H. N. H.

Do not itself unkennel in one speech   90
It is a damned ghost that we have seen,
And my imaginations are as foul
As Vulcan's stithy.   Give him heedful note;
For I mine eyes will rivet to his face,
And after we will both our judgments join
In censure of his seeming.

Hor.   Well, my lord:
If he steal aught the whilst this play is playing,
And 'scape detecting, I will pay the theft.

Ham. They are coming to the play: I must be idle:
Get you a place.   100

*Danish march.   A flourish.   Enter King, Queen,
Polonius, Ophelia, Rosencrantz, Guildenstern,
and other Lords attendant, with the Guard carrying torches.*

King. How fares our cousin Hamlet?

Ham. Excellent, i' faith; of the chameleon's
dish: I eat the air, promise-crammed: you
cannot feed capons so.

King. I have nothing with this answer, Hamlet; these words are not mine.

Ham. No, nor mine now. [*To Polonius*]
My lord, you played once i' the university,
you say?

Pol. That did I, my lord, and was accounted a 110
good actor.

Ham. What did you enact?

Pol. I did enact Julius Cæsar: I was killed i'
the Capitol; Brutus killed me.

113. *"I was killed i' the capitol"*; a Latin play on Cæsar's death

Ham. It was a brute part of him to kill so capital a calf there.   Be the players ready?

Ros. Aye, my lord; they stay upon your patience.

Queen. Come hither, my dear Hamlet, sit by
me.   120

Ham. No, good mother, here's metal more at-
tractive.

Pol. [*To the King*] O, ho! do you mark that?

Ham. Lady, shall I lie in your lap?

> [*Lying down at Ophelia's feet.*

Oph. No, my lord.

Ham. I mean, my head upon your lap?

Oph. Aye, my lord.

Ham. Do you think I meant country matters?

Oph. I think nothing, my lord.

Ham. That's a fair thought to lie between 130
maids' legs.

Oph. What is, my lord?

Ham. Nothing.

Oph. You are merry, my lord.

Ham. Who, I?

Oph. Aye, my lord.

Ham. O God, your only jig-maker.   What
should a man do but be merry? for, look you,

---

was performed at Christ Church, Oxford, in 1582. Malone thinks
that there was an English play on the same subject previous to
Shakespeare's. Cæsar was killed in *Pompey's portico,* and not in the
Capitol: but the error is at least as old as Chaucer's time.—H. N. H.

117. *"stay upon your patience";* that is, they *wait* upon your *suffer-*
ance or *will.* Johnson would have changed the word to *pleasure;*
but Shakespeare has it in a similar sense in *The Two Gentlemen of*
Verona, Act iii. sc. 1: "And think my *patience* more than thy desert
is privilege for thy departure hence."—H. N. H.

how cheerfully my mother looks, and my
father died within 's two hours.   140

Oph. Nay, 'tis twice two months, my lord.

Ham. So long? Nay then, let the devil wear
black, for I 'll have a suit of sables. O
heavens! die two months ago, and not forgotten yet? Then there's hope a great
man's memory may outlive his life half a
year: but, by 'r lady, he must build churches
then; or else shall he suffer not thinking on,
with the hobby-horse, whose epitaph is, 'For,
O, for, O, the hobby-horse is forgot.'   150

Hautboys play. The dumb-show enters.

*Enter a King and a Queen very lovingly; the
Queen embracing him and he her. She kneels,
and makes show of protestation unto him. He
takes her up, and declines his head upon her
neck: lays him down upon a bank of flowers:
she, seeing him asleep, leaves him. Anon comes
in a fellow, takes off his crown, kisses it, and
pours poison in the King's ears, and exit. The
Queen returns; finds the King dead, and makes
passionate action. The Poisoner, with some two
or three Mutes, comes in again, seeming to lament with her. The dead body is carried away.
The Poisoner wooes the Queen with gifts: she*

150. *"the hobby-horse is forgot";* alluding to the expulsion of the
hobby-horse from the May-games, where he had long been a favorite.
—H. N. H.

151. Much has been said to explain the introduction of the dumb-
show; from the historical point of view its place in a court-play
is not surprising, *vide* Glossary, "DUMB SHOW."—I. G.

*seems loath and unwilling awhile, but in the end
accepts his love.* [*Exeunt.*

Oph. What means this, my lord?

Ham. Marry, this is miching mallecho; it means
mischief.

Oph. Belike this show imports the argument of
the play.

Enter Prologue.

Ham. We shall know by this fellow: the players cannot keep counsel; they 'll tell all.

Oph. Will he tell us what this show meant?

Ham. Aye, or any show that you 'll show him:
be not you ashamed to show, he 'll not shame 160
to tell you what it means.

Oph. You are naught, you are naught: I 'll
mark the play.

Pro.   For us, and for our tragedy,
       Here stooping to your clemency,
       We beg your hearing patiently.

Ham. Is this a prologue, or the posy of a ring?

Oph. 'Tis brief, my lord.

Ham. As woman's love.

Enter two Players, King and Queen.

P. King. Full thirty times hath Phœbus' cart gone
       round   170
    Neptune's salt wash and Tellus' orbed ground,
    And thirty dozen moons with borrowed sheen
    About the world have times twelve thirties been,
    Since love our hearts and Hymen did our hands
    Unite commutual in most sacred bands.

100

P. Queen. So many journeys may the sun and
    moon
  Make us again count o'er ere love be done!
  But, woe is me, you are so sick of late,
  So far from cheer and from your former state,
  That I distrust you. Yet, though I distrust,
  Discomfort you, my lord, it nothing must: 181
  For women's fear and love holds quantity,
  In neither aught, or in extremity.
  Now, what my love is, proof hath made you
    know,
  And as my love is sized, my fear is so:
  Where love is great, the littlest doubts are fear,
  Where little fears grow great, great love grows
    there.

P. King. Faith, I must leave thee, love, and shortly
    too;
  My operant powers their functions leave to do:
  And thou shalt live in this fair world behind, 190
  Honor'd, beloved; and haply one as kind
  For husband shalt thou—

P. Queen.   O, confound the rest!
  Such love must needs be treason in my breast:
  In second husband let me be accurst!
  None wed the second but who kill'd the first.

Ham. [*Aside*] Wormwood, wormwood.

---

182. The reading of the Ff.; Qq. is:—

> *"For women feare too much, even as they love,*
> *And women's fear and love holds quantity."*

Johnson believed that a line was lost rhyming with *"love."*—I. G.

183. *"In neither aught, or in extremity";* Malone's emendation;
Ff., *"In neither ought,"* &c.; Qq., *"Eyther none, in neither ought,"*
&c.—I. G.

P. Queen. The instances that second marriage
    move
    Are base respects of thrift, but none of love:
    A second time I kill my husband dead,
    When second husband kisses me in bed.   200
P. King. I do believe you think what now you
    speak,
    But what we do determine oft we break.
    Purpose is but the slave to memory,
    Of violent birth but poor validity:
    Which now, like fruit unripe, sticks on the
    tree,
    But fall unshaken when they mellow be.
    Most necessary 'tis that we forget
    To pay ourselves what to ourselves is debt:
    What to ourselves in passion we propose,
    The passion ending, doth the purpose lose. 210
    The violence of either grief or joy
    Their own enactures with themselves destroy:
    Where joy most revels, grief doth most lament;
    Grief joys, joy grieves, on slender accident.
    This world is not for aye, nor 'tis not strange
    That even our loves should with our fortunes
    change,
    For 'tis a question left us yet to prove,
    Whether love lead fortune or else fortune love.
    The great man down, you mark his favorite
    flies;
    The poor advanced makes friends of enemies:
    And hitherto doth love on fortune tend;   221

219. *"favorite"*; F. 1, *"favorites,"* a reading for which much is
to be said.—I. G.

For who not needs shall never lack a friend,
And who in want a hollow friend doth try
Directly seasons him his enemy.
But, orderly to end where I begun,
Our wills and fates do so contrary run,
That our devices still are overthrown,
Our thoughts are ours, their ends none of our
    own:
So think thou wilt no second husband wed,
But die thy thoughts when thy first lord is dead.

P. Queen. Nor earth to me give food nor heaven
    light!   231
Sport and repose lock from me day and night!
To desperation turn my trust and hope!
An anchor's cheer in prison be my scope!
Each opposite, that blanks the face of joy,
Meet what I would have well and it destroy!
Both here and hence pursue me lasting strife,
If, once a widow, ever I be wife!

Ham. If she should break it now!

P. King. 'Tis deeply sworn. Sweet, leave me here
    a while;   240
My spirits grow dull, and fain I would beguile
The tedious day with sleep.   *[Sleeps.*

P. Queen.   Sleep rock thy brain;
And never come mischance between us twain!
                            [Exit.

Ham. Madam, how like you this play?

Queen. The lady doth protest too much, methinks.

Ham. O, but she 'll keep her word.

King. Have you heard the argument? Is there
no offense in 't?

Ham. No, no, they do but jest, poison in jest; 250
no offense i' the world.

King. What do you call the play?

Ham. The Mouse-trap. Marry, how? Tropically. This play is the image of a murder
done in Vienna: Gonzago is the duke's name;
his wife, Baptista: you shall see anon; 'tis a
knavish piece of work; but what o' that? your majesty, and we that have free souls,
it touches us not: let the galled jade wince,
our withers are unwrung.   260

Enter Lucianus.

This is one Lucianus, nephew to the king.

Oph. You are as good as a chorus, my lord.

Ham. I could interpret between you and your
love, if I could see the puppets dallying.

Oph. You are keen, my lord, you are keen.

Ham. It would cost you a groaning to take off
my edge.

Oph. Still better and worse.

255. *"Vienna";* Q. 1, *"Guyana";* for *"Gonzago,"* Q. 1 reads *Alber-
tus,* who is throughout called Duke; in Q. 2 it is always *King;*
except here where Hamlet says *"Gonzago is the Duke's name."*—I. G.

255. *"Gonzago is the duke's name";* all the old copies read thus.
Yet in the dumb show we have, "Enter a *King* and Queen"; and at
the end of this speech, "Lucianus, nephew to the *king."* This seeming inconsistency, however, may be reconciled. Though the interlude
is the *image* of the murder of the *duke* of Vienna, or in other words
founded upon that story, the Poet might make the principal person
in *his fable* a *king.* *Baptista* is always the name of a man.—
H. N. H.

Ham. So you must take your husbands. Begin, murderer; pox, leave thy damnable 270
faces, and begin.   Come: the croaking raven
doth bellow for revenge.

Luc. Thoughts black, hands apt, drugs fit, and
time agreeing;
Confederate season, else no creature seeing;
Thou mixture rank, of midnight weeds col-
lected,
With Hecate's ban thrice blasted, thrice in-
fected,
Thy natural magic and dire property,
On wholesome life usurp immediately.

        [*Pours the poison into the sleeper's ear.*

Ham. He poisons him i' the garden for his
estate.   His name's Gonzago: the story is 280
extant, and written in very choice Italian:
you shall see anon how the murderer gets
the love of Gonzago's wife.

Oph. The king rises.

Ham. What, frighted with false fire!

Queen. How fares my lord?

Pol. Give o'er the play.

269. *"take your husbands"*; alluding, most likely, to the language
of the Marriage service: "To have and to hold from this day forward, *for better, for worse,* for richer, for poorer," &c.—All the old
copies, but the first quarto, have *mistake;* which Theobald conjectured should be *must take,* before any authority for it was known.
—H. N. H.

271. *"The croaking raven doth bellow for revenge"*;
      cp. *"The screeking raven sits croaking for revenge,*
            Whole herds of beasts comes bellowing for revenge."
                        The True Tragedy of Rich. III.—I. G.

274. *"midnight weeds"*; that is, weeds collected at midnight; as in
Macbeth: "Root of hemlock, *digg'd i'the dark.*"—H. N. H.

King. Give me some light.   Away!

Pol. Lights, lights, lights!

          [*Exeunt all but Hamlet and Horatio.*

Ham. Why, let the stricken deer go weep,   290
    The hart ungalled play;
  For some must watch, while some must sleep:
    Thus runs the world away.
Would not this, sir, and a forest of feathers
—if the rest of my fortunes turn Turk with
me—with two Provincial roses on my razed
shoes, get me a fellowship in a cry of
players, sir?

Hor. Half a share.

Ham. A whole one, I.   300
    For thou dost know, O Damon dear,
      This realm dismantled was
    Of Jove himself; and now reigns here
      A very, very—pajock.

Hor. You might have rhymed.

Ham. O good Horatio, I'll take the ghost's
word for a thousand pound. Didst perceive?

Hor. Very well, my lord.

Ham. Upon the talk of the poisoning?   310

Hor. I did very well note him.

Ham. Ah, ha!   Come, some music! come, the
recorders!
      For if the king like not the comedy,
        Why then, belike, he likes it not, perdy.
    Come, some music!

---

299. *"half a share";* the players were paid not by salaries, but by
shares or portions of the profit, according to merit.—H. N. H.

Re-enter Rosencrantz and Guildenstern.

Guil. Good my lord, vouchsafe me a word with
    you.

Ham. Sir, a whole history.

Guil. The king, sir,—   320

Ham. Aye, sir, what of him?

Guil. Is in his retirement marvelous distem-
    pered.

Ham. With drink, sir?

Guil. No, my lord, rather with choler.

Ham. Your wisdom should show itself more
    richer to signify this to the doctor; for, for
    me to put him to his purgation would per-
    haps plunge him into far more choler.

Guil. Good my lord, put your discourse into 330
    some frame, and start not so wildly from
    my affair.

Ham. I am tame, sir: pronounce.

Guil. The queen, your mother, in most great
    affliction of spirit, hath sent me to you.

Ham. You are welcome.

Guil. Nay, good my lord, this courtesy is not of
    the right breed. If it shall please you to
    make me a wholesome answer, I will do your
    mother's commandment: if not, your pardon 340
    and my return shall be the end of my busi-
    ness.

Ham. Sir, I cannot.

Guil. What, my lord?

Ham. Make you a wholesome answer; my wit's
    diseased: but, sir, such answer as I can make,

you shall command; or rather, as you say, my mother: therefore no more, but to the matter: my mother, you say,—

Ros. Then thus she says; your behavior hath 350 struck her into amazement and admiration.

Ham. O wonderful son, that can so astonish a mother! But is there no sequel at the heels of this mother's admiration? Impart.

Ros. She desires to speak with you in her closet, ere you go to bed.

Ham. We shall obey, were she ten times our mother. Have you any further trade with us?

Ros. My lord, you once did love me. 360

Ham. So I do still, by these pickers and stealers.

Ros. Good my lord, what is your cause of distemper? you do surely bar the door upon your own liberty, if you deny your griefs to your friend.

Ham. Sir, I lack advancement.

Ros. How can that be, when you have the voice of the king himself for your succession in Denmark? 370

Ham. Aye, sir, but 'while the grass grows,'— the proverb is something musty.

Re-enter Players with recorders.

O, the recorders! let me see one. To withdraw with you:—why do you go about to recover the wind of me, as if you would drive me into a toil?

376. *"toil"*; net.—C. H. H.

Guil. O, my lord, if my duty be too bold, my
  love is too unmannerly.

Ham. I do not well understand that. Will
  you play upon this pipe?   380

Guil. My lord, I cannot.

Ham. I pray you.

Guil. Believe me, I cannot.

Ham. I do beseech you.

Guil. I know no touch of it, my lord.

Ham. It is as easy as lying: govern these ven~tages~
  tages with your fingers and thumb, give it
  breath with your mouth, and it will discourse
  most eloquent music. Look you, these are
  the stops.   390

Guil. But these cannot I command to any utter-
  ance of harmony; I have not the skill.

Ham. Why, look you now, how unworthy a *Expressio*
  thing you make of me! You would play
  upon me; you would seem to know my stops;
  you would pluck out the heart of my
  mystery; you would sound me from my lowest note to the top of my compass: and there
  is much music, excellent voice, in this little
  organ; yet cannot you make it speak. 400
  'Sblood, do you think I am easier to be
  played on than a pipe? Call me what instrument you will, though you can fret me,
  yet you cannot play upon me.

  379. Hamlet may say with propriety, "I do not well understand
that." Perhaps Guildenstern means, "If my duty to the king makes
me too bold, my love to you makes me importunate even to rudeness."
—H. N. H.

109

Re-enter Polonius.

God bless you, sir!

Pol. My lord, the queen would speak with you,
and presently.

Ham. Do you see yonder cloud that's almost
in shape of a camel?

Pol. By the mass, and 'tis like a camel, indeed. 410

Ham. Methinks it is like a weasel.

Pol. It is backed like a weasel.

Ham. Or like a whale?

Pol. Very like a whale.

Ham. Then I will come to my mother by and
by.   They fool me to the top of my bent.
I will come by and by.

Pol. I will say so.   [*Exit Polonius.*

Ham. 'By and by' is easily said.   Leave me,
friends.   [*Exeunt all but Hamlet.*
'Tis now the very witching time of night, 420
When churchyards yawn, and hell itself breathes
out
Contagion to this world: now could I drink hot
blood,
And do such bitter business as the day
Would quake to look on.   Soft! now to my
mother.
O heart, lose not thy nature; let not ever
The soul of Nero enter this firm bosom:
Let me be cruel, not unnatural:
I will speak daggers to her, but use none;
My tongue and soul in this be hypocrites;

423. *"bitter business as the day"*; so Ff.; Qq. read *"business as
the bitter day."*—I. G.

How in my words soever she be shent,   43
To give them seals never, my soul, consent!

[*Exit.*

Scene III

A room in the castle.

Enter King, Rosencrantz, and Guildenstern.

King. I like him not, nor stands it safe with us
    To let his madness range.   Therefore prepare
        you;
    I your commission will forthwith dispatch,
    And he to England shall along with you:
    The terms of our estate may not endure
    Hazard so near us as doth hourly grow
    Out of his lunacies.
Guil.   We will ourselves provide:
    Most holy and religious fear it is
    To keep those many many bodies safe
    That live and feed upon your majesty.   10
Ros. The single and peculiar life is bound
    With all the strength and armor of the mind
    To keep itself from noyance; but much more
    That spirit upon whose weal depends and rests
    The lives of many.   The cease of majesty
    Dies not alone, but like a gulf doth draw
    What 's near it with it; it is a massy wheel,
    Fix'd on the summit of the highest mount,
    To whose huge spokes ten thousand lesser
        things

7. *"lunacies"*; so Ff.; Qq., *"browes."*—I. G.

Are mortised and adjoin'd; which, when it falls,　20
Each small annexment, petty consequence,
Attends the boisterous ruin.　Never alone
Did the king sigh, but with a general groan.

King. Arm you, I pray you, to this speedy voyage,
For we will fetters put about this fear,
Which now goes too free-footed.

Ros. ⎱
Guil. ⎰　　　　　　　　　We will haste us.

[*Exeunt Rosencrantz and Guildenstern.*

Enter Polonius

Pol. My lord, he's going to his mother's closet:
Behind the arras I'll convey myself,
To hear the process: I'll warrant she'll tax him home:
And, as you said, and wisely was it said,　30
'Tis meet that some more audience than a mother,
Since nature makes them partial, should o'er-
hear
The speech, of vantage.　Fare you well, my liege:
I'll call upon you ere you go to bed,
And tell you what I know.

King.　　　　　　　　　Thanks, dear my lord.

[*Exit Polonius.*

---

30. *"as you said."* Polonius astutely (or obliviously) attributes his own suggestion to the king.—C. H. H.

33. *"speech of vantage"* probably means "speech having the advantage of a mother's partiality."—H. N. H.

O, my offense is rank, it smells to heaven;
It hath the primal eldest curse upon 't,
A brother's murder. Pray can I not,
Though inclination be as sharp as will:
My stronger guilt defeats my strong intent,   40
And like a man to double business bound,
I stand in pause where I shall first begin,
And both neglect. What if this cursed hand
Were thicker than itself with brother's blood,
Is there not rain enough in the sweet heavens
To wash it white as snow? Whereto serves
    mercy
But to confront the visage of offense?
And what 's in prayer but this twofold force,
To be forestalled ere we come to fall,
Or pardon'd being down? Then I 'll look
    up;   50
My fault is past. But O, what form of prayer
Can serve my turn? 'Forgive me my foul
    murder?'
That cannot be, since I am still possess'd
Of those effects for which I did the murder,
My crown, mine own ambition and my queen.
May one be pardon'd and retain the offense?
In the corrupted currents of this world
Offense's gilded hand may shove by justice,
And oft 'tis seen the wicked prize itself
Buys out the law: but 'tis not so above;   60
There is no shuffling, there the action lies
In his true nature, and we ourselves compell'd

---

38. *"pray can I not"*; that is, "though I were not only willing, but strongly inclined to pray, my guilt would prevent me."—H. N. H.

Even to the teeth and forehead of our faults
To give in evidence.   What then? what rests?
Try what repentance can: what can it not?
Yet what can it when one can not repent?
O wretched state!   O bosom black as death;
O limed soul, that struggling to be free
Art more engaged!   Help, angels! make assay!
Bow, stubborn knees, and, heart with strings of
    steel,   70
Be soft as sinews of the new-born babe!
All may be well.   [*Retires and kneels.*

Enter Hamlet

Ham. Now might I do it pat, now he is praying;
And now I 'll do 't: and so he goes to heaven:
And so am I revenged.   That would be
    scann'd;
A villain kills my father; and for that,
I, his sole son, do this same villain send
To heaven.
O, this is hire and salary, not revenge.
He took my father grossly, full of bread,   80
With all his crimes broad blown, as flush as
    May;

71–76, 78–81, 161–165, 167–170, 202–210, omitted in Ff.—I. G.

72. *"All may be well";* "This speech well marks the difference between crime and guilt of habit. The conscience here is still ad-
mitted to audience.   Nay, even as an audible soliloquy, it is far less
improbable than is supposed by such as have watched men only
in the beaten road of their feelings.   But the final—"All may be
well!" is remarkable;—the degree of merit attributed by the self-
flattering soul to its own struggles, though baffled, and to the indefinite half promise, half command, to persevere in religious duties"
(Coleridge).—H. N. H.

79. *"hire and salary";* so Ff.; Qq. misprint, *"base and silly."*—
I. G.

And how his audit stands, who knows, save
    heaven?
But in our circumstance and course of thought,
'Tis heavy with him: and am I then revenged,
To take him in the purging of his soul,
When he is fit and season'd for his passage?
No.
Up, sword, and know thou a more horrid hent:
When he is drunk asleep, or in his rage,
Or in the incestuous pleasure of his bed;   90
At game, a-swearing, or about some act
That has no relish of salvation in 't;
Then trip him, that his heels may kick at heaven
And that his soul may be as damn'd and black
As hell, whereto it goes.   My mother stays:
This physic but prolongs thy sickly days. [*Exit.*

King. [*Rising*] My words fly up, my thoughts re-
    main below:
    Words without thoughts never to heaven go.
                            [*Exit.*

Scene IV

The Queen's closet.

Enter Queen and Polonius.

Pol. He will come straight.   Look you lay home to
    him:
    Tell him his pranks have been too broad to bear
    with,

83. "So far as we can judge by inference."—C. H. H.

And that your grace hath screen'd and stood
between

Much heat and him.   I 'll sconce me even here.

Pray you, be round with him.

Ham.   [*Within*] Mother, mother, mother!

Queen. I 'll warrant you; fear me not.   Withdraw,
I hear him coming.

[*Polonius hides behind the arras.*

Enter Hamlet.

Ham. Now, mother, what 's the matter?

Queen. Hamlet, thou hast thy father much offended.

Ham. Mother, you have my father much offended.

Queen. Come, come, you answer with an idle
tongue.

Ham. Go, go, you question with a wicked tongue.

Queen. Why, how now, Hamlet!

Ham.   What 's the matter now?

Queen. Have you forget me?

Ham.   No, by the rood, not so:

You are the queen, your husband's brother's
wife;

And—would it were not so!—you are my
mother.

Queen. Nay, then, I 'll set those to you that can
speak.

Ham. Come, come, and sit you down; you shall
not budge;

You go not till I set you up a glass —

Where you may see the inmost part of you.   20
Queen. What wilt thou do? thou wilt not murder
   me?
   Help, help, ho!
Pol. [*Behind*] What, ho! help, help, help!
Ham. [*Drawing*] How now! a rat? Dead, for a
   ducate, dead!
                    [*Makes a pass through the arras.*
Pol. [*Behind*] O, I am slain!   [*Falls and dies.*
Queen.   O me, what hast thou done?
Ham. Nay, I know not: is it the king?
Queen. O, what a rash and bloody deed is this!
Ham. A bloody deed! almost as bad, good mother,
   As kill a king, and marry with his brother.
Queen. As kill a king!
Ham.   Aye, lady, 'twas my word.   30
      [*Lifts up the arras and discovers Polonius.*
   Thou wretched, rash, intruding fool, farewell!
   I took thee for thy better: take thy fortune;
   Thou find'st to be too busy is some danger.
   Leave wringing of your hands: peace! sit you
      down,
   And let me wring your heart: for so I shall,
   If it be made of penetrable stuff;
   If damned custom have not brass'd it so,
   That it be proof and bulwark against sense.
Queen. What have I done, that thou darest wag
      thy tongue
   In noise so rude against me?
Ham.   Such an act   40
   That blurs the grace and blush of modesty,

Calls virtue hypocrite, takes off the rose
From the fair forehead of an innocent love,
And sets a blister there; makes marriage vows
As false as dicers' oaths: O, such a deed
As from the body of contraction plucks
The very soul, and sweet religion makes
A rhapsody of words: heaven's face doth glow;
Yea, this solidity and compound mass,
With tristful visage, as against the doom,   50
Is thought-sick at the act.

Queen. Aye me, what act,
That roars so loud and thunders in the index?

Ham. Look here, upon this picture, and on this,
The counterfeit presentment of two brothers.
See what a grace was seated on this brow;
Hyperion's curls, the front of Jove himself,
An eye like Mars, to threaten and command;
A station like the herald Mercury
New-lighted on a heaven-kissing hill;
A combination and a form indeed,   60
Where every god did seem to set his seal
To give the world assurance of a man:
This was your husband. Look you now, what
follows:

49. *"solidity"*; the earth.—C. H. H.

53. *"Look here, upon this picture, and on this."* It has been
doubted whether Hamlet here points to two portraits hung on the
walls or takes a miniature of his father from his pocket. Irving and
Salvini even suppose the pictures to be drawn only to the imagination. That the Elizabethans understood actual paintings of considerable size may probably be gathered from the German version,
where Hamlet says: *"Aber sehet, dort in jener Gallerie hängt das
Conterfait Eures ersten Ehegemahls, und da hängt das Conterfait
des itzigen"* (iii. 5.).—C. H. H.

Here is your husband; like a mildew'd ear,
Blasting his wholesome brother. Have you
    eyes?
Could you on this fair mountain leave to feed,
And batten on this moor?   Ha! have you eyes?
You cannot call it love, for at your age
The hey-day in the blood is tame, it 's humble,
And waits upon the judgment:/and what judg-
    ment   70
Would step from this to this?   Sense sure you
    have,
Else could you not have motion: but sure that
    sense
Is apoplex'd: for madness would not err,
Nor sense to ecstasy was ne'er so thrall'd
But it reserved some quantity of choice,
To serve in such a difference. What devil
    was 't
That thus hath cozen'd you at hoodman-blind?
Eyes without feeling, feeling without sight,
Ears without hands or eyes, smelling sans all,
Or but a sickly part of one true sense   80
Could not so mope.
O shame! where is thy blush? Rebellious hell,
If thou canst mutine in a matron's bones,
To flaming youth let virtue be as wax
And melt in her own fire: proclaim no shame
When the compulsive ardor gives the charge,
Since frost itself as actively doth burn,
And reason pandars will.
Queen.   O Hamlet, speak no more:
Thou turn'st mine eyes into my very soul,

And there I see such black and grained spots 9
As will not leave their tinct.

Ham.   Nay, but to live
In the rank sweat of an enseamed bed,
Stew'd in corruption, honeying and making
    love
Over the nasty sty,—

Queen.   O, speak to me no more
These words like daggers enter in my ears;
No more, sweet Hamlet!

Ham.   A murderer and a villain
A slave that is not twentieth part the tithe
Of your precedent lord; a vice of kings;
A cutpurse of the empire and the rule,—
That from a shelf the precious diadem stole 10
And put it in his pocket!

Queen.   No more!

Ham. A king of shreds and patches—

Enter Ghost.

Save me, and hover o'er me with your wings,
You heavenly guards! What would you
    gracious figure?

Queen. Alas, he's mad!

Ham. Do you not come your tardy son to chide,
That, lapsed in time and passion, lets go by
The important acting of your dread command
O, say!

2. *"Enter ghost";* when the Ghost goes out, Hamlet says,—"Look
how it steals away! my father, *in his habit as he liv'd."* It has
been much argued what is meant by this; that is, whether the Ghost
should wear armor here, as in former scenes, or appear in a different dress. The question is set at rest by the stage-direction in the
quarto: "Enter the Ghost, *in his night-gown."*—H. N. H.

Ghost. Do not forget: this visitation   110
    Is but to whet thy almost blunted purpose.
    But look, amazement on thy mother sits:
    O, step between her and her fighting soul:
    Conceit in weakest bodies strongest works:
    Speak to her, Hamlet.
Ham.   How is it with you, lady?
Queen. Alas, how is 't with you,
    That you do bend your eye on vacancy
    And with the incorporal air do hold discourse?
    Forth at your eyes your spirits wildly peep;
    And, as the sleeping soldiers in the alarm,   120
    Your bedded hairs, like life in excrements,
    Stand up and stand an end. O gentle son,
    Upon the heat and flame of thy distemper
    Sprinkle cool patience. Whereon do you
    look?
Ham. On him, on him! Look you how pale he
    glares!
    His form and cause conjoin'd, preaching to
    stones,___
    Would make them capable. Do not look upon
    me,
    Lest with this piteous action you convert___
    My stern effects: then what I have to do
    Will want true color; tears perchance for
    blood.   130

129. *"my stern effects"; affects* was often used for *affections;* as in
Othello, "the young *affects* in me defunct." The old copies read
ffects, which was a frequent misprint for *affects.* Singer justly
remarks, that "the 'piteous action' of the Ghost could not alter
things already *effected,* but might move Hamlet to a less stern *mood
of mind."*—H. N. H.

Queen. To whom do you speak this?

Ham.   Do you see nothing there

Queen. Nothing at all; yet all that is I see.

Ham. Nor did you nothing hear?

Queen.   No, nothing but ourselves

Ham. Why, look you there! look, how it steals
  away!

My father, in his habit as he lived!

Look, where he goes, even now, out at the por
  tal!   [*Exit Ghost*

Queen. This is the very coinage of your brain:

This bodiless creation ecstasy

Is very cunning in.

Ham.   Ecstasy!

My pulse, as yours, doth temperately keep
  time,——   14

And makes as healthful music: it is not madnes

That I have utter'd: bring me to the test,

And I the matter will re-word, which madness

Would gambol from. Mother, for love o
  grace,——

Lay not that flattering unction to your soul,

That not your trespass but my madness speaks

Pause It will but skin and film the ulcerous place,

Whiles rank corruption, mining all within,

Infects unseen. Confess yourself to heaven

Repent what's past, avoid what is to come, 15

---

144. *"would gambol from";* science has found the Poet's test
correct one. Dr. Ray, of Providence, in his work on the *Jurispru*
dence of Insanity, thus states the point: "In simulated mania, th
imposter, when requested to repeat his disordered idea, will generall
do it correctly; while the genuine patient will be apt to wande
from the track, or introduce ideas that had not presented themselve
before."—H. N. H.

And do not spread the compost on the weeds,
To make them ranker. Forgive me this my
    virtue,
For in the fatness of these pursy times
Virtue itself of vice must pardon beg,   *Pause*
Yea, curb and woo for leave to do him good.

Queen. O Hamlet, thou hast cleft my heart in
    twain.

Ham. O, throw away the worser part of it,
And live the purer with the other half.
Good night: but go not to my uncle's bed; \
Assume a virtue, if you have it not. √   160
That monster, custom, who all sense doth eat,
Of habits devil, is angel yet in this,
That to the use of actions fair and good
He likewise gives a frock or livery,
That aptly is put on. Refrain to-night,
And that shall lend a kind of easiness

162. *"is angel yet in this"*; a very obscure and elliptical passage,
if indeed it be not corrupt. We have adopted Caldecott's pointing,
which gives the meaning somewhat thus: "That monster, custom,
who devours or eats out all sensibility or feeling as to what we do,
though he be the devil or evil genius of our habits, is yet our good
angel in this." Collier and Verplanck order the pointing thus:
"Who all sense doth eat of habits, devil, is angel yet in this." Where
the meaning is,—"That monster, custom, who takes away all sense
of habits, devil though he be, is still an angel in this respect."
This also pleads a fair title to preference, and we find it not easy
to choose between the two. Dr. Thirlby proposed to read, "Of
habits *evil*"; which would give the clear and natural sense, that by
custom we lose all feeling or perception of bad habits, and become
reconciled to them as if they were nature. The probability, however, that an antithesis was meant between *devil* and *angel*, is
against this reading; otherwise, we should incline to think it right.
—The whole sentence is omitted in the folio; as is also the passage
beginning with "the next more easy," and ending with "wondrous
potency."—H. N. H.

To the next abstinence; the next more easy;
For use almost can change the stamp of nature,
And either . . . the devil, or throw him
    out
With wondrous potency. Once more, good
    night: 170
And when you are desirous to be blest,
I 'll blessing beg of you. For this same lord,
                            [*Pointing to Polonius.*
I do repent: but heaven hath pleased it so,
To punish me with this, and this with me,
That I must be their scourge and minister.
I will bestow him, and will answer well
The death I gave him. So, again, good night.
I must be cruel, only to be kind:
Thus bad begins, and worse remains behind.
One word more, good lady.
Queen.   What shall I do?   180
Ham. Not this, by no means, that I bid you do:
Let the bloat king tempt you again to bed;
Pinch wantom on your cheek, call you his
    mouse;
And let him, for a pair of reechy kisses,
Or paddling in your neck with his damn'd
    fingers,
Make you to ravel all this matter out,
That I essentially am not in madness,

169. *"And either . . . the devil"*; some such word as *"master,"*
"quell," "shame," has been omitted in Qq., which read *"and either
the devil."*—I. G.

184. *"reechy kisses"*; *reeky* and *reechy* are the same word, and
always applied to any vaporous exhalation, even to the fumes of a
dunghill.—H. N. H.

But mad in craft. / 'Twere good you let him
    know;
For who, that 's but a queen, fair, sober, wise,
Would from a paddock, from a bat, a gib, 190
Such dear concernings hide? who would do so?
No, in despite of sense and secrecy,
Unpeg the basket on the house's top,
Let the birds fly, and like the famous ape,
To try conclusions, in the basket creep
And break your own neck down.

Queen. Be thou assured, if words be made of
    breath
And breath of life, I have no life to breathe
What thou hast said to me.

Ham. I must to England; you know that?

Queen.   Alack, 200
I had forgot: 'tis so concluded on.

Ham. There 's letters seal'd: and my two school-
    fellows,
Whom I will trust as I will adders fang'd,

---

199. *"What thou hast said to me";* "I confess," says Coleridge,
"that Shakespeare has left the character of the Queen in an un-
pleasant perplexity. Was she, or was she not, conscious of the
fratricide?" This "perplexity," whatever it be, was doubtless designed by the Poet; for in the original form of the play she stood
perfectly clear on this score; as appears from several passages in the
quarto of 1603, which were afterwards disciplined out of the text.
Thus, in one place of this scene, she says to Hamlet,—

> "But, as I have a soul, I swear to Heaven,
> I never knew of this most horrid murder."

And in this place she speaks thus:

> "Hamlet, I vow by that Majesty,
> That knows our thoughts and looks into our hearts,
> I will conceal, consent, and do my best,
> What stratagem soe'er thou shalt devise."—H. N. H.

They bear the mandate; they must sweep my
    way,
And marshal me to knavery.   Let it work;
For 'tis the sport to have the enginer
Hoist with his own petar: and 't shall go hard
But I will delve one yard below their mines,
And blow them at the moon: O, 'tis most
    sweet
When in one line two crafts directly meet.   210
This man shall set me packing:
I 'll lug the guts into the neighbor room.
Mother, good night.   Indeed this counselor
Is now most still, most secret and most grave,
Who was in life a foolish prating knave.
Come, sir, to draw toward an end with you.
Good night, mother.
[*Exeunt severally; Hamlet dragging in Polonius.*

ACT FOURTH

SCENE I

A room in the castle.

*Enter King, Queen, Rosencrantz, and
Guildenstern.*

King. There 's matter in these sighs, these pro-
    found heaves:
  You must translate: 'tis fit we understand them.
  Where is your son?
Queen. Bestow this place on us a little while.
          [*Exeunt Rosencrantz and Guildenstern.*
  Ah, mine own lord, what have I seen to-night!
King. What, Gertrude?   How does Hamlet?
Queen. Mad as the sea and wind, when both con-
    tend
  Which is the mightier: in his lawless fit,
  Behind the arras hearing something stir,
  Whips out his rapier, cries 'A rat, a rat!'   10
  And in this brainish apprehension kills
  The unseen good old man.
King.   O heavy deed!
  It had been so with us, had we been there:
  His liberty is full of threats to all,
  To you yourself, to us, to every one.

4. Omitted in Ff.—I. G.

Alas, how shall this bloody deed be answer'd?
It will be laid to us, whose providence
Should have kept short, restrain'd and out of
haunt,
This mad young man: but so much was our
love,
We would not understand what was most fit, 20
But, like the owner of a foul disease,
To keep it from divulging, let it feed
Even on the pith of life.   Where is he gone?
Queen. To draw apart the body he hath kill'd:
O'er whom his very madness, like some ore
Among a mineral of metals base,
Shows itself pure; he weeps for what is done.
King. O Gertrude, come away!
The sun no sooner shall the mountains touch,
But we will ship him hence: and this vile deed
We must, with all our majesty and skill,   31
Both countenance and excuse.   Ho, Guilden-
stern!

Re-enter Rosencrantz and Guildenstern.

Friends both, go join you with some further
aid:
Hamlet in madness hath Polonius slain,
And from his mother's closet hath he dragg'd
him:
Go seek him out; speak fair, and bring the
body
Into the chapel.   I pray you, haste in this.
         [*Exeunt Rosencrantz and Guildenstern.*

128

Come, Gertrude, we'll call up our wisest
    friends;
And let them know, both what we mean to do,
And what's untimely done. . . .   40
Whose whisper o'er the world's diameter
As level as the cannon to his blank
Transports his poison'd shot, may miss our
    name
And hit the woundless air. O, come away!
My soul is full of discord and dismay. [*Exeunt*

SCENE II

Another room in the castle.

Enter Hamlet.

Ham. Safely stowed.

Ros.
Guil. } [*Within*] Hamlet! Lord Hamlet.

Ham. But soft, what noise? who calls on Ham-
    let?
    O, here they come.

Enter Rosencrantz and Guildenstern.

Ros. What have you done, my lord, with the dead
    body?

Ham. Compounded it with dust, whereto 'tis kin.

40–44. F. 1 omits these lines, and ends scene with the words—
        "*And what's untimely done. Oh, come away,
        My soul is full of discord and dismay.*"

Theobald proposed to restore the line by adding "*for, haply, slander.*"
—I. G.

Ros. Tell us where 'tis, that we may take it thence
　　And bear it to the chapel.

Ham. Do not believe it.

Ros. Believe what?　　　　　　　　　　　　10

Ham. That I can keep your counsel and not
　　mine own. Besides, to be demanded of a
　　sponge! what replication should be made by
　　the son of a king?

Ros. Take you me for a sponge, my lord?

Ham. Aye, sir; that soaks up the king's coun-
　　tenance, his rewards, his authorities. But
　　such officers do the king best service in the
　　end: he keeps them, like an ape, in the corner
　　of his jaw; first mouthed, to be last swal-　20
　　lowed: when he needs what you have
　　gleaned, it is but squeezing you, and, sponge,
　　you shall be dry again.

Ros. I understand you not, my lord.

Ham. I am glad of it: a knavish speech sleeps
　　in a foolish ear.

Ros. My lord, you must tell us where the body
　　is, and go with us to the king.

Ham. The body is with the king, but the king
　　is not with the body. The king is a thing—　30

Guil. A thing, my lord?

Ham. Of nothing: bring me to him. Hide
　　fox, and all after.　　　　　　　　　*[Exeunt.*

19. *"like an ape";* so Ff.; Qq., *"like an apple";* Farmer conj. *"like
an ape, an apple";* Singer, from Q. 1, *"like an ape doth nuts";* Hudson (1879), *"as an ape doth nuts."*—I. G.

25. *"A knavish speech sleeps in a foolish ear";* a sentence proverbial since Shakespeare's time, but not known earlier.—I. G.

32. *cp.* Psalm cxliv., *"Man is like a thing of naught";* 32–33, *"Hide
fox, and all after,"* the reading of Ff.; omitted in Qq.—I. G.

Scene III

Another room in the castle.

Enter King, attended.

King. I have sent to seek him, and to find the body.
    How dangerous is it that this man goes loose!
    Yet must not we put the strong law on him:
    He 's loved of the distracted multitude,
    Who like not in their judgment, but their eyes;
    And where 'tis so, the offender's scourge is
        weigh'd,
    But never the offense.   To bear all smooth and
        even,
    This sudden sending away must seem
    Deliberate pause: diseases desperate grown
    By desperate appliance are relieved,   10
    Or not at all.

Enter Rosencrantz.

                    How now! what hath befall'n?
Ros. Where the dead body is bestow'd, my lord,
    We cannot get from him.
King.   But where is he?
Ros. Without, my lord; guarded, to know your
        pleasure.
King. Bring him before us.
Ros. Ho, Guildenstern! bring in my lord.

Enter Hamlet and Guildenstern.

King. Now, Hamlet, where 's Polonius?

Ham. At supper.

King. At supper! where?

Ham. Not where he eats, but where he is eaten: 20
a certain convocation of public worms are
e'en at him. Your worm is your only emperor for diet: we fat all creatures else to
fat us, and we fat ourselves for maggots:
your fat king and your lean beggar is but
variable service, two dishes, but to one table:
that's the end.

King. Alas, alas!

Ham. A man may fish with the worm that hath
eat of a king, and eat of the fish that hath 30
fed of that worm.

King. What dost thou mean by this?

Ham. Nothing but to show you how a king
may go a progress through the guts of a
beggar.

King. Where is Polonius?

Ham. In heaven; send thither to see: if your
messenger find him not there, seek him i' the
other place yourself. But indeed, if you
find him not within this month, you shall 40
nose him as you go up the stairs into the
lobby.

King. Go seek him there.   [*To some Attendants.*

Ham. He will stay till you come.

[*Exeunt Attendants.*

21–23. There is a punning allusion to the Diet of Worms.—
C. H. H.

28–31. Omitted in Ff.—I. G.

29–30. Probably pure mystification.—C. H. H.

King. Hamlet, this deed, for thine especial safety,
   Which we do tender, as we dearly grieve
   For that which thou hast done, must send thee
      hence
   With fiery quickness: therefore prepare thy-
      self;
   The bark is ready and the wind at help,
   The associates tend, and every thing is bent 50
   For England.
Ham.   For England?
King.   Aye, Hamlet.
Ham.   Good.
King. So is it, if thou knew'st our purposes.
Ham. I see a cherub that sees them. But,
   come; for England! Farewell, dear mother.
King. Thy loving father, Hamlet.
Ham. My mother: father and mother is man
   and wife; man and wife is one flesh, and so,
   my mother. Come, for England!   [*Exit.*
King. Follow him at foot; tempt him with speed
      abroad;
   Delay it not; I 'll have him hence to-night: 60
   Away! for every thing is seal'd and done
   That else leans on the affair: pray you, make
      haste.
         [*Exeunt Rosencrantz and Guildenstern.*
   And, England, if my love thou hold'st at
      aught—
   As my great power thereof may give thee sense,

45. *"this deed, for thine"; so* Qq.; Ff., *"deed of thine, for thine."*
—I. G.
48. *"with fiery quickness"; so* Ff.; *omitted in* Qq.—I. G.

Since yet thy cicatrice looks raw and red
After the Danish sword, and thy free awe
Pays homage to us—thou mayst not coldly set
Our sovereign process; which imports at full,
By letters congruing to that effect,
The present death of Hamlet.   Do it, Eng-
    land;   70
For like the hectic in my blood he rages,
And thou must cure me; till I know 'tis done,
Howe'er my haps, my joys were ne'er begun.
                           [*Exit.*

SCENE IV

A plain in Denmark.

Enter Fortinbras, a Captain and Soldiers,
marching.

For. Go, captain, from me greet the Danish king;
Tell him that by his license Fortinbras
Craves the conveyance of a promised march
Over his kingdom.   You know the rendezvous.
If that his majesty would aught with us,
We shall express our duty in his eye;

73. *"my haps, my joys were ne'er begun";* so Ff.; Qq., *"my haps, my joyes will nere begin";* Johnson conj. *"my hopes, my joys are not begun";* Heath conj. *"'t may hap, my joys will ne'er begin";* Collier MS., *"my hopes, my joyes were ne're begun";* Tschischwitz, *"my joys will ne'er begun."*—I. G.

3. *"Craves";* so Qq.; Ff. 1, 2, *"Claimes."*—I. G.

6. *"express our duty in his eye";* in the *Regulations for the Establishment of the Queen's Household,* 1627: "All such as doe service *in the queen's eye."* And in *The Establishment of Prince Henry's Household,* 1610: "All such as doe service *in the prince's eye."*—H. N. H.

And let him know so.

Cap.   I will do 't, my lord.

For. Go softly on.

[*Exeunt Fortinbras and Soldiers.*

*Enter Hamlet, Rosencrantz, Guildenstern,
and others.*

Ham. Good sir, whose powers are these?

Cap. They are of Norway, sir.   10

Ham. How purposed, sir, I pray you?

Cap. Against some part of Poland.

Ham. Who commands them, sir?

Cap. The nephew to old Norway, Fortinbras.

Ham. Goes it against the main of Poland, sir,
Or for some frontier?

Cap. Truly to speak, and with no addition,
We go to gain a little patch of ground
That hath in it no profit but the name.
To pay five ducats, five, I would not farm it; 20
Nor will it yield to Norway or the Pole
A ranker rate, should it be sold in fee.

Ham. Why, then the Polack never will defend it.

Cap. Yes, it is already garrison'd.

Ham. Two thousand souls and twenty thousand
ducats
Will not debate the question of this straw:
This is the imposthume of much wealth and
peace,
That inward breaks, and shows no cause without
Why the man dies.   I humbly thank you, sir.

8. *"Go softly on";* these words are probably spoken to the troops.
The folio has *safely* instead of *softly.*—H. N. H.

9–66. the reading of the Qq.; omitted in Ff.—I. G.

Cap. God be wi' you, sir.   [*Exit.*
Ros.   Will 't please you go, my lord?
Ham. I 'll be with you straight. Go a little be-
        fore.   31
                    [*Exeunt all but Hamlet.*
How all occasions do inform against me,
And spur my dull revenge! What is a man,
If his chief good and market of his time
Be but to sleep and feed? a beast, no more.
Sure, he that made us with such large discourse,
Looking before and after, gave us not
That capability and god-like reason
To fust in us unused. Now, whether it be
Bestial oblivion, or some craven scruple   40
Of thinking too precisely on the event,—
A thought which, quarter'd, hath but one part
        wisdom
And ever three parts coward,—I do not know
Why yet I live to say 'this thing 's to do,'
Sith I have cause, and will, and strength, and
        means,
To do 't. Examples gross as earth exhort me:
Witness this army, of such mass and charge,
Led by a delicate and tender prince,
Whose spirit with divine ambition puff'd
Makes mouths at the invisible event,   50
Exposing what is mortal and unsure
To all that fortune, death and danger dare,
Even for an egg-shell. Rightly to be great
It not to stir without great argument,
But greatly to find quarrel in a straw

50. *"Makes mouths at"*; mocks at.—C. H. H.

When honor 's at the stake. ∧ How stand I then,
That have a father kill'd, a mother stain'd,
Excitements of my reason and my blood,
And let all sleep, while to my shame I see
The imminent death of twenty thousand men, 60 *pause*
That for a fantasy and trick of frame
Go to their graves like beds, fight for a plot
Whereon the numbers cannot try the cause,
Which is not tomb enough and continent —
To hide the slain?   O, from this time forth,
My thoughts be bloody, or be nothing worth!
                                        [*Exit.*

SCENE V

Elsinore.   A room in the castle.

Enter Queen, Horatio, and a Gentleman.

Queen. I will not speak with her.
Gent. She is importunate, indeed distract:
  Her mood will needs be pitied.
Queen.   What would she have?
Gent. She speaks much of her father, says she
    hears
  There 's tricks i' the world, and hems and beats
    her heart,
  Spurns enviously at straws; speaks things in
    doubt,
  That carry but half sense: her speech is nothing,
  Yet the unshaped use of it doth move
  The hearers to collection; they aim at it,

And botch the words up fit to their own
　　thoughts;　　　　　　　　　　　　10
Which, as her winks and nods and gestures yield
　　them,
Indeed would make one think there might be
　　thought,
Though nothing sure, yet much unhappily.

Hor. 'Twere good she were spoken with, for she
　　may strew
Dangerous conjectures in ill-breeding minds.

Queen. Let her come in.　　　　*[Exit Gentleman.*
　　[Aside] To my sick soul, as sin's true nature is,
Each toy seems prologue to some great amiss:
So full of artless jealousy is guilt,
It spills itself in fearing to be spilt.　　　　20

Re-enter Gentleman, with Ophelia.

Oph. Where is the beauteous majesty of Den-
　　mark?

Queen. How now, Ophelia!

Oph. *[Sings]* How should I your true love know
　　　　From another one?
　　　　By his cockle hat and staff
　　　　And his sandal shoon.

Queen. Alas, sweet lady, what imports this song?

13. *"Unhappily"* is here used in the sense of *mischievously.*—
H. N. H.

14–16; Qq. and Ff. assign these lines to Horatio; Blackstone re-
arranged the lines as in the text.—I. G.

22. *"Ophelia";* in the quarto of 1603, this stage-direction is curious
as showing that Ophelia was originally made to play an accompani-
ment to her singing. It reads thus: "Enter Ophelia, playing on a
lute, and her hair down, singing."—H. N. H.

Oph. Say you? nay, pray you, mark.

[*Sings*]   He is dead and gone, lady,
        He is dead and gone;   30
        At his head a grass-green turf,
        At his heels a stone.
  Oh, oh!

Queen.   Nay, but Ophelia,—

Oph.   Pray you, mark.

[*Sings*] White his shroud as the mountain snow,—

Enter King.

Queen. Alas, look here, my lord.

Oph. [*Sings*] Larded with sweet flowers;
        Which bewept to the grave did go
        With true-love showers.

King. How do you, pretty lady?   40

Oph. Well, God 'ild you! They say the owl was a baker's daughter. Lord, we know

33. *Nay, but Ophelia";* "There is no part of this play in its representation on the stage more pathetic than this scene; which, I suppose, proceeds from the utter insensibility Ophelia has to her own misfortunes. A great sensibility, or none at all, seems to produce the same effects. In the latter case the audience supply what is wanting, and with the former they sympathize" (Sir J. Reynolds).— H. N. H.

38. *"grave,"* so Q. 1, Ff.; Qq., *"ground"; "did go";* Pope's emendation of Qq.; Ff., *"did not go."*—I. G.

41. *"The owl was a baker's daughter";* this is said to be a common tradition in Gloucestershire. Mr. Douce relates it thus: "Our Saviour went into a baker's shop where they were baking, and asked for some bread to eat. The mistress of the shop immediately put a piece of dough in the oven to bake for him; but was reprimanded by her daughter, who, insisting that the piece of dough was too large, reduced it to a very small size. The dough, however, immediately began to swell, and presently became of a most enormous size,

what we are, but know not what we may be.
God be at your table!

King. Conceit upon her father.

Oph. Pray you, let's have no words of this;
but when they ask you what it means, say
you this:

    [*Sings*] To-morrow is Saint Valentine's day
        All in the morning betime,   50
        And I a maid at your window,
        To be your Valentine.
    Then up he rose, and donn'd his clothes,
        And dupp'd the chamber-door;
    Let in the maid, that out a maid
        Never departed more.

King. Pretty Ophelia!

Oph. Indeed, la, without an oath, I'll make an
end on 't:

Whereupon the baker's daughter cried out, 'Heugh, heugh, heugh,'
which owl-like noise probably induced our Saviour to transform
her into that bird for her wickedness." The story is told to deter
children from illiberal behavior to the poor.—H. N. H.

49–56. Song in Qq.; omitted in Ff.—I. G.

49. *"Saint Valentine's day"*; the origin of the choosing of Valen-
tines has not been clearly developed. Mr. Douce traces it to a Pagan
custom of the same kind during the Lupercalia feasts in honor of
Pan and Juno, celebrated in the month of February by the Romans.
The anniversary of the good bishop, or Saint Valentine, happening
in this month, the pious early promoters of Christianity placed this
popular custom under the patronage of the saint, in order to eradi-
cate the notion of its pagan origin. In France the *Valantin* was a
movable feast, celebrated on the first Sunday in Lent, which was
called the *jour des brandons,* because the boys carried about lighted
torches on that day. It is very probable that the saint has nothing
to do with the custom; his legend gives no clue to any such supposi-
tion. The popular notion that the birds choose their mates about
this period has its rise in the poetical world of fiction.—H. N. H.

[*Sings*] By Gis and by Saint Charity,   60
      Alack, and fie for shame!
     Young men will do 't, if they come to 't;
      By cock, they are to blame.
    Quoth she, before you tumbled me,
     You promised me to wed.

He answers:

    So would I ha' done, by yonder sun,
     An thou hadst not come to my bed.

King. How long hath she been thus?
Oph. I hope all will be well. We must be   70
patient: but I cannot choose but weep, to
think they should lay him i' the cold ground.
My brother shall know of it: and so I thank
you for your good counsel. Come, my
coach! Good night, ladies; good night,
sweet ladies; good night, good night.   [*Exit.*
King. Follow her close; give her good watch,
    I pray you.   [*Exit Horatio.*
O, this is the poison of deep grief; it springs
All from her father's death. O Gertrude,
    Gertrude,
When sorrows come, they come not single
    spies,   80
But in battalions! First, her father slain:
Next, your son gone; and he most violent author
Of his own just remove: the people muddied,
Thick and unwholesome in their thoughts and
    whispers,

79. *"Death, O"; Qq., "death, and now behold, &."*—I. G.

For good Polonius' death; and we have done
    but greenly,
In hugger-mugger to inter him: poor Ophelia
Divided from herself and her fair judgment,
Without the which we are pictures, or mere
    beasts:
Last, and as much containing as all these,
Her brother is in secret come from France,   90
Feeds on his wonder, keeps himself in clouds,
And wants not buzzers to infect his ear
With pestilent speeches of his father's death;
Wherein necessity, of matter beggar'd,
Will nothing stick our person to arraign
In ear and ear. O my dear Gertrude, this,
Like to a murdering-piece, in many places
Gives me superfluous death. [*A noise within.*

Queen.   Alack, what noise is this?
King. Where are my Switzers? Let them guard
    the door.

Enter another Gentleman.

What is the matter?
Gent.   Save yourself, my lord: 100
The ocean, overpeering of his list,
Eats not the flats with more impetuous haste
Than young Laertes, in a riotous head,
O'erbears your officers. The rabble call him
    lord;

91. *"Feeds on his wonder"*; Johnson's emendation; Qq., *"Feeds on this wonder"*; Ff., *"Keepes on his wonder"*; Hanmer, *"Feeds on his anger."*—I. G.
96. *"Alack, what noise is this"*; omitted in Qq.—I. G.

And, as the world were now but to begin,
Antiquity forgot, custom not known,
The ratifiers and props of every word,
They cry 'Choose we; Laertes shall be king!'
Caps, hands and tongues applaud it to the
    clouds,
'Laertes shall be king, Laertes king!'   110
Queen. How cheerfully on the false trail they cry!
O, this is counter, you false Danish dogs!
                              [*Noise within.*
King. The doors are broke.

Enter Laertes, armed: Danes following.

Laer. Where is this king? Sirs, stand you all
    without.
Danes. No, let's come in.
Laer.   I pray you, give me leave.
Danes. We will, we will.
                    [*They retire without the door.*
Laer. I thank you: keep the door. O thou vile
    king,
    Give me my father!
Queen.   Calmly, good Laertes.
Laer. That drop of blood that's calm proclaims me
    bastard;   119
    Cries cuckold to my father; brands the harlot
    Even here, between the chaste unsmirched brows
    Of my true mother.

105. *"as the world"; as* has here the force of *as if.* The explanation sometimes given of the passage is, that the rabble are the
ratifiers and props of every *idle* word. The plain sense is, that
antiquity and custom are the ratifiers and props of every *sound*
word touching the matter in hand, the ordering of human society
and the State.—H. N. H.

King.   What is the cause, Laertes,
    That thy rebellion looks so giant-like?
    Let him go, Gertrude; do not fear our person:
    There 's such divinity doth hedge a king,
    That treason can but peep to what it would,
    Acts little of his will.   Tell me, Laertes,
    Why thou art thus incensed: let him go,
       Gertrude:
    Speak, man.
Laer. Where is my father?
King.   Dead.
Queen.   But not by him.   130
King. Let him demand his fill.
Laer. How came he dead?   I 'll not be juggled
    with:
    To hell, allegiance! vows, to the blackest devil!
    Conscience and grace, to the profoundest pit!
    I dare damnation: to this point I stand,
    That both the worlds I give to negligence,
    Let come what comes; only I 'll be revenged
    Most throughly for my father.
King.   Who shall stay you?
Laer. My will, not all the world:
    And for my means, I 'll husband them so well,
    They shall go far with little.   141
King.   Good Laertes.
    If you desire to know the certainty

121. *"unsmirched brows";* Grant White's emendation; F. 1, *"unsmirched brow."*—I. G.

127. *"Acts little of his will";* "Proofs," says Coleridge, "as indeed
all else is, that Shakespeare never intended us to see the King with
Hamlet's eyes; though, I suspect, the managers have long done so."
—H. N. H.

Of your dear father's death, is 't writ in your re-
    venge
That, swoopstake, you will draw both friend
    and foe,
Winner and loser?

Laer. None but his enemies.

King.   Will you know them then?

Laer. To his good friends thus wide I 'll ope my
    arms;
And, like the kind life-rendering pelican,
Repast them with my blood.

King.   Why, now you speak
Like a good child and a true gentleman.   150
That I am guiltless of your father's death,
And am most sensibly in grief for it,
It shall as level to your judgment pierce
As day does to your eye.

Danes. [*Within*]   Let her come in.

Laer. How now! what noise is that?

Re-enter Ophelia.

O heat, dry up my brains! tears seven times salt,
Burn out the sense and virtue of mine eye!
By heaven, thy madness shall be paid with
    weight,
Till our scale turn the beam.   O rose of May!

153. *"your judgment pierce";* the folio has *pierce;* the quartos,
pear, meaning, of course, *appear.* The latter is both awkward in
language and tame in sense. Understanding *level* in the sense of
direct, pierce gives an apt and clear enough meaning.—H. N. H.

156. *"Re-enter Ophelia";* modern editions commonly add here,
"fantastically dressed with Straws and Flowers." There is no authority, and not much occasion, for any such stage-direction.—
H. N. H.

Dear maid, kind sister, sweet Ophelia!   16(

O heavens! is 't possible a young maid's wits

Should be as mortal as an old man's life?

Nature is fine in love, and where 'tis fine

It sends some precious instance of itself

After the thing it loves.

Oph. [*Sings*] They bore him barefaced on the
bier:

    Hey non nonny, nonny, hey nonny

    And in his grave rain'd many a
tear,—

Fare you well, my dove!

Laer. Hadst thou thy wits, and didst persuade revenge,   17(

It could not move thus.

Oph. [*Sings*] You must sing down a-down,

    An you call him a-down-a.

O, how the wheel becomes it! It is the false

steward, that stole his master's daughter.

Laer. This nothing 's more than matter.

Oph. There 's rosemary, that 's for remem-

162–165, 167, omitted in Qq.—I. G.

168. *"rain'd"*; so Qq.; Ff. 1, 2, *"raines."*—I. G.

174–175. *"It is the false steward,"* &c.; the story has not yet been
identified.—I. G.

177. *"There's rosemary"*; our ancestors gave to almost every
flower and plant its emblematic meaning, and, like the ladies of the
east, made them almost as expressive as written language. Perdita
in *The Winter's Tale,* distributes her flowers in the same manner as
Ophelia, and some of them with the same meaning. *The Handfull of
Pleasant Delites,* 1584, has a ballad called "A Nosegaie alwaies
sweet for Lovers to send for Tokens," where we find,—

   "Rosemarie is for *remembrance*
   Betweene us day and night."

Rosemarie had this attribute because it was said to strengthen the

OPHELIA: There's rosemary, that's for remembrance—
Act IV, Scene 5.

brance: pray you, love, remember: and there
is pansies, that's for thoughts.

Laer. A document in madness; thoughts and 180
remembrance fitted.

Oph. There's fennel for you, and columbines:
there's rue for you: and here's some for me:
we may call it herb of grace o' Sundays: O,
you must wear your rue with a difference.
There's a daisy: I would give you some
violets, but they withered all when father
died: they say a' made a good end,—
[*Sings*] For bonnie sweet Robin is all my
joy.   190

Laer. Thought and affliction, passion, hell itself,
She turns to favor and to prettiness.

memory, and was therefore used as a token of remembrance and
affection between lovers. Why *pansies* (pensées) are emblems of
thoughts is obvious. *Fennel* was emblematic of *flattery*. Browne,
in his *Britannia's Pastorals*, says,—

"The *columbine,* in tawny often taken,
    Is then ascrib'd to such as are *forsaken.*"

Rue was for *ruth* or *repentance.* It was also commonly called
herb grace, probably from being accounted "a present remedy
against all poison, and a potent auxiliary in exorcisms, all evil
things fleeing from it." Wearing it with a difference was an heraldic term for a mark of distinction. The *daisy* was emblematic
of a *dissembler.* The *violet* is for *faithfulness,* and is thus characterized in *The Lover's Nosegaie.*—H. N. H.

190. Poor Ophelia in her madness remembers the ends of many
old popular ballads. "Bonny Robin" appears to have been a favorite, for there were many others written to that tune. This last
stanza is quoted with some variation in *Eastward Ho!* 1605, by
Jonson, Marston, and Chapman.—H. N. H.

191. *"Thought"* was used for *grief, care, pensiveness.* "Curarum
volvere in pectore. He will die for sorrow and *thought*" (Baret).
—H. N. H.

Oph. [*Sings*] And will a' not come again?
              And will a' not come again?
                 No, no, he is dead,
                 Go to thy death-bed,
         He never will come again.
         His beard was as white as snow,
         All flaxen was his poll:
              He is gone, he is gone,   200
              And we cast away moan:
             God ha' mercy on his soul!
   And of all Christian souls, I pray God. God
     be wi' you.   [*Exit.*

Laer. Do you see this, O God?

King. Laertes, I must commune with your grief,
   Or you deny me right. Go but apart,
   Make choice of whom your wisest friends you
     will.
   And they shall hear and judge 'twixt you and
     me:
   If by direct or by collateral hand   209
   They find us touched, we will our kingdom give,
   Our crown, our life, and all that we call ours,
   To you in satisfaction; but if not,
   Be you content to lend your patience to us,
   And we shall jointly labor with your soul
   To give it due content.

Laer.   Let this be so;
   His means of death, his obscure funeral,
   No trophy, sword, nor hatchment o'er his bones,

198. *cp.* "*Eastward Hoe*" (1604), by Jonson, Marston, and Chap-
m*'*n, for a travesty of the scene and this song (Act III. Sc. i.).—
G.

No noble rite nor formal ostentation,
Cry to be heard, as 'twere from heaven to earth,
That I must call 't in question.   220
King.   So you shall;
And where the offense is let the great axe fall.
I pray you, go with me.   [*Exeunt.*

SCENE VI

Another room in the castle.

Enter Horatio and a servant.

Hor. What are they that would speak with me?
Serv. Sea-faring men, sir: they say they have let-
     ters for you.
Hor. Let them come in.   [*Exit Servant.*
I do not know from what part of the world
I should be greeted, if not from Lord Hamlet.

Enter Sailors.

First Sail. God bless you, sir.
Hor. Let him bless thee too.
First Sail. He shall, sir, an 't please him.
     There 's a letter for you, sir; it comes from
     the ambassador that was bound for Eng-   10

220. *"call it in question";* the funerals of knights and persons of
rank were made with great ceremony and ostentation formerly. Sir
John Hawkins observes that "the sword, the helmet, the gauntlet,
spurs, and tabard are still hung over the grave of every knight."—
H. N. H.
   2. *"Sea-faring men";* so Qq.; Ff. read *"Sailors."*—I. G.

land; if your name be Horatio, as I am let
to know it is.

Hor. [*Reads*] 'Horatio, when thou shalt have
overlooked this, give these fellows some
means to the king: they have letters for him.
Ere we were two days old at sea, a pirate of
very warlike appointment gave us chase.
Finding ourselves too slow of sail, we put on
a compelled valor, and in the grapple I
boarded them: on the instant they got clear   20
of our ship; so I alone became their prisoner.
They have dealt with me like thieves of
mercy: but they knew what they did; I am
to do a good turn for them. Let the king
have the letters I have sent; and repair thou
to me with as much speed as thou wouldst
fly death. I have words to speak in thine
ear will make thee dumb; yet are they much
too light for the bore of the matter. These
good fellows will bring thee where I am.   30
Rosencrantz and Guildenstern hold their
course for England: of them I have much to
tell thee. Farewell.

'He that thou knowest thine, HAMLET.'

Come, I will make you way for these your let-
ters;
And do 't the speedier, that you may direct me
To him from whom you brought them.

                          [*Exeunt.*

Scene VII

Another room in the castle.

Enter King and Laertes.

King. Now must your conscience my acquittance
seal,
  And you must put me in your heart for friend,
  Sith you have heard, and with a knowing ear,
  That he which hath your noble father slain
  Pursued my life.
Laer.   It well appears: but tell me
  Why you proceeded not against these feats,
  So crimeful and so capital in nature,
  As by your safety, wisdom, all things else,
  You mainly were stirr'd up.
King.   O, for two special reasons,
  Which may to you perhaps seem much un-
sinew'd,   10
  But yet to me they 're strong. The queen his
mother
  Lives almost by his looks; and for myself—
  My virtue or my plague, be it either which—
  She 's so conjunctive to my life and soul,
  That, as the star moves not but in his sphere,
  I could not but by her. The other motive,
  Why to a public count I might not go,
  Is the great love the general gender bear him;

9. *"mainly were stirr'd up"*; had the strongest motive to do.—
C. H. H.
  14. *"She's so conjunctive"*; so Ff.; Qq. read *"She is so concline"*;
Q., 1676, *"She is so precious."*—I. G.

Who, dipping all his faults in their affection,
Would, like the spring that turneth wood to
    stone,   20
Convert his gyves to graces; so that my arrows,
Too slightly timber'd for so loud a wind,
Would have reverted to my bow again
And not where I had aim'd them.

Laer. And so have I a noble father lost;
A sister driven into desperate terms,
Whose worth, if praises may go back again,
Stood challenger on mount of all the age
For her perfections: but my revenge will come.

King. Break not your sleeps for that: you must
    not think   30
That we are made of stuff so flat and dull
That we can let our beard be shook with danger
And think it pastime.   You shortly shall hear
    more:
I loved your father, and we love ourself;
And that, I hope, will teach you to imagine—

Enter a Messenger, with letters.

How now! what news?

Mess.   Letters, my lord, from Hamlet:
This to your majesty; this to the queen.

King. From Hamlet! who brought them?

Mess. Sailors, my lord, they say; I saw them not:
They were given me by Claudio; he received
    them   40
Of him that brought them.

22. *"loud a wind,"* so Ff.; Qq. 2, 3, *"loued Arm'd"*; Qq. 4, 5,
"loued armes."—I. G.

King.   Laertes, you shall hear them.
    Leave us.   [*Exit Messenger.*
[*Reads*] 'High and mighty, You shall know I
    am set naked on your kingdom.   To-mor-
    row shall I beg leave to see your kingly
    eyes: when I shall, first asking your pardon
    thereunto, recount the occasion of my sud-
    den and more strange return.
                              'HAMLET.'
    What should this mean?   Are all the rest come
        back?   50
    Or is it some abuse, and no such thing?
Laer. Know you the hand?
King. 'Tis Hamlet's character.   'Naked'!
    And in a postscript here, he says 'alone.'
    Can you advise me?
Laer. I 'm lost in it, my lord.   But let him come;
    It warms the very sickness in my heart,
    That I shall live and tell him to his teeth,
    'Thus didest thou.'
King.   If it be so, Laertes,—
    As how should it be so? how otherwise?—
    Will you be ruled by me?
Laer.   Aye, my lord;   60
    So you will not o'errule me to a peace.
King. To thine own peace.   If he be now return'd,
    As checking at his voyage, and that he means
    No more to undertake it, I will work him
    To an exploit now ripe in my device,
    Under the which he shall not choose but fall:

59. *"As how should it be so? how otherwise?"* It is incompre-
hensible, and yet, on the evidence, beyond question.—C. H. H.

  And for his death no wind of blame shall
   breathe;
  But even his mother shall uncharge the practice,
  And call it accident.

Laer.   My lord, I will be ruled;
  The rather, if you could devise it so   70
  That I might be the organ.

King.   It falls right.
  You have been talk'd of since your travel much,
  And that in Hamlet's hearing, for a quality
  Wherein, they say, you shine: your sum of parts
  Did not together pluck such envy from him,
  As did that one, and that in my regard
  Of the unworthiest siege.

Laer.   What part is that, my lord?
King. A very riband in the cap of youth,
  Yet needful too; for youth no less becomes
  The light and careless livery that it wears 80
  Than settled age his sables and his weeds,
  Importing health and graveness. Two months
   since,
  Here was a gentleman of Normandy:—
  I 've seen myself, and served against, the
   French,
  And they can well on horseback: but this gallant
  Had witchcraft in 't; he grew unto his seat,
  And to such wondrous doing brought his horse
  As had he been incorpsed and demi-natured

  69–82. *"my lord . . . graveness";* omitted in Ff.; so, too, ll.
115–124.—I. G.

  78. *"A very riband";* we have elsewhere found *very* used in the
sense of *mere.*—H. N. H.

With the brave beast: so far he topp'd my
    thought
That I, in forgery of shapes and tricks,   90
Come short of what he did.

Laer.   A Norman was 't?

King. A Norman.

Laer. Upon my life, Lamond.

King.   The very same.

Laer. I know him well: he is the brooch indeed
And gem of all the nation.

King. He made confession of you,
And gave you such a masterly report,
For art and exercise in your defense,
And for your rapier most especial,
That he cried out, 'twould be a sight indeed 100
If one could match you: the scrimers of their
    nation,
He swore, had neither motion, guard, nor eye,
If you opposed them. Sir, this report of his
Did Hamlet so envenom with his envy
That he could nothing do but wish and beg
Your sudden coming o'er, to play with him.
Now, out of this—

Laer.   What out of this, my lord?

King. Laertes, was your father dear to you?
Or are you like the painting of a sorrow,
A face without a heart?

Laer.   Why ask you this?   110

King. Not that I think you did not love your
    father,

---

97. *"gave you such a masterly report";* i. e. reported him to be
uch a master.—C. H. H.

But that I know love is begun by time,
And that I see, in passages of proof,
Time qualifies the spark and fire of it.
There lives within the very flame of love
A kind of wick or snuff that will abate it;
And nothing is at a like goodness still,
For goodness, growing to a plurisy,
Dies in his own too much: that we would do
We should do when we would; for this 'would'
    changes   120
And hath abatements and delays as many
As there are tongues, are hands, are accidents,
And then this 'should' is like a spendthrift sigh,
That hurts by easing. But, to the quick o' the
    ulcer:
Hamlet comes back: what would you undertake,
To show yourself your father's son indeed
More than in words?
Laer.   To cut his throat i' the church.
King. No place indeed should murder sanctuarize;
    Revenge should have no bounds. But, good
      Laertes,
    Will you do this, keep close within your cham-
      ber.   130

112. As *"love is begun by time,"* and has its gradual increase, so *time* qualifies and abates it. *"Passages of proof"* are transactions of daily experience.—H. N. H.

123. *"a spendthrift sigh"*; Mr. Blakeway justly observes, that "Sorrow for neglected opportunities and time abused seems most aptly compared to *the sigh of a spendthrift;*—good resolutions not carried into effect are deeply injurious to the moral character. Like sighs, *they hurt by easing;* they unburden the mind and satisfy the conscience, without producing any effect upon the conduct."— H. N. H.

> Hamlet return'd shall know you are come home:
> We 'll put on those shall praise your excellence
> And set a double varnish on the fame
> The Frenchman gave you; bring you in fine to-
>   gether
> And wager on your heads: he, being remiss,
> Most generous and free from all contriving,
> Will not peruse the foils, so that with ease,
> Or with a little shuffling, you may choose
> A sword unbated, and in a pass of practice
> Requite him for your father.

Laer.   I will do 't;   140
> And for that purpose I 'll anoint my sword.
> I bought an unction of a mountebank,
> So mortal that but dip a knife in it,
> Where it draws blood no cataplasm so rare,
> Collected from all simples that have virtue
> Under the moon, can save the thing from death
> That is but scratch'd withal: I 'll touch my
>   point
> With this contagion, that, if I gall him slightly,
> It may be death.

141. *"anoint my sword":* Warburton having pronounced Laertes "a *good* character," Coleridge thereupon makes the following note: "Mercy on Warburton's notion of goodness! Please to refer to the seventh scene of this Act;—'I will do't; and, for this purpose, I'll anoint my sword,'—uttered by Laertes after the King's description of Hamlet: 'He, being remiss, most generous, and free from all contriving, will not peruse the foils.' Yet I acknowledge that Shakespeare evidently wishes, as much as possible, to spare the character of Laertes,—to break the extreme turpitude of his consent to become an agent and accomplice of the King's treachery;—and to this end he re-introduces Ophelia at the close of this scene, to afford a probable stimulus of passion in her brother."—H. N. H.

149. *"it may be death";* Ritson has exclaimed against the villainous treachery of Laertes in this horrid plot: he observes "there is more

King.   Let's further think of this;
    Weigh what convenience both of time and
       means   150
    May fit us to our shape: if this should fail,
    And that our drift look through our bad per-
       formance,
    'Twere better not assay'd: therefore this pro-
       ject
    Should have a back or second, that might hold
    If this did blast in proof.   Soft! let me see:
    We'll make a solemn wager on your cunnings:
    I ha't:
    When in your motion you are hot and dry—
    As make your bouts more violent to that end—
    And that he calls for drink, I'll have prepared
       him   160
    A chalice for the nonce; whereon but sipping,
    If he by chance escape your venom'd stuck,
    Our purpose may hold there.   But stay, what
       noise?

Enter Queen.

How now, sweet queen!

occasion that he should be pointed out for an object of abhorrence,
as he is a character we are led to respect and admire in some preceding scenes." In the quarto of 1603 this contrivance originates
with the king.—H. N. H.

163. *"But stay, what noise?"*; the reading of Qq.; omitted in Ff.
—I. G.

164. *"How now, sweet queen"*; "That Laertes," says Coleridge,
"might be excused in some degree for not cooling, the Act con-
cludes with the affecting death of Ophelia; who in the beginning
lay like a little projection of land into a lake or stream, covered
with spray-flowers, quietly reflected in the quiet waters; but at
length is undermined or loosened, and becomes a faery isle, and
after a brief vagrancy sinks almost without an eddy."—H. N. H.

Queen. One woe doth tread upon another's heel,
     So fast they follow: your sister's drown'd,
     Laertes.
Laer. Drown'd!   O, where?
Queen. There is a willow grows aslant a brook,
     That shows his hoar leaves in the glassy stream;
     There with fantastic garlands did she come
     Of crow-flowers, nettles, daisies, and long pur-
          ples,   170
     That liberal shepherds give a grosser name,
     But our cold maids do dead men's fingers call
          them:
     There, on the pendent boughs her coronet weeds
     Clambering to hang, an envious sliver broke;
     When down her weedy trophies and herself
     Fell in the weeping brook.   Her clothes spread
          wide,
     And mermaid-like a while they bore her up:
     Which time she chanted snatches of old tunes,
     As one incapable of her own distress,
     Or like a creature native and indued   180
     Unto that element: but long it could not be
     Till that her garments, heavy with their drink,
     Pull'd the poor wretch from her melodious lay
     To muddy death.
Laer.   Alas, then she is drown'd!
Queen. Drown'd, drown'd.
Laer. Too much of water hast thou, poor Ophelia,

167. *"There is a willow"*; this exquisite passage is deservedly celebrated. Nothing could better illustrate the Poet's power to make
the description of a thing better than the thing itself, by giving us his
eyes to see it with.—H. N. H.
   178. *"tunes"*; so F. and Q. 1; Q. 2, *"lauds"* (*i. e.* chants).—I. G.

And therefore I forbid my tears: but yet
It is our trick; nature her custom holds,
Let shame say what it will: when these are gone,
The woman will be out.   Adieu, my lord: 190
I have a speech of fire that fain would blaze,
But that this folly douts it.   *[Exit.*
King.   Let 's follow, Gertrude:
How much I had to do to calm his rage!
Now fear I this will give it start again;
Therefore let 's follow.   *[Exeunt.*

192. *"douts";* Knight's emendation; F. 1, *"doubts";* Qq., *"drownes."*
—I. G.

ACT FIFTH

Scene I

A churchyard.

Enter two Clowns, with spades, &c.

First Clo. Is she to be buried in Christian
burial that willfully seeks her own salvation?

Sec. Clo. I tell thee she is; and therefore make
her grave straight: the crowner hath sat on
her, and finds it Christian burial.

First Clo. How can that be, unless she
drowned herself in her own defense?

Sec. Clo. Why, 'tis found so.

First Clo. It must be 'se offendendo;' it cannot
be else.   For here lies the point: if I drown   10
myself wittingly, it argues an act: and an
act hath three branches; it is, to act, to do, to
perform: argal, she drowned herself wittingly.

13. *"wittingly";* Shakespeare's frequent and correct use of legal
terms and phrases has led to the belief that he must have served
something of an apprenticeship in the law. Among the legal authorities studied in his time, were Plowden's *Commentaries,* a black-
letter book, written in the old law French. One of the cases reported by Plowden, is that of Dame Hales, regarding the forfeiture
of a lease, in consequence of the suicide of Sir James Hales; and
Sir John Hawkins has pointed out, that this rich burlesque of
"crowner's-quest law" was probably intended as a ridicule on certain passages in that case. He produces the following speech of

Sec. Clo. Nay, but hear you, goodman delver.

First Clo. Give me leave. Here lies the
water; good: here stands the man; good: if
the man go to this water and drown himself,
it is, will he, nill he, he goes; mark you that;
but if the water come to him and drown him,   20
he drowns not himself: argal, he that is not
guilty of his own death shortens not his own
life.

Sec. Clo. But is this law?

First Clo. Aye, marry, is 't; crowner's quest
law.

Sec. Clo. Will you ha' the truth on 't? If this

one of the counsel: "Walsh said that the act consists of three
parts. The first is the imagination, which is a reflection or meditation of the mind, whether or no it is convenient for him to destroy
himself, and what way it can be done. The second is the resolution,
which is a determination of the mind to destroy himself, and to do
it in this or that particular way. The third is the perfection,
which is the execution of what the mind has resolved to do. And
this perfection consists of two parts, the beginning and the end.
The beginning is the doing of the act which causes the death; and
the end is the death, which is only a sequel to the act."—H. N. H.

22. *"shortens not his own life";* we must here produce another passage from Plowden, as given by Hawkins. It is the reasoning of
one of the judges, and is nearly as good as that in the text: "Sir
James Hales was dead, and how came he to his death? It may be
answered, by drowning; and who drowned him? Sir James Hales.
And when did he drown him? in his life-time. So that Sir James
Hales, being alive, caused Sir James Hales to die; and the act of
the living man was the death of the dead man. And then for this
offence it is reasonable to punish the living man who committed the
offence, and not the dead man. But how can he be said to be
punished alive, when the punishment comes after his death? Sir,
this can be done no other way but by divesting out of him, from the
time of the act done in his life which was the cause of his death,
the title and property of those things which he had in his life-time."
—H. N. H.

had not been a gentlewoman, she should have
been buried out o' Christian burial.

First Clo. Why, there thou say'st: and the 30
more pity that great folk should have countenance in this world to drown or hang themselves, more than their even Christian.
Come, my spade. There is no ancient gentlemen but gardeners, ditchers and grave-
makers: they hold up Adam's profession.

Sec. Clo. Was he a gentleman?

First Clo. A' was the first that ever bore arms.

Sec. Clo. Why, he had none.

First Clo. What, art a heathen? How dost 40
thou understand the Scripture? The Scripture says Adam digged: could he dig without arms? I 'll put another question to
thee: if thou answerest me not to the purpose, confess thyself—

Sec. Clo. Go to.

First Clo. What is he that builds stronger than
either the mason, the shipwright, or the carpenter?

Sec. Clo. The gallows-maker; for that frame 50
out-lives a thousand tenants.

First Clo. I like thy wit well, in good faith: the
gallows does well; but how does it well? it
does well to those that do ill: now, thou dost
ill to say the gallows is built stronger than
the church: argal, the gallows may do well
to thee. To 't again, come.

Sec. Clo. 'Who builds stronger than a mason,
a shipwright, or a carpenter?'
First Clo. Aye, tell me that, and unyoke.   60
Sec. Clo. Marry, now I can tell.
First Clo. To 't.
Sec. Clo. Mass, I cannot tell.

Enter Hamlet and Horatio, afar off.

First Clo. Cudgel thy brains no more about it,
for your dull ass will not mend his pace with
beating, and when you are asked this question next, say 'a grave-maker:' the houses
that he makes last till doomsday. Go, get
thee to Yaughan; fetch me a stoup of liquor.

> [*Exit Sec. Clown.*
> [*He digs, and sings.*

In youth, when I did love, did love,   70
    Methought it was very sweet,
To contract, O, the time, for-a my behove,
    O, methought, there-a was nothing-a meet.

---

70. *"In youth when I did love"*; the original ballad from whence
these stanzas are taken is printed in Tottel's *Miscellany,* or *Songes
and Sonnettes* by Lord Surrey and others, 1575. The ballad is
attributed to Lord Vaux, and is printed by Dr. Percy in his
Reliques of Ancient Poetry. The *ohs* and the *ahs* are caused by
the forcible emission of the digger's breath at each stroke of the mat-
tock. The original runs thus:

> "I lothe that I did love,
>   In youth that I thought swete:
> As time requires for my behove,
>   Methinks they are not mete.

> "For age with stealing steps
>   Hath claude me with his crowch;
> And lusty youthe away he leaps,
>   As there had bene none such."—H. N. H.

Ham. Has this fellow no feeling of his business, that he sings at grave-making?

Hor. Custom hath made it in him a property
of easiness.

Ham. 'Tis e'en so: the hand of little employ-
ment hath the daintier sense.

First Clo. [*Sings*] But age, with his stealing steps,
　　　Hath claw'd me in his clutch,　　　　81
　　　And hath shipped me intil the land,
　　　As if I had never been such.
　　　　　　　　　　　　　　[*Throws up a skull.*

Ham. That skull had a tongue in it, and could
sing once: how the knave jowls it to the
ground, as if it were Cain's jaw-bone, that
did the first murder! It might be the pate
of a politician, which this ass now o'er-
reaches; one that would circumvent God,
might it not?　　　　　　　　　　　　90

Hor. It might, my lord.

Ham. Or of a courtier, which could say 'Good
morrow, sweet lord! How dost thou, sweet
lord?' This might be my lord such-a-one,
that praised my lord such-a-one's horse,
when he meant to beg it; might it not?

Hor. Aye, my lord.

Ham. Why, e'en so: and now my Lady
Worm's; chapless, and knocked about the
mazzard with a sexton's spade: here 's fine 100

86. *"Cain's jaw-bone";* alluding to the ancient tradition that Cain
slew Abel with the jaw-bone of an ass.—C. H. H.

98. *"now my lady Worm's";* the skull that was *my lord such-a-
one's* is now *my lady worm's.*—H. N. H.

revolution, an we had the trick to see 't.
Did these bones cost no more the breeding,
but to play at loggats with 'em? mine ache
to think on 't.

First Clo. [*Sings*] A pick-axe, and a spade, a
      spade,
    For and a shrouding sheet:
  O, a pit of clay for to be made
    For such a guest is meet.

               [*Throws up another skull.*

Ham. There 's another: why may not that be 110
the skull of a lawyer?   Where be his quiddities now, his quillets, his cases, his tenures,
and his tricks? why does he suffer this rude
knave now to knock him about the sconce
with a dirty shovel, and will not tell him of
his action of battery?   Hum! This fellow
might be in 's time a great buyer of land,
with his statutes, his recognizances, his fines,
his double vouchers, his recoveries: is this
the fine of his fines and the recovery of his 120
recoveries, to have his fine pate full of fine
dirt? will his vouchers vouch him no more
of his purchases, and double ones too, than
the length and breadth of a pair of inden-
tures?   The very conveyances of his lands
will hardly lie in this box; and must the inheritor himself have no more, ha?

Hor. Not a jot more, my lord.

Ham. Is not parchment made of sheep-skins?

Hor. Aye, my lord, and of calf-skins too.   130

119–121. *"is this . . . recoveries"*; omitted in Qq.—I. G.

166

Ham. They are sheep and calves which seek out
    assurance in that. I will speak to this fel-
    low. Whose grave's this, sirrah?

First Clo. Mine, sir.
    [*Sings*] O, a pit of clay for to be made
               For such a guest is meet.

Ham. I think it be thine indeed, for thou liest
    in 't.

First Clo. You lie out on 't, sir, and therefore
    'tis not yours: for my part, I do not lie in 't, 140
    and yet it is mine.

Ham. Thou dost lie in 't, to be in 't and say it is
    thine: 'tis for the dead, not for the quick;
    therefore thou liest.

First Clo. 'Tis a quick lie, sir; 'twill away
    again, from me to you.

Ham. What man dost thou dig it for?

First Clo. For no man, sir.

Ham. What woman then?

First Clo. For none neither.   150

Ham. Who is to be buried in 't?

First Clo. One that was a woman, sir; but, rest
    her soul, she's dead.

Ham. How absolute the knave is! we must
    speak by the card, or equivocation will undo
    us. By the Lord, Horatio, this three years
    I have taken note of it; the age is grown
    so picked that the toe of the peasant comes
    so near the heel of the courtier, he galls his
    kibe. How long hast thou been a grave- 160
    maker?

136, omitted in Qq.—I. G.

First Clo. Of all the days i' the year, I came
to 't that day that our last King Hamlet
o'ercame Fortinbras.

Ham. How long is that since?

First Clo. Cannot you tell that? every fool can
tell that: it was that very day that young
Hamlet was born: he that is mad, and sent
into England.

Ham. Aye, marry, why was he sent into Eng- 170
land?

First Clo. Why, because a' was mad; a' shall
recover his wits there: or, if a' do not, 'tis
no great matter there.

Ham. Why?

First Clo. 'Twill not be seen in him there;
there the men are as mad as he.

Ham. How came he mad?

First Clo. Very strangely, they say.

Ham. How 'strangely'?   180

First Clo. Faith, e'en with losing his wits.

Ham. Upon what ground?

First Clo. Why, here in Denmark: I have been
sexton here, man and boy, thirty years.

Ham. How long will a man lie i' the earth ere
he rot?

167. *"the very day that young Hamlet was born";* by this scene
it appears that Hamlet was then thirty years old, and knew Yorick
well, who had been dead twenty-three years. And yet in the beginning of the play he is spoken of as one that designed to go back
to the university of Wittenburgh.—H. N. H.

170. *"there the men are as mad as he."* The "madness" of Eng-
lishmen was a proverbial jest, like the gluttony of the Dutch and
the family pride of the Welsh.—C. H. H.

First Clo. I' faith, if a' be not rotten before a'
die—as we have many pocky corses now-a-
days, that will scarce hold the laying in—a'
will last you some eight year or nine year: 190
a tanner will last you nine year.

Ham. Why he more than another?

First Clo. Why, sir, his hide is so tanned with
his trade that a' will keep out water a great
while; and your water is a sore decayer of
your whoreson dead body. Here 's a skull
now: this skull has lain in the earth three and
twenty years.

Ham. Whose was it?

First Clo. A whoreson mad fellow's it was: 200
whose do you think it was?

Ham. Nay, I know not.

First Clo. A pestilence on him for a mad
rogue! a' poured a flagon of Rhenish on my
head once. This same skull, sir, was
Yorick's skull, the king's jester.

Ham. This?

First Clo. E'en that.

Ham. Let me see. [*Takes the skull.*] Alas,
poor Yorick! I knew him, Horatio: a fel- 210
low of infinite jest, of most excellent fancy:
he hath borne me on his back a thousand
times; and now how abhorred in my imagination it is! my gorge rises at it. Here
hung those lips that I have kissed I know not
how oft. Where be your gibes now? your
gambols? your songs? your flashes of merri-

209, omitted in Qq.—I. G.

ment, that were wont to set the table on a
roar? Not one now, to mock your own
grinning? quite chop-fallen? Now get you 220
to my lady's chamber, and tell her, let her
paint an inch thick, to this favor she must
come; make her laugh at that. Prithee,
Horatio, tell me one thing.

Hor. What's that, my lord?

Ham. Dost thou think Alexander looked o'
this fashion i' the earth?

Hor. E'en so.

Ham. And smelt so? pah!   [*Puts down the skull.*

Hor. E'en so, my lord.   230

Ham. To what base uses we may return, Horatio! Why may not imagination trace the
noble dust of Alexander, till he find it stop-
ping a bunghole?

Hor. 'Twere to consider too curiously, to consider so.

Ham. No, faith, not a jot; but to follow him
thither with modesty enough and likelihood
to lead it: as thus: Alexander died, Alexander was buried, Alexander returneth into 240
dust; the dust is earth; of earth we make
loam; and why of that loam, whereto he was
converted, might they not stop a beer-barrel?

Imperious Cæsar, dead and turn'd to clay,
Might stop a hole to keep the wind away:
O, that that earth, which kept the world in awe,
Should patch a wall to expel the winter's flaw!

But soft! but soft! aside: here comes the
king.

*Enter Priests &c, in procession; the Corpse of
Ophelia, Laertes and Mourners following;
King, Queen, their trains, &c.*

The queen, the courtiers: who is this they fol-
low?   250
And with such maimed rites? This doth be-
token
The corse they follow did with desperate hand
Fordo its own life: 'twas of some estate.
Couch we awhile, and mark.
                             [*Retiring with Horatio.*
Laer. What ceremony else?
Ham. That is Laertes, a very noble youth: mark.
Laer. What ceremony else?
First Priest. Her obsequies have been as far en-
larged
As we have warranty: her death was doubtful;
And, but that great command o'ersways the
order   260
She should in ground unsanctified have lodged
Till the last trumpet; for charitable prayers,
Shards, flints and pebbles should be thrown on
her:
Yet here she is allow'd her virgin crants,
Her maiden strewments and the bringing home
Of bell and burial.
Laer. Must there no more be done?
First Priest.   No more be done:
We should profane the service of the dead

266. *"of bell and burial"; of* has here the force of *with.*—H. N. H.

171

To sing a requiem and such rest to her
As to peace-parted souls.

Laer.   Lay her i' the earth: 270
And from her fair and unpolluted flesh
May violets spring! I tell thee, churlish priest,
A ministering angel shall my sister be,
When thou liest howling.

Ham.   What, the fair Ophelia!

Queen. [*Scattering flowers*] Sweets to the sweet:
      farewell!
    I hoped thou shouldst have been my Hamlet's
      wife;
    I thought thy bride-bed to have deck'd, sweet
      maid,
    And not have strew'd thy grave.

Laer.   O, treble woe
Fall ten times treble on that cursed head
Whose wicked deed thy most ingenious sense 280
Deprived thee of! Hold off the earth a while,
Till I have caught her once more in mine arms:
                    [*Leaps into the grave.*
Now pile your dust upon the quick and dead,
Till of this flat a mountain you have made
To o'ertop old Pelion or the skyish head
Of blue Olympus.

Ham. [*Advancing*] What is he whose grief
    Bears such an emphasis? whose phrase of sorrow

269. *"a requiem"* is a mass sung for the rest of the soul. So
called from the words, "Requiem æternam dona eis, Domine."—
H. N. H.

278. *"treble woe";* the reading of Qq. 2, 3, 6; F. 1, *"terrible woer"*;
Ff. 2, 3, 4, *"terrible wooer."*—I. G.

Conjures the wandering stars and makes them
    stand
Like wonder-wounded hearers?   This is I,
Hamlet the Dane.   [*Leaps into the grave.* 290
Laer. The devil take thy soul!
                          [*Grappling with him.*
Ham.   Thou pray'st not well.
    I prithee, take thy fingers from my throat;
    For, though I am not splenitive and rash,
    Yet have I in me something dangerous,
    Which let thy wisdom fear.   Hold off thy
        hand.
King. Pluck them asunder.
Queen.   Hamlet, Hamlet!
All.   Gentlemen,—
Hor. Good my lord, be quiet.
        [*The Attendants part them, and they
                come out of the grave.*
Ham. Why, I will fight with him upon this theme
    Until my eyelids will no longer wag.
Queen. O my son, what theme?   300
Ham. I loved Ophelia: forty thousand brothers
    Could not, with all their quantity of love,
    Make up my sum.   What wilt thou do for her?
King. O, he is mad, Laertes.
Queen. For love of God, forbear him.
Ham. 'Swounds, show me what thou 'lt do:
    Woo 't weep? woo 't fight? woo 't fast? woo 't
        tear thyself?
    Woo 't drink up eisel? eat a crocodile?

308. *"woo't drink up eisel"; vide* Glossary, *"eisel";* the various
emendations *"Weissel," "Vssel,"* (a northern branch of the Rhine),
"Nile," "Nilus," are all equally unnecessary.—I. G.

173

I 'll do 't. Dost thou come here to whine?
To outface me with leaping in her grave? 310
Be buried quick with her, and so will I:
And, if thou prate of mountains, let them throw
Millions of acres on us, till our ground,
Singeing his pate against the burning zone,
Make Ossa like a wart! Nay, an thou 'lt
        mouth,
I 'll rant as well as thou.

Queen.   This is mere madness:
And thus a while the fit will work on him;
Anon, as patient as the female dove
When that her golden couplets are disclosed,
His silence will sit drooping.

Ham.   Hear you, sir; 320
What is the reason that you use me thus?
I loved you ever: but it is no matter;
Let Hercules himself do what he may,
The cat will mew, and dog will have his day.
                                    [*Exit.*

King. I pray thee, good Horatio, wait upon him.
                              [*Exit Horatio.*
[*To Laertes*] Strengthen your patience in our
        last night's speech;
We 'll put the matter to the present push.
Good Gertrude, set some watch over your son.
This grave shall have a living monument:
An hour of quiet shortly shall we see; 330
Till then, in patience our proceeding be.
                                  [*Exeunt.*

Scene II

A hall in the castle.

Enter Hamlet and Horatio.

Ham. So much for this, sir: now shall you see the
　　other;
　　You do remember all the circumstance?
Hor. Remember it, my lord!
Ham. Sir, in my heart there was a kind of fight-
　　ing,
　　That would not let me sleep: methought I lay
　　Worse than the mutines in the bilboes.　Rashly,
　　And praised be rashness for it, let us know,
　　Our indiscretion sometime serves us well
　　When our deep plots do pall; and that should
　　　　learn us
　　There's a divinity that shapes our ends,　　10
　　Rough-hew them how we will.
Hor.　　　　　　　　　That is most certain.
Ham. Up from my cabin,
　　My sea-gown scarf'd about me, in the dark
　　Groped I to find out them; had my desire,
　　Finger'd their packet, and in fine withdrew
　　To mine own room again; making so bold,
　　My fears forgetting manners, to unseal
　　Their grand commission; where I found, Ho-
　　　　ratio,—
　　O royal knavery!— an exact command,
　　Larded with many several sorts of reasons,　　20

9. *"yall"; so Q. 2; F. 1, "parle"; Pope, "fail."—I. G.*

Importing Denmark's health and England's
    too,
With, ho! such bugs and goblins in my life,
That, on the supervise, no leisure bated,
No, not to stay the grinding of the axe,
My head should be struck off.

Hor.   Is 't possible?

Ham. Here 's the commission: read it at more leis-
    ure,
But wilt thou hear now how I did proceed?

Hor. I beseech you.

Ham. Being thus be-netted round with villainies,—
    Or I could make a prologue to my brains,   30
    They had begun the play,—I sat me down;
    Devised a new commission; wrote it fair:
    I once did hold it, as our statists do,
    A baseness to write fair, and labor'd much
    How to forget that learning; but, sir, now
    It did me yeoman's service: wilt thou know
    The effect of what I wrote?

Hor.   Aye, good my lord.

Ham. An earnest conjuration from the king,
    As England was his faithful tributary,
    As love between them like the palm might flour-
    ish,   40
    As peace should still her wheaten garland wear
    And stand a comma 'tween their amities,
    And many such-like 'As' es of great charge,

23. *"the supervise, no leisure bated"; the supervise* is the looking
over; *no leisure bated* means without any abatement or intermission
of time.—H. N. H.

31. *"they," i. e.* my brains.—I. G.

That, on the view and knowing of these con-
    tents,
Without debatement further, more or less,
He should the bearers put to sudden death,
Not shriving-time allow'd.

Hor.   How was this seal'd?

Ham. Why, even in that was heaven ordinant.
I had my father's signet in my purse,
Which was the model of that Danish seal: 50
Folded the writ up in the form of the other;
Subscribed it; gave 't the impression; placed it
    safely,
The changeling never known. Now, the next
    day
Was our sea-fight; and what to this was se-
    quent
Thou know'st already.

Hor. So Guildenstern and Rosencrantz go to 't.

Ham. Why, man, they did make love to this em-
    ployment;
They are not near my conscience; their defeat
Does by their own insinuation grow:
'Tis dangerous when the baser nature comes 60
Between the pass and fell incensed points
Of mighty opposites.

Hor.   Why, what a king is this!

Ham. Does it not, think'st thee, stand me now
    upon—
He that hath kill'd my king, and whored my
    mother;
Popp'd in between the election and my hopes;

Thrown out his angle for my proper life,
And with such cozenage—is 't not perfect con-
    science,
To quit him with this arm? and is 't not to be
    damn'd,
To let this canker of our nature come
In further evil?   70

Hor. It must be shortly known to him from Eng-
    land
What is the issue of the business there.

Ham. It will be short: the interim is mine;
And a man's life 's no more than to say 'One.'
But I am very sorry, good Horatio,
That to Laertes I forgot myself;
For, by the image of my cause, I see
The portraiture of his: I 'll court his favors:
But, sure, the bravery of his grief did put me
Into a towering passion.

Hor.   Peace! who comes here?   80

Enter Osric.

Osr. Your lordship is right welcome back to
    Denmark.

Ham. I humbly thank you, sir. Dost know
this water-fly?

Hor. No, my good lord.

Ham. Thy state is the more gracious, for 'tis a
vice to know him. He hath much land, and
fertile: let a beast be lord of beasts, and his
crib shall stand at the king's mess: 'tis a

78. *"court"*; Rowe's emendation of Ff., *"count."*—I. G.

chough, but, as I say, spacious in the posses- 90
sion of dirt.

Osr. Sweet lord, if your lordship were at leisure, I should impart a thing to you from
his majesty.

Ham. I will receive it, sir, with all diligence of
spirit. Put your bonnet to his right use;
'tis for the head.

Osr. I thank your lordship, it is very hot.

Ham. No, believe me, 'tis very cold; the wind
is northerly.   100

Osr. It is indifferent cold, my lord, indeed.

Ham. But yet methinks it is very sultry and
hot, or my complexion—

Osr. Exceedingly, my lord; it is very sultry,
as 'twere,—I cannot tell how. But, my
lord, his majesty bade me signify to you that
he has laid a great wager on your head: sir,
this is the matter—

Ham. I beseech you, remember—

> [*Hamlet moves him to put on his hat.*

Osr. Nay, good my lord; for mine ease, in good 110
faith. Sir, here is newly come to court
Laertes; believe me, an absolute gentleman,
full of most excellent differences, of very
soft society and great showing: indeed, to
speak feelingly of him, he is the card or cal-
endar of gentry, for you shall find in him

---

102. *"or my complexion—"*; some such words as "deceives me" are
understood. But Hamlet must be supposed to break off, as in his
next speech, not to be *interrupted* by Osric.—H. N. H.

111–150. These lines are omitted in Ff., which read, *"Sir, you are
not ignorant of what excellence Laertes is at his weapon."*—I. G.

the continent of what part a gentleman
would see.

Ham. Sir, his definement suffers no perdition
in you; though, I know, to divide him inven- 120
torially would dizzy the arithmetic of memory, and yet but yaw neither, in respect of
his quick sail.   But in the verity of extolment, I take him to be a soul of great article,
and his infusion of such dearth and rareness,
as, to make true diction of him, his semblable
is his mirror, and who else would trace him,
his umbrage, nothing more.

Osr. Your lordship speaks most infallibly of
him.   130

Ham. The concernancy, sir? why do we wrap
the gentleman in our more rawer breath?

Osr. Sir?

Hor. Is 't not possible to understand in another
tongue?   You will do 't, sir, really.

Ham. What imports the nomination of this
gentleman?

Osr. Of Laertes?

Hor. His purse is empty already; all 's golden
words are spent.   140

Ham. Of him, sir.

Osr. I know you are not ignorant—

Ham. I would you did, sir; yet, in faith, if you
did, it would not much approve me.   Well,
sir?

134. *"another tongue";* Johnson conj. *"a mother tongue";* Heath
conj. *"a mother tongue?"* No change is necessary; it's a bit of
sarcasm.—I. G.

Osr. You are not ignorant of what excellence
    Laertes is—

Ham. I dare not confess that, lest I should com-
    pare with him in excellence; but, to know a
    man well, were to know himself.   150

Osr. I mean, sir, for his weapon; but in the im-
    putation laid on him by them, in his meed
    he's unfellowed.

Ham. What's his weapon?

Osr. Rapier and dagger.

Ham. That's two of his weapons: but, well.

Osr. The king, sir, hath wagered with him six
    Barbary horses: against the which he has im-
    poned, as I take it, six French rapiers and
    poniards, with their assigns, as girdle, 160
    hanger, and so: three of the carriages, in
    faith, are very dear to fancy, very responsive
    to the hilts, most delicate carriages, and of
    very liberal conceit.

Ham. What call you the carriages?

Hor. I knew you must be edified by the mar-
    gent ere you had done.

Osr. The carriages, sir, are the hangers.

Ham. The phrase would be more germane to
    the matter if we could carry a cannon by our 170
    sides: I would it might be hangers till then.
    But, on: six Barbary horses against six
    French swords, their assigns, and three lib-

150. *"to know a man well were to know himself";* I dare not pretend to know him, lest I should pretend to an equality: no man
can completely know another, but by knowing himself, which is the
utmost of human wisdom.—H. N. H.

165–166. Omitted in Ff.—I. G.

eral-conceited carriages; that's the French
bet against the Danish. Why is this 'imponed, as you call it?

Osr. The king, sir, hath laid, sir, that in a dozen
passes between yourself and him, he shall not
exceed you three hits: he hath laid on twelve
for nine; and it would come to immediate 180
trial if your lordship would vouchsafe the
answer.

Ham. How if I answer 'no'?

Osr. I mean, my lord, the opposition of your
person in trial.

Ham. Sir, I will walk here in the hall: if it
please his majesty, it is the breathing time of
day with me; let the foils be brought, the
gentleman willing, and the king hold his
purpose, I will win for him an I can; if not, 190
I will gain nothing but my shame and the
odd hits.

Osr. Shall I redeliver you e'en so?

Ham. To this effect, sir, after what flourish
your nature will.

Osr. I commend my duty to your lordship.

Ham. Yours, yours. [*Exit Osric.*] He does
well to commend it himself; there are no
tongues else for 's turn.

Hor. This lapwing runs away with the shell on 200
his head.

Ham. He did comply with his dug before he
sucked it. Thus has he—and many more of
the same breed that I know the drossy age

dotes on—only got the tune of the time and
outward habit of encounter; a kind of yesty
collection, which carries them through and
through the most fond and winnowed opinions; and do but blow them to their trial, the
bubbles are out. 210

Enter a Lord.

Lord. My lord, his majesty commended him to
you by young Osric, who brings back to him,
that you attend him in the hall: he sends to
know if your pleasure hold to play with
Laertes, or that you will take longer time.

Ham. I am constant to my purposes; they follow the king's pleasure: if his fitness speaks,
mine is ready; now or whensoever, provided
I be so able as now.

Lord. The king and queen and all are coming 220
down.

Ham. In happy time.

Lord. The queen desires you to use some gentle
entertainment to Laertes before you fall to
play.

Ham. She well instructs me.   [*Exit Lord.*

Hor. You will lose this wager, my lord.

Ham. I do not think so; since he went into
France, I have been in continual practice;
I shall win at the odds.   But thou wouldst 230
not think how ill all 's here about my heart:
but it is no matter.

"*mine more of the same Beauty*"; Ff. 2, 3, 4, "*nine more of the
same Beavy.*"—I. G.

210–225. Omitted in Ff.—I. G.

Hor. Nay, good my lord,—

Ham. It is but foolery; but it is such a kind of gain-giving as would perhaps trouble a woman.

Hor. If your mind dislike anything, obey it. I will forestall their repair hither, and say you are not fit.

Ham. Not a whit; we defy augury: there is 240 special providence in the fall of a sparrow. If it be now, 'tis not to come; if it be not to come, it will be now; if it be not now, yet it will come: the readiness is all; since no man has aught of what he leaves, what is 't to leave betimes? Let be.

Enter King, Queen, Laertes, and Lords, Osric and other Attendants with foils and gauntlets; a table and flagons of wine on it.

King. Come, Hamlet, come, and take this hand from me.

  [*The King puts Laertes' hand into Hamlet's.*

Ham. Give me your pardon, sir: I 've done you wrong;

244–245. *"Since no man has aught of what he leaves, what is 't to leave betimes? Let be."* The reading is taken partly from the Folios and partly from the Quartos; a long list of proposed emendations is given by the Cambridge editors.—I. G.

Johnson thus interprets the passage: "Since *no man knows* aught of the state which *he leaves;* since he cannot judge what other years may produce; why should we be afraid of *leaving* life betimes?" Warburton's explanation is very ingenious, but perhaps strains the Poet's meaning: "It is true that by death we lose all the goods of life; yet seeing this loss is no otherwise an evil than as we are sensible of it; and since death removes all sense of it; what matters it how soon we lose them?"—H. N. H.

But pardon 't, as you are a gentleman.
This presence knows,   250
And you must needs have heard, how I am
    punish'd
With sore distraction.   What I have done,
That might your nature, honor and exception
Roughly awake, I here proclaim was madness.
Was 't Hamlet wrong'd Laertes? Never Ham-
    let:
If Hamlet from himself be ta'en away,
And when he 's not himself does wrong Laertes,
Then Hamlet does it not, Hamlet denies it.
Who does it then?   His madness: if 't be so,
Hamlet is of the faction that is wrong'd;   260
His madness is poor Hamlet's enemy.
Sir, in this audience,
Let my disclaiming from a purposed evil
Free me so far in your most generous thoughts,
That I have shot mine arrow o'er the house,
And hurt my brother.
Laer.   I am satisfied in nature,
Whose motive, in this case, should stir me most
To my revenge: but in my terms of honor
I stand aloof, and will no reconcilement,
Till by some elder masters of known honor   270
I have a voice and precedent of peace,
To keep my name ungored.   But till that time
I do receive your offer'd love like love
And will not wrong it.
Ham.   I embrace it freely,

262. Omitted in Qq.—I. G.
266. *"brother"*; so Qq.; Ff. read *"mother."*—I. G.

And will this brother's wager frankly play.
Give us the foils. Come on.

Laer.   Come, one for me.

Ham. I 'll be your foil, Laertes: in mine ignorance
Your skill shall, like a star i' the darkest night,
Stick fiery off indeed.

Laer.   You mock me, sir.

Ham. No, by this hand.   280

King. Give them the foils, young Osric. Cousin
Hamlet,
You know the wager?

Ham.   Very well, my lord;
Your grace has laid the odds o' the weaker side.

King. I do not fear it; I have seen you both:
But since he is better'd, we have therefore odds.

Laer. This is too heavy; let me see another.

Ham. This likes me well. These foils have all a
length?   [*They prepare to play.*

Osr. Aye, my good lord.

King. Set me the stoups of wine upon that table.
If Hamlet give the first or second hit,   290
Or quit in answer of the third exchange,
Let all the battlements their ordnance fire;
The king shall drink to Hamlet's better breath;
And in the cup an union shall he throw,
Richer than that which four successive kings
In Denmark's crown have worn. Give me the
cups;

---

283. *"laid the odds";* the king had wagered *six Barbary horses* to
a few *rapiers, poniards,* &c.; that is, about *twenty* to one. These
are the *odds* here meant. The odds the king means in the next
speech were *twelve* to *nine* in favor of Hamlet, by Laertes giving
him three.—H. N. H.

And let the kettle to the trumpet speak,
The trumpet to the cannoneer without,
The cannons to the heavens, the heaven to
    earth,
'Now the king drinks to Hamlet.'   Come, be-
    gin;   300
And you, the judges, bear a wary eye.

Ham. Come on, sir.

Laer.   Come, my lord.   [*They play.*

Ham.   One.

Laer.   No.

Ham.   Judgment.

Osr. A hit, a very palpable hit.

Laer.   Well; again.

King. Stay; give me drink. Hamlet, this pearl is
    thine;
    Here 's to thy health..
        [*Trumpets sound, and cannon shot off within.*
                Give him the cup.

Ham. I 'll play this bout first; set it by awhile.
    Come. [*They play.*]   Another hit; what say
    you?

Laer. A touch, a touch, I do confess.

King. Our son shall win.

Queen.   He 's fat and scant of breath.
    Here, Hamlet, take my napkin, rub thy brows:
    The queen carouses to thy fortune, Hamlet. 311

Ham. Good madam!

King.   Gertrude, do not drink.

Queen. I will, my lord; I pray you, pardon me.

King. [*Aside*] It is the poison'd cup; it is too late.

---

309. *"He's fat and scant of breath"; vide* Glossary, "FAT."—I. G.

Ham. I dare not drink yet, madam; by and by.

Queen. Come, let me wipe thy face.

Laer. My lord, I 'll hit him now.

King.   I do not think 't.

Laer. [*Aside*] And yet it is almost against my
    conscience.

Ham. Come, for the third, Laertes: you but dally;
    I pray you, pass with your best violence;   320
    I am afeard you make a wanton of me.

Laer. Say you so? come on.   [*They play.*

Osr. Nothing, neither way.

Laer. Have at you now!

  [*Laertes wounds Hamlet; then, in scuffling, they
      change rapiers, and Hamlet wounds Laertes.*

King.   Part them; they are incensed.

Ham. Nay, come, again.   [*The Queen falls.*

Osr.   Look to the queen there, ho!

Hor. They bleed on both sides. How is it, my
    lord?

Osr. How is 't, Laertes?

Laer. Why, as a woodcock to mine own springe,
    Osric;
    I am justly kill'd with mine own treachery.

Ham. How does the queen?

King.   She swounds to see them bleed.

Queen. No, no, the drink, the drink,—O my dear
    Hamlet,—   331
    The drink, the drink! I am poison'd.   [*Dies.*

Ham. O villainy! Ho! let the door be lock'd:
    Treachery! seek it out.   [*Laertes falls.*

Laer. It is here, Hamlet: Hamlet, thou art slain;
    No medicine in the world can do thee good,

188

In thee there is not half an hour of life;
The treacherous instrument is in thy hand,
Unbated and envenom'd: the foul practice
Hath turn'd itself on me; lo, here I lie,   340
Never to rise again: thy mother 's poison'd:
I can no more: the king, the king 's to blame.

Ham. The point envenom'd too!
Then, venom, to thy work.   [*Stabs the King.*

All. Treason! treason!

King. O, yet defend me, friends; I am but hurt.

Ham. Here, thou incestuous, murderous, damned
          Dane,
Drink off this potion: is thy union here?
Follow my mother.   [*King dies.*

Laer.   He is justly served;
It is a poison temper'd by himself.   350
Exchange forgiveness with me, noble Hamlet:
Mine and my father's death come not upon thee,
Nor thine on me!   [*Dies.*

Ham. Heaven make thee free of it! I follow
          thee.
I am dead, Horatio. Wretched queen, adieu!
You that look pale and tremble at this chance,
That are but mutes or audience to this act,
Had I but time—as this fell sergeant, death,
Is strict in his arrest—O, I could tell you—
But let it be. Horatio, I am dead;   360
Thou livest; report me and my cause aright
To the unsatisfied.

Hor.   Never believe it.
I am more an antique Roman than a Dane:
Here 's yet some liquor left.

Ham.   As thou 'rt a man,
  Give me the cup: let go; by heaven, I 'll have 't.
  O good Horatio, what a wounded name,
  Things standing thus unknown, shall live be-
      hind me!
  If thou didst ever hold me in thy heart,
  Absent thee from felicity a while,
  And in this harsh world draw thy breath in
      pain,   370
  To tell my story.
                    [*March afar off, and shot within.*
              What warlike noise is this?
Osr. Young Fortinbras, with conquest come from
      Poland,
  To the ambassadors of England gives
  This warlike volley.
Ham.   O, I die, Horatio;
  The potent poison quite o'er-crows my spirit:
  I cannot live to hear the news from England;
  But I do prophesy the election lights
  On Fortinbras: he has my dying voice;
  So tell him, with the occurrents, more and less,
  Which have solicited.   The rest is silence.   380
                                          [*Dies.*
Hor. Now cracks a noble heart. Good night,
      sweet prince,
  And flights of angels sing thee to thy rest!
                                  [*March within.*
  Why does the drum come hither?

*Enter Fortinbras, and the English Ambassadors,
    with drum, colors, and Attendants.*

367. "*live*"; so Ff.; Qq., "*I leave.*"—I. G.

Fort. Where is this sight?

Hor.   What is it you would see?
   If aught of woe or wonder, cease your search.

Fort. This quarry cries on havoc.   O proud death,
   What feast is toward in thine eternal cell,
   That thou so many princes at a shot
   So bloodily hast struck?

First Amb.   The sight is dismal;
   And our affairs from England come too late:
   The ears are senseless that should give us hear-
       ing,   391
   To tell him his commandment is fulfill'd,
   That Rosencrantz and Guildenstern are dead:
   Where should we have our thanks?

Hor.   Not from his mouth
   Had it the ability of life to thank you:
   He never gave commandment for their death.
   But since, so jump upon this bloody question,
   You from the Polack wars, and you from Eng-
       land,
   Are here arrived, give order that these bodies
   High on a stage be placed to the view;   400
   And let me speak to the yet unknowing world
   How these things came about: so shall you hear
   Of carnal, bloody and unnatural acts,
   Of accidental judgments, casual slaughters,
   Of deaths put on by cunning and forced cause,
   And, in this upshot, purposes mistook
   Fall'n on the inventors' heads: all this can I
   Truly deliver.

Fort.   Let us haste to hear it,

405. *"forced cause";* so Ff.; Qq. read *"for no cause."*—I. G.

And call the noblest to the audience.
For me, with sorrow I embrace my fortune: 410
I have some rights of memory in this kingdom,
Which now to claim my vantage doth invite me.

Hor. Of that I shall have also cause to speak,
And from his mouth whose voice will draw on
more:
But let this same be presently perform'd,
Even while men's minds are wild; lest more
mischance
On plots and errors happen.

Fort.   Let four captains
Bear Hamlet, like a soldier, to the stage;
For he was likely, had he been put on,
To have proved most royally: and, for his pas-
sage,   420
The soldiers' music and the rites of war
Speak loudly for him.
Take up the bodies: such a sight as this
Becomes the field, but here shows much amiss.
Go, bid the soldiers shoot.

[*A dead march.   Exeunt, bearing off the bodies:
after which a peal of ordnance is shot off.*

GLOSSARY

By Israel Gollancz, M.A.

A', he; (Ff. *"he"*); II. i. 58.

About, get to your work! II. ii. 638.

Above; "more a," moreover; II. ii. 128.

Abridgement (Ff. *'Abridgements'*), entertainment for pastime (with perhaps a secondary idea of that which makes one brief and shortens tedious conversation); II. ii. 453.

Absolute, positive; V. i. 154; perfect, faultless (used by Osric); V. ii. 111.

Abstract, summary, or epitome; (Ff. *"abstracts"*); II. ii. 566.

Abuse, delusion; IV. vii. 51.

Abuses, deceives; II. ii. 653.

Acquittance, acquittal; IV. vii. 1.

Act, operation; (Warburton *"effect"*); I. ii. 205.

Addition, title; I. iv. 20.

Address, prepare; I. ii. 216.

Admiration, wonder, astonishment; I. ii. 192.

Adulterate, adulterous; I. v. 42.

Æneas' tale to Dido; burlesque lines from an imaginary play written after the grandiloquent manner of quasi-classical plays (*e. g.* Nash's contributions to Marlowe's *Dido, Queen of Carthage*); II. ii. 486.

Afeard, afraid; V. ii. 321.

Affection, affectation; (Ff. *"affectation"*); II. ii. 482.

Affront, confront, encounter; III. i. 31.

A-foot, in progress; III. ii. 87.

After, according to; II. ii. 570.

Against, in anticipation of; III. iv. 50.

Aim, guess; IV. v. 9.

Allowance, permission (according to some, "regards of a."= allowable conditions); II. ii. 79.

Amaze, confound, bewilder; II. ii. 612.

Amazement, astonishment; III. ii. 351.

Ambition, attainment of ambition; III. iii. 55.

Amble, move in an affected manner; III. i. 153.

Amiss, misfortune; IV. v. 18.

Anchor's, Anchorite's, hermit's; III. ii. 233.

"And will he not come again," etc.; a well-known song found in song-books of the period, called *The Milkmaid's Dumps;* IV. v. 193.

An end, on end; (Q. 1, *"on end"*); I. v. 19.

Angle, angling-line; V. ii. 66.

An if, if; I. v. 177.

Annexment, appendage; III. iii. 21.

Anon, soon, presently; II. ii. 525.

ANSWER, reply to a challenge;
V. ii. 183.

ANSWER'D, explained; IV. i. 16.

ANTIC, disguised, fantastic; I. v.
172.

ANTIQUE, ancient; V. ii. 363.

APART, aside, away; IV. i. 24.

APE; "the famous ape," etc., a
reference to an old fable which
has not yet been identified;
III. iv. 193–196

APOPLEX'D, affected with apo-
plexy; III. iv. 73.

APPOINTMENT, equipment; IV. vi.
17.

APPREHENSION, conception, perception; II. ii. 327.

APPROVE, affirm, confirm, I. i. 29;
credit, make approved, V. ii.
144.

APPURTENANCE, proper accom-
paniment; II. ii. 399.

ARGAL, Clown's blunder for *ergo;*
V. i. 13.

ARGUMENT, subject, plot of a
play; II. ii. 382.

——, subject in dispute; IV. iv.
54.

ARM YOU, prepare yourselves;
III. iii. 24.

ARRAS, tapestry (originally made
at Arras); II. ii. 165.

ARTICLE, clause in an agreement,
I. i. 94; "a soul of great a."
i. e. a soul with so many qualities that its inventory would
be very large; V. ii. 124.

AS, as if; II. i. 91.

——, as if, as though; IV. v. 105;
so; IV. vii. 159; namely; I. iv.
25.

AS'ES, used quibblingly, (Ff. *"As-
sis"*; Qq. *"as sir"*); V. ii. 43.

ASLANT, across; IV. vii. 168.

ASSAULT; "of general a.", "incident to all men"; II. i. 35.

ASSAY, trial, test; II. ii. 71.

——, try; III. i. 14.

——, "make a.", "throng to the
rescue"; III. iii. 69.

ASSAYS OF BIAS, indirect aims,
(such as one takes in the game
of bowls, taking into account
the bias side of the bowl); II.
i. 65.

ASSIGNS, appendages; V. ii. 160.

ASSISTANT, helpful; I. iii. 3.

ASSURANCE, security; with play
upon the legal sense of the
word; V. i. 132.

ATTENT, attentive; I. ii. 193.

ATTRIBUTE, reputation; I. iv. 22.

AUGHT; "hold'st at a.", holds of
any value, values at all; IV.
iii. 63.

AUTHORITIES, offices of authority,
attributes of power; IV. ii. 17.

AVOUCH, declaration; I. i. 57.

A-WORK, at work; II. ii. 527.

BACK, "support in reserve"; IV.
vii. 154.

BAKED-MEATS, pastry; "funeral
b.", cold entertainment prepared for the mourners at a
funeral; I. ii. 180.

BAN, curse; III. ii. 276.

BAPTISTA, used as a woman's
name (properly a man's, *cf.
Tam. of Shrew*); III. ii. 256.

BARE, mere; III. i. 76.

BARK'D ABOUT, grew like bark
around; I. v. 71.

BARREN, barren of wit, foolish;
III. ii. 50.

BARR'D, debarred, excluded; I. ii.
14.

BATTEN, grow fat; III. iv. 67.

BEATEN, well-worn, familiar; II.
ii. 283.

BEATING, striking; (Q. 1, *"towl-*

194

ing"; Collier MS., *"tolling"*);
I. i. 39.

BEAUTIED, beautified; III. i. 51.

BEAUTIFIED, beautiful, endowed
with beauty, (Theobald *"beati-
fied"*); II. ii. 110.

BEAVER, visor; movable part of
the helmet covering the face;
I. ii. 230.

BEDDED, lying flat, (?) matted;
III. iv. 121.

BED-RID, bed-ridden; (Qq. 2–5
"bed red"); I. ii. 29.

BEETLES, projects, juts over; I.
iv. 71.

BEHOVE, behoof, profit; V. i. 72.

BENT, straining, tension; (properly an expression of archery);
II. ii. 30.

——, "to the top of my b.", to
the utmost; III. ii. 416.

BESHREW, a mild oath; II. i. 113.

BESMIRCH, soil, sully; I. iii. 15.

BESPEAK, address, speak to; II.
ii. 142.

BEST; "in all my b.", to the utmost of my power; I. ii. 120.

BESTOWED, placed, lodged; II. ii.
565.

BETEEM, allow, permit; I. ii. 141.

BETHOUGHT, thought of; I. iii. 90.

BILBOES, stocks or fetters used
for prisoners on board ship;
V. ii. 6.

BISSON; 'b. rheum,' *i. e.* blinding
tears; II. ii. 527.

B L A N K, "the *white* mark at
which shot or arrows were
aimed" (Steevens); IV. i. 42.

BLANKS, blanches, makes pale;
III. ii. 235.

BLAST IN PROOF, "a metaphor
taken from the trying or prov-
ing of firearms or cannon,
which blast or burst in the
proof" (Steevens); IV. vii. 155.

BLASTMENTS, blighting influences;
I. iii. 42.

BLAZON; "eternal b.", publication
of eternal mysteries; (perhaps
'eternal'= infernal, or used 'to
express extreme abhorrence');
I. v. 21.

BLENCH, start aside; II. ii.
647.

BLOAT (Qq. *'blowt;'* Ff. *'blunt'*),
bloated; III. iv. 182.

BLOOD, passion; IV. iv. 58; "b.
and judgement," passion and
reason; III. ii. 78.

BLOWN, full blown, in its bloom;
III. i. 169.

BOARD, address; II. ii. 172.

BODES, forebodes, portends; I. i.
69.

BODKIN, the old word for dagger; III. i. 76.

BODYKINS, diminutive of body;
"the reference was originally
to the sacramental bread;" II.
ii. 572.

"BONNIE SWEET ROBIN," the first
words of a well-known song
of the period (found in Hol-
borne's *Cittharn Schoole,* 1597,
etc.); IV. v. 190.

BORE, calibre, importance of a
question; IV. vi. 29.

BORNE IN HAND, deceived with
false hopes; II. ii. 67.

BOUND, ready, prepared; I. v. 6.

——, was bound; I. ii. 90.

BOURN, limit, boundary; III. i.
79.

BRAINISH, imaginary, brain-sick;
IV. i. 11.

BRAVE, glorious; II. ii. 320.

BRAVERY, ostentation, bravado;
V. ii. 79.

BREATHE, whisper; II. i. 31.

BREATHING, whispering; I. iii.
130.

BREATHING TIME, time for exercise; V. ii. 187.

BRINGING HOME, strictly, the bridal procession from church; applied to a maid's funeral; V. i. 266.

BROAD, unrestrained; III. iv. 2.

BROKE, broken; IV. v. 111.

BROKERS, go betweens; I. iii. 127.

BROOCH, an ornament worn in the hat; IV. vii. 94.

BROOD; "on b.", brooding; III. i. 175.

BRUIT, proclaim abroad; I. ii. 127.

BUDGE, stir, move; III. iv. 18.

BUGS, bugbears; V. ii. 22.

B U L K, body; (according to some = breast); II. i. 95.

BUSINESS, do business; I. ii. 37.

BUTTONS, buds; I. iii. 40.

BUZ, BUZ! an interjection used to interrupt the teller of a story already well known; II. ii. 425.

BUZZERS, whisperers; (Q. 1676, "whispers"); IV. v. 92.

BY AND BY, immediately; III. ii. 415.

BY'R LADY, by our lady; a slight oath; III. ii. 147.

CAN, can do; III. iii. 65.

CANDIED, sugared, flattering; III. ii. 69.

CANKER, canker worm; I. iii. 39.

CANON, divine law; I. ii. 132.

CAPABLE, capable of feeling, susceptible; III. iv. 127.

CAP-A-PE, from head to foot (Old Fr. 'de cap a pie'); I. ii. 200.

CAPITOL; "I was killed i' the C." (an error repeated in *Julius Cæsar;* Cæsar was killed in the Curia Pompeii, near the theatre of Pompey in the Campus Martius); III. ii. 114.

CARD; "by the c.", with precision (alluding probably to the shipman's card); V. i. 155.

CARNAL, sensual; V. ii. 403.

CAROUSES, drinks; V. ii. 310.

CARRIAGE, tenor, import; I. i. 94.

CARRY IT AWAY, gain the victory; II. ii. 387.

CART, car, chariot; III. ii. 170.

CARVE FOR, choose for, please; I. iii. 20.

CAST, casting, moulding; I. i. 73.

——, contrive; 'c. beyond ourselves', to be over suspicious (? to be mistaken); II. i. 115.

CATAPLASM, plaster; IV. vii. 144.

CAUTEL, deceit, falseness; I. iii. 15.

CAVIARE; "a Russian condiment made from the roe of the sturgeon; at that time a new and fashionable delicacy not obtained nor relished by the vulgar, and therefore used by Shakespeare to signify anything above their comprehension" (Nares); II. ii. 474.

CEASE, extinction; (Qq. "cesse"; Pope "decease"); III. iii. 15.

CENSURE, opinion; I. iii. 69.

CENTRE, *i. e.* of the Earth; II. ii. 159.

C E R E M E N T S, cloths used as shrouds for dead bodies; I. iv. 48.

CHAMELEON, an animal supposed to feed on air; III. ii. 102.

CHANGE, exchange; I. ii. 163.

CHANSON, song (used affectedly; not found elsewhere in Shakespeare; 'pious chanson;' so Qq.; Ff. 'pons Chanson'; 'pans chanson'); II. ii. 452.

CHARACTER, hand-writing; IV. vii. 53.

CHARACTER, write, imprint; I. iii. 59.

CHARGE, expense; IV. iv. 47; load, weight; V. ii. 43.

CHARIEST, most scrupulous; I. iii. 36.

CHECKING AT; "to check at," a term in falconry, applied to a hawk when she forsakes her proper game and follows some other; (Qq. 2, 3, "the King at"; Qq. 4, 5, 6, "liking not"); IV. vii. 63.

CHEER, fare; III. ii. 232.

CHIEF, chiefly, especially; I. iii. 74.

CHOPINE, a high cork shoe; II. ii. 462.

CHORUS, interpreter of the action of a play; III. ii. 262.

CHOUGH, a sordid and wealthy boor; (chuff according to some, ="chattering crow"); V. ii. 89.

CICATRICE, scar; IV. iii. 65.

CIRCUMSTANCE, circumlocution, detail; I. v. 127.

——, "c. of thought", details of thought which lead to a conclusion; III. iii. 83.

CLAPPED, applauded; II. ii. 366.

CLEPE, call; I. iv. 19.

CLIMATURES, regions; I. i. 125.

CLOSELY, secretly; III. i. 29.

CLOSES WITH, agrees with; II. i. 45.

COAGULATE, coagulated, clotted; II. ii. 502.

COCKLE HAT; a mussel-shell in the hat was the badge of pilgrims bound for places of devotion beyond sea; IV. v. 25.

COIL; "mortal c.", mortal life, turmoil of mortality; III. i. 67.

COLD, chaste; IV. vii. 173.

COLDLY, lightly; IV. iii. 67.

COLLATERAL, indirect; IV. v. 209.

COLLEAGUED, leagued; I. ii. 21.

COLLECTION, an attempt to collect some meaning from it; IV. v. 9.

COLUMBINES, flowers emblematic of faithlessness; IV. v. 182.

COMBAT, duel; I. i. 84.

COMMA, "a c. 'tween their amities," the smallest break or separation; V. ii. 42.

COMMANDMENT, command; III. ii. 340.

COMMENT; "the very c. of thy soul," "all thy powers of observation"; (Ff. "my soul"); III. ii. 88.

COMMERCE, intercourse; III. i. 110.

COMPELLED, enforced; IV. vi. 19.

COMPLETE STEEL, full armor; I. iv. 52.

COMPLEXION, temperament, natural disposition; I. iv. 27.

COMPLY, use ceremony; II. ii. 401.

COMPULSATORY, compelling; (Ff. "compulsatiue"); I. i. 103.

COMPULSIVE, compulsory, compelling; III. iv. 86.

CONCEIT, imagination; III. iv. 114.

——, design; "liberal c.", tasteful, elaborate design; V. ii. 164.

CONCERNANCY, import, meaning; V. ii. 131.

CONCLUSIONS, experiments; III. iv. 195.

CONDOLEMENT, sorrow; I. ii. 93.

CONFEDERATE, conspiring, favoring; III. ii. 274.

CONFINE, boundary, territory; I. i. 155.

CONFINES, places of confinement, prisons; II. ii. 257.

CONFRONT, outface; III. iii. 47.

CONFUSION, confusion of mind; (Rowe *"confesion"*; Pope (in margin), *"confession"*); III. i. 2.

CONGREGATION, collection; II. ii. 323.

CONGRUING, agreeing; (Ff. *"coniuring"*); IV. iii. 69.

CONJUNCTIVE, closely joined; IV. vii. 14.

CONSEQUENCE; "in this c."; in the following way; or, 'in thus following up your remarks' (Schmidt); II. i. 45.

CONSIDER'D, fit for reflection; "at our more c. time," when we have more time for consideration; II. ii. 81.

CONSONANCY, accord, friendship; II. ii. 301.

CONSTANTLY, fixedly; I. ii. 235.

CONTAGION, contagious thing; IV. vii. 148.

CONTENT, please, gratify; III. i. 24.

CONTINENT, that which contains; IV. iv. 64; inventory; V. ii. 107.

CONTRACTION, the making of the marriage contract; III. iv. 46.

CONTRIVING, plotting; IV. vii. 136.

CONVERSATION, intercourse; III. ii. 64.

CONVERSE, conversation; II. i. 42.

CONVOY, conveyance; I. iii. 3.

COPED WITHAL, met with; III. ii. 64.

CORSE, corpse; I. iv. 52.

COTED, overtook, passed by (a term in hunting); II. ii. 339.

COUCHED, concealed; II. ii. 494.

COUCH WE, let us lie down, conceal ourselves; V. i. 254.

COUNT, account, trial; IV. vii. 17.

COUNTENANCE, favor; IV. ii. 16.

COUNTER; hounds *"run counter"* when they follow the scent in the wrong direction; a term of the chase; IV. v. 112.

COUNTERFEIT PRESENTMENT, portrait; III. iv. 54.

COUPLE, join, add; I. v. 93.

COUPLETS; "golden c.", "the pigeon lays only two eggs, at a time, and the newly hatched birds are covered with yellow down"; V. i. 319.

COUSIN, used of a nephew; I. ii. 64.

COZENAGE, deceit, trickery; V. ii. 67.

COZEN'D, cheated; III. iv. 77.

CRACKED WITHIN THE RING; "there was formerly a ring or circle on the coin, within which the sovereign's head was placed; if the crack extended from the edge beyond this ring, the ring was rendered unfit for currency" (Douce); II. ii. 464.

CRANTS, garland, used for the chaplet carried before a maiden's coffin, and afterwards hung up in the church; (Ff. *'rites'*; *'Crants'* occurs in the form *corance* in Chapman's *Alphonsus, (cf.* Lowland Scotch *crance*); otherwise unknown in English); V. i. 264.

CREDENT, credulous, believing; I. iii. 30.

CREW, did crow; I. i. 147.

CRIED; "c. in the top of mine," were higher than mine; II. ii. 476.

CRIES ON, cries out; V. ii. 386.

CRIMEFUL, criminal; (Qq. *"criminall"*); IV. vii. 7.

CROCODILE; "woo't eat a c.", referring probably to the toughness of its skin; V. i. 308.

CROOK, make to bend; III. ii. 70.

CROSS, go across its way; (to cross the path of a ghost was to come under its evil influence); I. i. 127.

CROW-FLOWERS, (probably) buttercups; IV. vii. 171.

CROWNER, coroner; V. i. 25.

CRY, company; (literally, a pack of hounds); III. ii. 297.

CUE, catch-word, call; (a technical stage term); II. ii. 608.

CUFFS, fisticuffs, blows; II. ii. 383.

CUNNINGS, respective skill; IV. vii. 156.

CURB, cringe; "c. and woo", bow and beg, "bend and truckle"; III. iv. 155.

CURIOUSLY, fancifully; V. i. 235.

CURRENTS, courses; III. iii. 57.

DAINTIER, more delicate; V. i. 79.

DAISY, emblem of faithlessness; IV. v. 186.

DANE, King of Denmark; I. i. 15.

DANSKERS, Danes; II. i. 7.

DAY AND NIGHT, an exclamation; I. v. 164.

DEAREST, greatest, intensest; I. ii. 182.

DEARLY, heartily, earnestly; IV. iii. 46.

DEARTH, high value; V. ii. 125.

DECLINE UPON, sink down to; I. v. 50.

DECLINING, falling, going from bad to worse; II. ii. 517.

DEFEAT, destruction; II. ii. 619.

DEFEATED, disfigured, marred; I. ii. 10.

DEFENSE, skill in weapons, "science of defense"; IV. vii. 98.

DEFINEMENT, definition; V. ii. 119.

DEJECT, dejected; III. i. 165.

DELATED, set forth in detail, prob. ="dilated," (the reading of the folios, properly "delated"= entrusted, delegated); I. ii. 38.

DELIVER, relate; I. ii. 193.

DELVER, digger; V. i. 15.

DEMANDED OF, questioned by; IV. ii. 12.

DENOTE, mark, portray; I. ii. 83.

DESIRES, good wishes; II. ii. 60.

DEXTERITY, nimbleness, celerity; (S. Walker, "celerity"); I. ii. 157.

DIET; "your worm is your only emperor for d.", a grim play of words upon "the Diet of Worms"; IV. iii. 23.

DIFFERENCE, properly a term in heraldry for a slight mark of distinction in the coats of arms of members of the same family; hence = a slight difference; IV. v. 185.

DIFFERENCES; "excellent d.", distinguishing qualities; V. ii. 113.

DISAPPOINTED, (?) unappointed, unprepared; (Pope "unanointed"; Theobald "unappointed"); I. v. 77.

DISCLOSE, hatching; III. i. 176.

DISCLOSED, hatched; V. i. 319.

DISCOURSE, conversation; III. i. 108.

——; "d. of reason," i. e. the reasoning faculty; I. ii. 150.

DISCOVERY, disclosure, confession; II. ii. 312.

DISJOINT, disjointed; I. ii. 20.

DISPATCH, hasten to get ready; III. iii. 3.

DISPATCH'D, deprived; I. v. 75.

DISPOSITION, nature; I. iv. 55.

DISTEMPER; "your cause of d.",

the cause of your disorder; III. ii. 363.

DISTEMPERED, disturbed; III. ii. 322.

DISTILL'D, dissolved, melted; (so Q. 2; F. 1, *"bestil'd"*); I. ii. 204.

DISTRACT, distracted; IV. v. 2.

DISTRUST; "I d. you," *i. e.* I am anxious about you; III. ii. 180.

DIVULGING, being divulged; IV. i. 22.

DO; "to do," to be done; IV. iv. 44.

DOCUMENT, precept, instruction; IV. v. 180.

DOLE, grief; I. ii. 13.

DOOM, Doomsday; III. iv. 50.

DOUBT, suspect, fear; I. ii. 257.

DOUTS, does out, extinguishes; (F. 1, *"doubts"*; Qq. F. 2, *"drownes"*; Ff. 3, 4, *"drowns"*); IV. vii. 193.

DOWN-GYVED, pulled down like gyves or fetters; (so F. 1; Qq. 2, 3, 6, *"downe gyved"*; Qq. 4, 5, *"downe gyred"*; Theobald *"down-gyred"*; *i. e.* rolled down); II. i. 80.

DRAB, strumpet; II. ii. 636.

DREADFUL, full of dread; I. ii. 207.

DRIFT; "d. of circumstance," round-about methods; (Qq. *"d. of conference"*; Collier conj. *"d. of confidence"*); III. i. 1.

DRIVES AT, rushes upon; II. ii. 511.

DUCATS, gold coins; II. ii. 393.

DULL THY PALM, *i. e.* "make callous thy palm by shaking every man by the hand" (Johnson); I. iii. 64.

DUMB SHOW, a show unaccompanied by words, preceding the dialogue and foreshadowing the action of a play, introduced originally as a compensatory addition to Senecan dramas, wherein declamation took the place of action; III. ii. 151–152.

DUPP'D, opened; IV. v. 54.

DYE, tinge; (F. 1, *"the eye;"* Qq. 2–5, *"that die"*); I. iii. 128.

EAGER, sharp, sour; (Ff. *"Aygre"*; Knight *"aigre"*); I. v. 69.

EALE, ? = e'ile (*i. e.* "evil"), *v.* Note; I. iv. 36.

EAR; "in the e.", within hearing; III. i. 195.

EASINESS, unconcernedness; V. i. 77.

EAT, eaten; IV. iii. 30.

ECSTASY, madness; II. i. 102.

EDGE, incitement; III. i. 26.

EFFECTS, purposes; III. iv. 129.

EISEL, vinegar; the term usually employed by older English writers for the bitter drink given to Christ (= late Lat. *acetillum*); [Q. (i.) *"vessels"*; Q. 2, *"Esill"*; Ff. *"Esile"*]; V. i. 208.

ELSINORE, the residence of the Danish kings, famous for the royal castle of Kronborg, commanding the entrance of the Sound; II. ii. 284.

EMULATE, emulous; I. i. 83.

ENACT, act; III. ii. 112.

ENACTURES, actions; III. ii. 212.

ENCOMPASSMENT, circumvention; II. i. 10.

ENCUMBER'D, folded; I. v. 174.

ENGAGED, entangled; III. iii. 69.

ENGINER, engineer; III. iv. 206.

ENSEAMED, defiled, filthy; III. iv. 90.

ENTERTAINMENT; "gentle e.", show of kindness; V. ii. 224.

ENTREATMENTS, solicitations; I. iii. 122.

ENVIOUSLY, angrily; IV. v. 6.

ERRING, wandering, roaming; I. i. 154.

ESCOTED, maintained; II. ii. 372.

ESPIALS, spies; III. i. 32.

ESTATE, rank; V. i. 253.

ETERNAL, ? = infernal; V. ii. 387; (*cp.* "(eternal) blazon)."

EVEN, honest, straightforward; II. ii. 304.

EVEN CHRISTIAN, fellow-Christian; V. i. 33.

EVENT, result, issue; IV. iv. 41.

EXCEPTION, objection; V. ii. 253.

EXCREMENTS, excrescences, outgrowth; (used of hair and nails); III. iv. 121.

EXPECTANCY, hope; (Qq. *"expectation"*); III. i. 162.

EXPOSTULATE, discuss; II. ii. 86.

EXPRESS, expressive, perfect; II. ii. 326.

EXTENT, behavior; II. ii. 401.

EXTOLMENT, praise; V. ii. 123.

EXTRAVAGANT, vagrant, wandering beyond its limit or confine; I. i. 154.

EXTREMITY; "in ex.", going to extremes; III. ii. 183.

EYASES, unfledged birds; properly, young hawks taken from the nest (Fr. niais); II. ii. 365.

EYE, presence; IV. iv. 6.

EYRIE, a brood of nestlings; properly, an eagle's nest; II. ii. 364.

FACULTIES, peculiar nature; (Ff. *"faculty"*); II. ii. 610.

FACULTY, ability, (Qq. *"faculties"*); II. ii. 325.

FAIR, gently; IV. i. 36.

FALLS, falls out, happens; IV. vii. 71.

FANCY; "express'd in f.", gaudy; I. iii. 71.

FANG'D, having fangs; (according to some, "deprived of fangs"); III. iv. 203.

FANTASY, imagination; I. i. 23; whim, caprice; IV. iv. 61.

FARDELS, packs, burdens; III. i. 76.

FARM, take the lease of it; IV. iv. 20.

FASHION, a mere temporary mood; I. iii. 6; "f. of himself," *i. e.* his usual demeanor; III. i. 185.

FAT, fatten; IV. iii. 23.

FAT; "f. and scant of breath," ? = out of training (but, probably, the words were inserted owing to the physical characteristics of Burbage, who sustained the part of Hamlet); V. ii. 309.

FAVOR, charm; IV. v. 192; appearance; V. i. 222.

FAWNING, cringing; (Ff. 1, 2, 3, *"faining"*; F. 4, *"feigning"*); III. ii. 71.

FAY, faith; (Ff. *"fey"*); II. ii. 278.

FEAR, object of fear; III. iii. 25. ——, fear for; I. iii. 51; IV. v. 124.

FEATURE, figure, form; (Qq. *"stature"*); III. i. 169.

FEE, payment, value; I. iv. 65; fee-simple; IV. iv. 22.

FELLIES, the outside of wheels; II. ii. 534.

FELLOWSHIP, partnership; III. ii. 297.

FENNEL, the symbol of flattery; iv. v. 182.

FETCH, artifice; "fetch of warrant," justifiable stratagem; (Qq. *"f. of wit"*); II. i. 38.

FEW; "in f.", in few words, in brief; I. iii. 126.

FIERCE, wild, terrible; I. i. 121.

FIERY QUICKNESS, hot haste; IV. iii. 48.

FIGURE, figure of speech; II. ii. 98.

FIND, find out, detect; III. i. 196.

FINE OF HIS FINES, end of his fines; with a play upon the other sense of the word; V. i. 120.

FIRE (dissyllabic); I. iii. 120.

FIRST, *i. e.* first request; II. ii. 61.

FISHMONGER, probably used in some cant coarse sense, (?) "seller of women's chastity"); II. ii. 176.

FIT, prepared, ready; V. ii. 239.

FITNESS, convenience; V. ii. 217.

FITS, befits; I. iii. 25.

FLAW, gust of wind; V. i. 247.

FLUSH, in full vigor; (Ff. *"fresh"*); III. iii. 81.

FLUSHING, redness; "had left the f.", *i. e.* had ceased to produce redness; I. ii. 155.

FOIL, used with play upon its two senses, (i.) blunted rapier, (ii.) gold-leaf used to set off a jewel; V. ii. 277.

FOND, foolish; I. v. 99.

FOND AND WINNOWED, foolish and over-refined; (so Ff.; Q. 2, *"prophane and trennowed"*; Johnson, *"sane and renowned"*; Warburton, *"fann'd and winnowed"*); V. ii. 208.

FOOLS OF NATURE, made fools of by nature; I. iv. 54.

FOOT; "at f." at his heels; IV. iii. 59.

FOR, as for; I. ii. 112; in place

of, instead; V. i. 262; "for all," once for all; I. iii. 131; "for and," and also; V. i. 106.

FORDO, destroy; V. i. 253.

FOREKNOWING, foreknowledge, prescience; I. i. 134.

FORESTALLED, prevented; III. iii. 49.

FORGED PROCESS, false statement of facts; I. v. 37.

FORGERY, invention, imagination; IV. vii. 90.

FORGONE, given up; II. ii. 315.

FORTUNE'S STAR, an accidental mark or defect; I. iv. 32.

FORWARD, disposed; III. i. 7.

FOUR; "f. hours", probably used for indefinite time; (Hanmer *"for"*); II. ii. 162.

FRAME, order, sense; III. ii. 331.

FREE, willing, not enforced; IV. iii. 66; innocent; II. ii. 608; III. ii. 258.

FRET, vex, annoy; with a play upon *'fret'*='small lengths of wire on which the fingers press the strings in playing the guitar'; III. ii. 403.

FRETTED, carved, adorned; II. ii. 321.

FRIENDING, friendliness; I. v. 186.

FRIGHTED, frightened, affrighted; III. ii. 285.

FROM, away from, contrary to; III. ii. 25.

FRONT, forehead; III. iv. 56.

FRUIT, dessert; (Ff. 1, 2, *"newes"*); II. ii. 52.

FRUITS, consequences; II. ii. 147.

FUNCTION, the whole action of the body; II. ii. 603.

FUST, becomes fusty, mouldy; (Rowe, *"rust"*); IV. iv. 39.

GAGED, pledged; I. i. 91.

GAIN-GIVING, misgiving; V. ii. 235.

GAIT, proceeding; I. ii. 31.

GALLED, wounded, injured; ("let the galled jade wince, our withers are unwrung," proverbial); III. ii. 259.

——, sore, injured by tears; I. ii. 155.

GALLS, hurts, injures; I. iii. 39.

GARB, fashion, manner; II. ii. 401.

GENDER; "general g.", common race of men; IV. vii. 18.

GENERAL, general public, common people; II. ii. 474.

GENTRY, courtesy; II. ii. 22; V. ii. 115.

GERMANE, akin; V. ii. 169.

GIB, a tom-cat, (a contraction of *Gilbert*); III. iv. 190.

GIBBER, gabble; I. i. 116.

GIBES, jeers; V. i. 216.

GIS, a corruption of Jesus; IV. v. 60.

GIVING OUT, profession, indication; I. v. 178.

GLIMPSES, glimmering light; I. iv. 53.

GLOBE, head; I. v. 97.

GO ABOUT, attempt; III. ii. 374.

GO BACK AGAIN, *i. e.* refers to what once was, but is no more; IV. vii. 27.

GOD-A-MERCY, God have mercy; II. ii. 174.

GOD BE WI'YE, good bye; (Qq. *"God buy ye"*; Ff. 1, 2, 3, *"God buy you"*; F. 4, *"God b' w' you"*); II. i. 69.

GOD 'ILD YOU, God yield, reward you; IV. v. 41.

GOD KISSING CARRION, said of "the sun breeding maggots in a dead dog"; (Warburton's

emendation of Qq. and Ff. *"good kissing carrion"*); II. ii. 184.

GOOD, good sirs; I. i. 70.

GOOD MY BROTHER, my good brother; I. iii. 46.

GOOSE-QUILLS; "afraid of g.", *i. e.* afraid of being satirized; II. ii. 370.

GO TO, an exclamation of impatience; I. iii. 112.

GRACE, honor; I. ii. 124.

GRACIOUS, *i. e.* Gracious king; III. i. 43.

——, benign, full of blessing; I. i. 164.

GRAINED, dyed in grain; III. iv. 90.

GRATING, offending, vexing; III. i. 3.

GREEN, inexperienced; I. iii. 101.

GREENLY, foolishly; IV. v. 85.

GROSS, great, palpable; IV. iv. 46.

——, "in the g.", *i. e.* in a general way; I. i. 68.

GROUNDLINGS, rabble who stood in the *pit* of the theatre, which had neither boarding nor benches; III. ii. 13.

GRUNT, groan; III. i. 77.

GULES, red; a term of heraldry; II. ii. 497.

GULF, whirlpool; III. iii. 16.

HABIT; "outward h.", external politeness; V. ii. 206.

HANDSAW = heronshaw, or hernsew,= heron; ("when the wind is southerly I know a hawk from a h.", for the birds fly with the wind, and when it is from the g. south, the sportsman would have his back to the sun and be able to distinguish them); II. ii. 410.

HANDSOME; "more h. than fine"; *"handsome* denotes genuine

natural beauty; *fine* artificial labored beauty" (Delius); II. ii. 484.

HAP, happen; I. ii. 249.

HAPLY, perchance, perhaps; III. i. 181.

HAPPILY, haply, perchance; (according to some = luckily); I. i. 134.

HAPPY; "in h. time", in good time (*à la bonne heure*); V. ii. 222.

HAPS, fortune; IV. iii. 73.

HATCHMENT, an armorial escutcheon used at a funeral; IV. v. 217.

HAUNT; "out of h.", from the haunts of men; IV. i. 18.

HAVE; "you h. me," you understand me; II. i. 68.

HAVE AFTER, let us go after, follow him; I. iv. 89.

HAVE AT YOU, I'll begin, I'll hit you; V. ii. 324.

HAVIOR, deportment; I. ii. 81.

HEAD, armed force; IV. v. 103.

HEALTH; "spirit of health", "healed or saved spirit"; I. iv. 40.

HEARSED, coffined; I. iv. 47.

HEAT, anger; III. iv. 4.

HEAVY; " 'tis h.", it goes hard; III. iii. 84.

HEBENON (so Ff.; Qq., "*hebona*"), probably henbane, but possibly (i.) the yew, or (ii.) the juice of ebony; I. v. 62.

HECATE, the goddess of mischief and revenge (dissyllabic); III. ii. 276.

HECTIC, continual fever; IV. iii. 71.

HEDGE, hedge round, encompass; IV. v. 125.

HEIGHT; "at h.", to the utmost; I. iv. 21.

HENT, hold, seizure; III. iii. 88.

HERALDRY; "law and h.", *i. e.* heraldic law; I. i. 87.

HERB OF GRACE, rue; IV. v. 184.

HERCULES AND HIS LOAD TOO; possibly an allusion to the Globe Theatre, the sign of which was Hercules carrying the Globe; II. ii. 388.

HEROD, a common character in the mystery plays, represented as a furious and violent tyrant; III. ii. 17.

HEY-DAY, frolicsome wildness; III. iv. 69.

HEY NON NONNY, meaningless refrain common in old songs; IV. v. 167.

HIC ET UBIQUE, here and everywhere; I. v. 156.

HIDE FOX, AND ALL AFTER, a children's hide-and-seek game; IV. ii. 32.

HIES, hastens; I. i. 154.

HILLO, a falconer's cry to recall his hawk; I. v. 116.

HIM, he whom; II. i. 42.

HIS, its; I. iii. 60.

HOAR LEAVES, the silvery-grey underside of willow leaves; IV. vii. 169.

HOBBY-HORSE, a principal figure in the old morris dances, suppressed at the Reformation; III. ii. 149.

HOIST, *i. e.* hoised, hoisted; III. iv. 207.

HOLDS QUANTITY, keep their relative proportion; III. ii. 182.

HOLD UP, continue; V. i. 36.

HOME, thoroughly; III. iii. 29.

HONEST, virtuous; III. i. 103.

HONESTY, virtue; III. i. 107.

HOODMAN-BLIND, blind man's buff; III. iv. 77.

Hoops, bands (Pope, *"hooks"*); I. iii. 63.

Hour (dissyllabic); I. iv. 3.

Hugger-mugger; "in h." *i. e.* in secrecy and in haste; IV. v. 86.

Humorous, full of humors or caprices; "the h. man", a standing character of many plays of the period; II. ii. 346.

Husband, manage; IV. v. 140.

Husbandry, thrift, economy; I. iii. 77.

Hush (used as adjective); II. ii. 525.

Hyperion, Phœbus Apollo; taken as the type of beauty; I. ii. 140.

Hyrcanian beast, the beast of Hyrcania, *i. e.* the tiger; II. ii. 490.

I,=(?) "ay"; III. ii. 300.

Idle, unoccupied (? frivolous, light-headed); III. ii. 99.

Ilium, the palace in Troy; II. ii. 513.

Ill-breeding, hatching mischief; IV. v. 15.

Illume, illumine; I. i. 37.

Image, representation, reproduction; III. ii. 254.

Immediate; "most i.", nearest; I. ii. 109.

Impart, (?) bestow myself, give all I can bestow; perhaps = "impart 't" *i. e.* impart it (the throne); I. ii. 112.

Impasted, made into paste; II. ii. 499.

Imperious, imperial; V. i. 244.

Implorators, implorers; I. iii. 129.

Imponed, staked; V. ii. 158.

Important, urgent, momentous; III. iv. 108.

Importing, having for import; I. ii. 23.

—— concerning; V. ii. 21.

Imposthume, abscess; IV. iv. 27.

Impress, impressment, enforced public service; I. i. 75.

Imputation, reputation; V. ii. 151.

In, into; III. iv. 95.

Incapable, insensible to, unable to realize; IV. vii. 180.

Incorporal, incorporeal, immaterial; (Q. 1676, *"incorporeal"*); III. iv. 118.

Incorpsed, incorporate; IV. vii. 88.

Incorrect, not subdued; I. ii. 95.

I n d e n t u r e s; "a pair of i.", "agreements were usually made in duplicate, both being written on the same sheet, which was cut in a crooked or *indented* line, so that the parts would tally with each other upon comparison"; V. i. 124.

Index, prologue, preface; III. iv. 52.

Indict, accuse; II. ii. 482.

Indifferent, ordinary, average; II. ii. 235.

——, indifferently, fairly; III. i. 124.

Indifferently, pretty well; III. ii. 45.

Indirections, indirect means; II. i. 66.

Individable; "scene ind.", probably a play in which the unity of place is preserved; II. ii. 432.

Induced, suited; IV. vii. 181.

I n e x p l i c a b l e, unintelligible, senseless; III. ii. 15.

Infusion, qualities; V. ii. 125.

Ingenious, intelligent, conscious; V. i. 280.

INHERITOR, possessor; V. i. 126.

INHIBITION, prohibition; a technical term for an order restraining or restricting theatrical performances; II. ii. 356.

INNOVATION, change (for the worse); "the late i." perhaps alludes to the license granted Jan. 30, 1603–4, to the children of the Revels to play at the Blackfriars Theatre, and elsewhere (according to some, the reference is to "the practice of introducing polemical matter on the stage"); II. ii. 357.

INQUIRE, enquiry; II. i. 4.

INSINUATION, artful intrusion, meddling; V. ii. 59.

INSTANCE, example; IV. v. 164.

INSTANCES, motives; III. ii. 196.

INSTANT, immediate, instantaneous; I. v. 71.

INTENTS, intentions, purposes; (Ff., *"events"*; Warburton *"advent"*); I. iv. 42.

IN THAT, inasmuch as; I. ii. 31.

INURN'D, entombed, interred; (Qq., *"interr'd"*); I. iv. 49.

INVESTMENTS, vestments, vestures; I. iii. 128.

"IN YOUTH, WHEN I DID LOVE," etc.; stanzas from a song attributed to Lord Vaux, printed in *Tottel's Miscellany* (1557); V. i. 70.

IT, its; (Qq. 2, 3, 4, Ff. 1, 2, *"it"*; Qq. 5, 6, Ff. 3, 4, *"its"*; Q. 1, *"his"*); I. ii. 216.

JEALOUSY, suspicion; II. i. 113.

"JEPHTHAH, JUDGE OF ISRAEL," etc., a quotation from an old ballad, to be found in Percy's *Reliques;* II. ii. 436.

JIG, a ludicrous ballad; II. ii. 539.

JIG, walk as if dancing a jig; III. i. 152.

JOHN-A-DREAMS, John of Dreams, John the Dreamer; II. ii. 616.

JOINTRESS, dowager; I. ii. 9.

JOWLS, knocks; V. i. 85.

JOYS, gladdens; III. ii. 214.

JUMP, just; (so Q. 2; Ff. *"just"*); I. i. 65.

KEEP, dwell; II. i. 8.

KETTLE, kettle-drum; V. ii. 297.

KIBE, chilblain or sore on the heel; V. i. 160.

KIND; "more than kin, and less than k."; used equivocally for (i.) natural, and (ii.) affectionate, with a play upon "kin"; I. ii. 65.

KINDLESS, unnatural; II. ii. 630.

KNOTTED, interwoven; (Ff. *"knotty"*); I. v. 18.

KNOW, acknowledge; V. ii. 7.

LABORSOME, laborious, assiduous; I. ii. 59.

LACK, be wanting; I. v. 187.

LAMOND, possibly a name suggested by that of Pietro Monte, a famous swordsman, instructor to Louis the Seventh's Master of the Horse, called "Peter Mount" in English (Ff. *"Lamound"*; Qq. *"Lamord"*); IV. vii. 92.

LAPSED; "l. in time and passion"; having let time slip by indulging in mere passion; III. iv. 107.

LAPWING, the symbol of a forward fellow; V. ii. 200.

LARDED, garnished; (Qq. *"Larded all"*); IV. v. 37.

LAWLESS, unruly; (Ff., *"Landlesse"*); I. i. 98.

LAZAR-LIKE, like a leper; I. v. 72.

LEANS ON, depends on; IV. iii. 62.

LEARN, teach; (Ff. *"teach"*); V. ii. 9.

LEAVE, permission; I. ii. 57.

——, leave off; II. i. 51; give up; III. iv. 91.

LENDS, gives; (Ff. *"giues"*); I. iii. 117 (*v.* Note).

LENTEN, meagre; II. ii. 338.

LETHE, the river of oblivion; ("L e t h e w h a r f"=Lethe's bank;) I. v. 33.

LETS, hinders; I. iv. 85.

LET TO KNOW, informed; IV. vi. 11.

LIBERAL, free-spoken; IV. vii. 172.

LIBERTY; *v.* "writ."

LIEF, gladly, willingly; III. ii. 4.

LIFE; "the single and peculiar l.", the private individual; III. iii. 11.

——, "in my l.", *i. e.* in my continuing to live; V. ii. 22.

LIGHTNESS, lightheadedness; II. ii. 151.

LIKE, likely; I. ii. 237.

LIKES, pleases; II. ii. 80.

LIMED, caught as with bird-lime; III. iii. 68.

LIST, muster-roll, (Q. 1, *"sight"*); I. i. 98.

——, boundary; IV. v. 101.

——, listen to; I. iii. 30.

LIVING, lasting (used perhaps equivocally); V. i. 329.

LOAM, clay; V. i. 242.

LOGGATS, a game somewhat resembling bowls; the *loggats* were small logs about two feet and a quarter long; V. i. 103.

LONG PURPLES, "the early *purple orchis* (*Orchis mascula*) which blossoms in April and May"; IV. vii. 171.

LOOK THROUGH, show itself; IV. vii. 152.

LOSE, waste, throw away; I. ii. 45.

LUXURY, lust; I. v. 83.

MACHINE, body; II. ii. 126.

MAIMED, imperfect; V. i. 251.

MAIN, main point, main cause; II. ii. 56.

——, the country as a whole; IV. iv. 15.

MAJESTICAL, majestic; I. i. 143.

MAKE, brings; II. ii. 284.

MANNER, fashion, custom; I. iv. 15.

MARGENT, margin; it was a common practice to write comment or gloss in the margins of old books; V. ii. 166.

MARK, watch; III. ii. 163.

MARKET OF HIS TIME, "that for which he sells his time" (Johnson); IV. iv. 34.

MART, marketing, traffic; I. i. 74.

MARVELLOUS, marvellously; II. i. 3.

MASSY, massive; III. iii. 17.

MATIN, morning; I. v. 89.

MATTER, sense; IV. v. 176.

MATTER, subject; (misunderstood wilfully by Hamlet to mean "cause of dispute"); II. ii. 198.

MAZZARD, skull; used contemptuously; (Qq. 2, 3, *"massene"*; Qq. 4, 5, 6, *"mazer"*); V. i. 100.

MEANS, means of access; IV. vi. 15.

MEED, merit; V. ii. 152.

MEET, proper; I. v. 107.

MERELY, absolutely; I. ii. 137.

METAL, mettle; I. i. 96.

MICHING MALLECHO, mouching

(*i. e.* skulking) mischief; (Span. *malhecho,* ill-done); III. ii. 152.

MIGHT, could; I. i. 56.

MIGHTIEST, very mighty; I. i. 114.

M I L C H, milk-giving = moist = tearful; (Pope *"melt"*); II. ii. 538.

MILKY, white; II. ii. 517.

MINCING, cutting in pieces; II. ii. 535.

MINERAL, mine; IV. i. 26.

MINING, undermining; (Ff. 3, 4, *"running"*); III. iv. 148.

MISTOOK, mistaken; V. ii. 406.

MOBLED, muffled; (*cp.* Prov. E. *mop,* to muffle; *"mob-cap,"* etc.); [Qq. *mobled"*; F. 1, *inobled;* Upton conj. *"mob-led"*; Capel, *ennobl'd, etc.*]; II. ii. 543.

MODEL, exact copy, counterpart; V. ii. 50.

MOIETY, portion; I. i. 90.

MOIST; "the moist star," *i. e.* the moon; I. i. 118.

MOLE OF NATURE, natural defect, blemish; I. iv. 24.

MOPE, be stupid; III. iv. 81.

MORTAL, deadly; IV. vii. 143.

MORTISED, joined with a mortise; III. iii. 20.

MOST, greatest; I. v. 180.

MOTE, atom; (Qq. 2, 3, 4, *"moth"*); I. i. 112.

MOTION, emotion, impulse; (Warburton, *"notion"*); III. iv. 72.

——, movement; I. ii. 217.

MOTION, "attack in fencing, opposed to guard or parrying"; IV. vii. 158.

MOULD OF FORM, the model on which all endeavored to form themselves; III. i. 163.

MOUSE, a term of endearment; III. iv. 183.

MOUTH, rant; V. i. 315.

MOWS, grimaces; II. ii. 392.

MUDDY-METTLED, dull-spirited, irresolute; II. ii. 615.

M U R D E R I N G-PIECE, a cannon loaded with case-shot, so as to scatter death more widely; IV. v. 97.

MUTES, dumb spectators; V. ii. 357.

MUTINE, mutiny, rebel; III. iv. 83.

MUTINES, mutineers; V. ii. 6.

NAPKIN, handkerchief; V. ii. 310.

NATIVE, kindred, related; I. ii. 47.

——, "n. hue," natural color; III. i. 84.

NATURE, natural affection; I. v. 81.

NATURE'S LIVERY, a natural blemish; I. iv. 32.

NAUGHT, naughty; III. ii. 162.

NEAR, is near; I. iii. 44.

NEIGHBOR, neighboring; III. iv. 212.

NEIGHBOR'D TO, intimate, friendly with; II. ii. 12.

NEMEAN LION, one of the monsters slain by Hercules; I. iv. 83.

NERO, the Roman Emperor, who murdered his mother Agrippina; III. ii. 426.

NERVE, sinew, muscle; I. iv. 83.

NEUTRAL, a person indifferent to both; II. ii. 520.

NEW-HATCH'D, newly hatched; (Ff. *"unhatch't"*); I. iii. 65.

NEW-LIGHTED, newly alighted; III. iv. 59.

NICK-NAME, misname; III. i. 153.

NIGHTED, dark, black as night; (Ff. *"nightly"*; Collier MS. *"nightlike"*); I. ii. 68.

NILL; "will he, nill he," *i. e.*

whether he will, or whether he will not; V. i. 19.

Niobe, daughter of Tantalus, whose children were slain by Apollo and Artemis, while she herself was turned into stone upon Mount Sipylus in Lydia, where she weeps throughout the summer months; I. ii. 149.

Nomination, naming; V. ii. 136.

No more, nothing more; III. i. 61.

Nonce, "for the n.", for that once, for the occasion; (Qq. 4, 5, *"once"*); IV. vii. 161.

Norway, King of Norway; I. i. 61.

Nose, smell; IV. iii. 41.

Note, notice, attention; III. ii. 93.

Noted, known; II. i. 23.

Nothing, not at all; I. ii. 41.

Noyance, injury, harm; III. iii. 13.

Obsequious, dutiful, with perhaps a reference to the other sense of the word ="funereal"; I. ii. 92.

Occulted, concealed, hidden; III. ii. 89.

Occurrents, occurrences; V. ii. 379.

Odds; "at the o.", with the advantage allowed; V. ii. 230.

O'er-crows, triumphs over; V. ii. 375.

O'er-raught, over-reached, overtook; (Qq. *"ore-raught"*; Ff. 1, 2, *"ore-wrought"*; Ff. 3, 4, *"o're-took"*; Warburton *"o'er-rode"*); III. i. 17.

O'er-reaches, outwits; (F. 1, *"o're Offices"*; F. 2, *"ore-Offices"*); V. i. 88.

O'er-sized, covered with size, a sort of glue; II. ii. 502.

O'er-teemed, worn out with child-bearing; II. ii. 529.

O'ertook, overcome by drink, intoxicated; II. i. 58.

O'erweigh, outweigh; III. ii. 34.

Of, resulting from; IV. iv. 41; by; I. i. 25; IV. iii. 4; in; I. v. 60; on; IV. v. 203; about, concerning; IV. v. 46; upon, (*"I have an eye of you"*); II. ii. 307; over; II. ii. 27.

Offence, advantages gained by offence; III. iii. 56.

Omen, fatal event portended by the omen; (Theobald *"omen'd"*); I. i. 123.

Ominous, fatal; II. ii. 494.

On, in; V. i. 218; in consequence of, following on; V. ii. 417.

Once, ever; I. v. 121.

On't, of it; III. i. 185.

Oped, opened; I. iv. 50.

Open'd, discovered, disclosed; II. ii. 18.

Operant, active; III. ii. 189.

Opposed, opponent; I. iii. 67.

Opposites, opponents; V. ii. 62.

Or, before, ere; V. ii. 30.

Orb, earth; II. ii. 524.

Orchard, garden; (Q. 1676, *"garden"*); I. v. 35.

Order, prescribed rule; V. i. 260.

Ordinant, ordaining; (Ff. *"ordinate"*); V. ii. 48.

Ordnance, cannon; (F. 1, *"Ordinance"*); V. ii. 292.

Ore, gold; IV. i. 25.

Or ere, before; I. ii. 147.

Organ, instrument; IV. vii. 71.

Orisons, prayers; III. i. 89.

Ossa; a reference to the story of the giants, who piled Olympus, Pelion, and Ossa, three mountains in Thessaly, upon each other, in their attempt to scale heaven; V. i. 315.

OSTENTATION, funeral pomp; IV. v. 218.

OUTSTRETCHED, puffed up; II. ii. 276.

OVERLOOKED, perused; IV. vi. 14.

OVERPEERING, overflowing, rising above; IV. v. 101.

OWL WAS A BAKER'S DAUGHTER; alluding to a story current among the folk telling how Christ went into a baker's shop, and asked for bread, but was refused by the baker's daughter, in return for which He transformed her into an owl; IV. v. 41.

PACKING, plotting, contriving; (?) going off in a hurry; used probably in the former sense, with play upon the latter; III. iv. 211.

PADDOCK, toad; III. iv. 190.

PAINTED; "p. tyrant," *i. e.* tyrant in a picture; II. ii. 519; unreal, fictitious; III. i. 53.

PAJOCK,= pea-jock (*i. e.* jack), peacock, (*cp.* Scotch "bubbly-jock"= a turkey); III. ii. 304.

PALL, become useless; (Qq. 3, 4, 6, "*fall*"; Pope, "*fail*"); V. ii. 9.

PANSIES, "love-in-idleness," the symbol of thought; (F. 1, "*Paconcies*"); IV. v. 179.

PARDON, permission to take leave; I. ii. 56.

PARLE, parley; I. i. 62.

PART, quality, gift; IV. vii. 77.

PARTISAN, a kind of halberd; I. i. 140.

PARTS, gifts, endowments; IV. vii. 74.

PARTY, person, companion; II. i. 42.

PASS, passage; II. ii. 77.

——, "p. of practice," treacherous thrust; IV. vii. 139.

PASSAGE; "for his p.", to accompany his departure, in place of the passing bell; V. ii. 420.

PASSETH, surpasseth; (Qq. "*passes*"); I. ii. 85.

PASSION, violent sorrow; II. ii. 560.

PASSIONATE, full of passion, feeling; II. ii. 469.

PATE, a contemptuous word for *head;* V. i. 121.

PATIENCE, permission; III. ii. 118.

PATRICK, invoked as being the patron saint of all blunders and confusion; (or perhaps as the Keeper of Purgatory); I. v. 136.

PAUSE, time for reflection; III. i. 68.

——, "deliberate p.", a matter for deliberate arrangement; IV. iii. 9.

——, "in p.", in deliberation, in doubt; III. iii. 42.

PEACE-PARTED, having departed in peace; V. i. 270.

PEAK, sneak, play a contemptible part; II. ii. 615.

PELICAN, a bird which is supposed to feed its young with its own blood; (F. 1, '*politician*'); IV. v. 148.

PERDY, a corruption of *par Dieu;* III. ii. 315.

PERIWIG-PATED, wearing a wig; (at this time wigs were worn only by actors); III. ii. 11.

PERPEND, consider; II. ii. 105.

PERUSAL, study, examination; II. i. 90.

PERUSE, examine closely; IV. vii. 137.

PETAR, petard, "an Engine (made like a Bell or Mortar) wherewith strong gates are burst open" (Cotgrave); III. iv. 207.

PICKED, refined, fastidious; V. i. 158.

PICKERS AND STEALERS, i. e. hands; (alluding to the catechism "Keep my hands from picking and stealing"); III. ii. 361.

PICTURE IN LITTLE, miniature; II. ii. 394.

PIGEON-LIVER'D, too mild tempered; II. ii. 626.

PIONER, pioneer; I. v. 163.

PITCH, height, importance; (originally, height to which a falcon soars); (Ff. *"pith"*); III. i. 86.

PITEOUS, pitiful, exciting compassion; II. i. 94.

PITH AND MARROW, the most valuable part; I. iv. 22.

PLAUSIVE, plausible, pleasing; I. iv. 30.

PLAUTUS; "P. too light," alluding to the fact that Plautus was taken as the word for comedy by the Academic play-wrights; II. ii. 433.

PLAYED I' THE UNIVERSITY; alluding to the old academic practice of acting Latin or English plays at Christmastide, or in honor of distinguished visitors; (a play on Cæsar's death was performed at Oxford in 1582); III. ii. 108.

PLAYED; "p. the desk or talebook", i. e. been the agent of their correspondence; II. ii. 138.

PLOT, piece of ground; IV. iv. 62.

PLURISY, plethora, a fulness of blood, (*as if* Latin *plus,* more, but really an affection of the lungs, Gk. πλευρα); IV. vii. 118.

POINT; 'at p.' completely; (so Qq.; Ff. *'at all points'*); I. ii. 200.

POLACK, Pole; II. ii. 75.

——, Polish; V. ii. 398.

POLACKS, Poles; (Qq. F. 1, *'pollax'*; *v.* note); I. i. 63.

POLE, pole-star; I. i. 36.

POLITICIAN, plotter, schemer; V. i. 88.

PORPENTINE, porcupine; I. v. 20.

POSSET, curdle; (Qq. *"possesse"*); I. v. 68.

POSY, motto, verse on a ring; III. ii. 167.

POWERS, armed force, troops; IV. iv. 9.

PRACTICE, artifice, plot; IV. vii. 68.

PRECEDENT, former; III. iv. 98.

PRECURSE, forerunning; I. i. 121.

PREGNANT, yielding, ready; III. ii. 70.

PRENOMINATE, aforesaid; II. i. 43.

PRESCRIPTS, orders; (Ff., *"precepts"*); II. ii. 144.

PRESENTLY, at once, immediately; II. ii. 172.

PRESENT PUSH, immediate proof; V. i. 327.

PRESSURE, impress, imprint; III. ii. 30.

PRESSURES, impressions; I. v. 100.

PREVENT, anticipate; II. ii. 312.

PRICK'D ON, incited, spurred on; I. i. 83.

PRIMAL, first; III. iii. 37.

PRIMY, spring-like; I. iii. 7.

PRIVATES, common *soldiers;* II. ii.
242.

PROBATION, proof; (quadrisylla-
bic); I. i. 156.

PROCESS, decree; IV. iii. 68.

PRODIGAL, prodigally; I. iii. 116.

PROFIT, advantage; II. ii. 24.

PROGRESS, journey made by a sovereign through his own country; IV. iii. 34.

PRONOUNCE, speak on; III. ii.
333.

PROOF, trial of strength; II. ii.
529.

PROPER, appropriate; II. i. 114.

——, own, very; V. ii. 66.

PROPERTY, kingly right, (? "own
person"); II. ii. 618.

PROPOSER, orator; II. ii. 303.

PROVINCIAL ROSES, properly, dou-
ble-damask roses; here, rosettes
of ribbon worn on shoes; the
name was derived either from
Provence or Provins near Paris,
both places being famous for
their roses; III. ii. 296.

PUFF'D, bloated; I. iii. 49.

PUPPETS; "p. dallying"; (?) the
figures in the puppet-show (in
which Ophelia and her lover
were to play a part); more
probably used in some wanton
sense; III. ii. 264.

PURGATION; "put him to his p.",
"a play upon the legal and
medical senses of the word";
III. ii. 328.

PURSY, fat with pampering; III.
iv. 153.

PUT ON, incite, instigate; IV. vii.
132; put to the test, tried; V.
ii. 419; assume; I. v. 172.

PUT ON ME, impressed upon me;
I. iii. 94.

QUAINTLY, artfully, skilfully; II.
i. 31.

QUALITY, profession, calling (especially the actor's profession);
II. ii. 373.

QUANTITY, measure, portion; III.
iv. 75.

QUARRY, heap of dead; V. ii. 386.

QUESTION, talk; III. i. 13.

——; "cry out on the top of q.",
i. e. speak in a high key, or in
a high childish treble; II. ii.
365.

QUESTIONABLE, inviting question;
I. iv. 43.

QUEST LAW, inquest law; V. i. 25.

QUICK, alive; V. i. 143.

QUIDDITIES, subtleties; (Ff.,
"quiddits"); V. i. 111.

QUIETUS, a law term for the offi-
cial settlement of an account;
III. i. 75.

QUILLETS, subtle arguments; V. i.
112.

QUINTESSENCE, the highest or
fifth essence; (a term in al-
chemy); II. ii. 330.

QUIT, requite; V. ii. 68.

QUOTED, observed, noted; II. i.
112.

RACK, mass of clouds in motion;
II. ii. 523.

RANGE, roam at large; III. iii. 2.

RANKER, richer, greater; IV. iv.
22.

RANKLY, grossly; I. v. 38.

RAPIER, a small sword used in
thrusting; V. ii. 155.

RASHLY, hastily; V. ii. 6.

RAVEL OUT, unravel; (Qq. 2-5,
"rouell"); III. iv. 186.

RAZED, slashed; III. ii. 296.

REACH, capacity; II. i. 64.

RECKS, cares, minds; (Qq.
"reck'st"); I. iii. 51.

RECOGNIZANCES; "a recognizance is a bond or obligation of record testifying the recognizer to owe to the recognizee a certain· sum of money" (Cowel); V. i. 118.

RECORDERS, a kind of flute or flageolet; III. ii. 313.

RECOVERIES, a law term; (*v.* "Vouchers"); V. i. 119.

REDE, counsel, advice; I. iii. 51.

REDELIVER, report; V. ii. 193.

REELS, dances wildly; I. iv. 9.

REGARDS, conditions; II. ii. 79.

REGION, air; ("originally a division of the sky marked out by the Roman augurs"); II. ii. 526.

RELATIVE, conclusive, to the purpose; II. ii. 654.

RELISH OF, have a taste, flavor; III. i. 121.

REMEMBER; "I beseech you, r.", the full saying is found in *Love's Labor's Lost;* V. i. 103; *"I do beseech thee remember thy courtesy; I beseech thee apparel thy head"*; V. ii. 109.

REMEMBRANCES, mementos; III. i. 93.

REMISS, careless; IV. vii. 135.

REMORSE, pity; II. ii. 530.

REMOVE, removal; IV. v. 83.

REMOVED, retired, secluded; I. iv. 61.

REPAST, feed; IV. v. 149.

REPLICATION, reply, answer; IV. ii. 13.

REQUITE, repay; I. ii. 251.

RESIDENCE, a fixed abode as opposed to strolling; used technically of theatrical companies; II. ii. 353.

RESOLUTES, desperadoes; I. i. 98.

RESOLVE, dissolve, melt; I. ii. 130.

RE-SPEAKING, re-echoing; I. ii. 128.

RESPECT, consideration, motive; III. i. 68.

REST, stay, abode; II. ii. 13.

RESTS, remains; III. iii. 64.

RETROGRADE, contrary; I. ii. 114.

RETURN'D; "had r.", would have returned; (Qq. *"returne"*); I. i. 91.

REVEREND, venerable; II. ii. 518.

REVOLUTION, change; V. i. 101.

RE-WORD, repeat in the very words; III. iv. 143.

RHAPSODY, a collection of meaningless words; III. iv. 48.

RHENISH, Rhenish wine; I. iv. 10.

RIBAND, ribbon, ornament; IV. vii. 78.

RIGHTS OF MEMORY, rights remembered; (Ff. *"Rites"*); V. ii. 411.

RITES, funeral service; V. i. 251.

RIVALS, partners, sharers; I. i. 13.

ROBUSTIOUS, sturdy; III. ii. 11.

ROMAGE, bustle, turmoil; I. i. 107.

ROOD, cross; "by the rood," an oath; III. iv. 14.

ROOTS ITSELF, takes root, grows; I. v. 33.

ROSCIUS, the most celebrated actor of ancient Rome; II. ii. 423.

ROSE, charm, grace; III. iv. 42.

ROSEMARY, a herb; the symbol of remembrance, particularly used at weddings and funerals; IV. v. 177.

ROUGH-HEW, make the rough, or first form; a technical term in carpentering; V. ii. 11.

ROUND, in a straightforward manner; II. ii. 141.

ROUSE, bumper, revel; ("the Danish *rousa"*); I. ii. 127.

ROW, stanza (properly,= line); II. ii. 452.

RUB, impediment; a term in the game of bowls; III. i. 65.

RUE, called also "herb of grace"; emblematic of repentance; (Ophelia is probably playing on *rue* = repentance, and "*rue, even for ruth*" = pity; the former signification for the queen, the latter for herself) (*cp.* Richard II.; III. iv. 104); IV. v. 183.

SABLES, fur used for the trimming of rich robes; perhaps with a play on "*sable*" = black; III. ii. 143.

SAFETY; trisyllabic; (so Qq.; Ff., "*sanctity*"; Theobald, "*sanity*"); I. iii. 21.

SALLETS, salads; used metaphorically for "relish"; (Pope "*salts*", later "*salt*"); II. ii. 480.

SANDAL SHOON, shoes consisting of soles tied to the feet; (*shoon,* archaic plural); (Qq., "*Sendall*"); IV. v. 26.

SANS, without; III. iv. 79.

SATE, satiate; I. v. 56.

SATYR, taken as a type of deformity; I. ii. 140.

SAWS, maxims; I. v. 100.

SAY'ST, say'st well; V. i. 30.

'SBLOOD, a corruption of "*God's blood*"; an oath; II. ii. 394.

SCANN'D, carefully considered; III. iii. 75.

'SCAPES, escapes; I. iii. 38.

SCARF'D, put on loosely like a scarf; V. ii. 13.

SCHOLAR, a man of learning, and hence versed in Latin, the language of exorcists; I. i. 42.

SCHOOL, university; I. ii. 113.

SCONCE, colloquial term for head; V. i. 114.

SCONCE, ensconce; (Qq., Ff., "*silence*"); III. iv. 4.

SCOPE, utmost aim; III. ii. 234.

SCOURGE, punishment; IV. iii. 6.

SCRIMERS, fencers; IV. vii. 101.

SCULLION, the lowest servant; used as a term of contempt; II. ii. 637.

SEA-GOWN; "esclavine; a sea-gowne; or a coarse, high-collared, and short-sleeved gowne, reaching downe to the mid-leg, and used most by seamen, and Saylors" (Cotgrave); V. ii. 13.

SEALS; "to give them s.", to ratify by action; III. ii. 431.

SEA OF TROUBLES, (*v.* "take arms,") *etc.*

SEASON, temper, restrain; I. ii. 192.

——, ripen; I. iii. 81.

——, qualify; II. i. 28.

SEASONS, matures, seasons; III. ii. 224.

SECURE, careless, unsuspicious; (Johnson, "*secret*"); I. v. 61.

SEEMING, appearance; III. ii. 96.

SEIZED OF, possessed of; I. i. 89.

SEMBLABLE, equal, like; V. ii. 126.

SENECA; "S. cannot be too heavy," alluding to the rhetorical Senecan plays taken as models for tragedy by the Academic play-wrights; II. ii. 432.

SENSE, feeling; sensibility; III. iv. 71.

SENSIBLY, feelingly; (F. 1, "*sensible*"); IV. v. 152.

SE OFFENDENDO, Clown's blunder for *se defendendo;* V. i. 9.

SEQUENT, consequent, following; V. ii. 54.

SERGEANT, sheriff's officer; V. ii. 358.

SET, regard, esteem; IV. iii. 67.

SEVERAL, different; V. ii. 20.

SHALL, will; III. i. 186.

SHALL ALONG, shall go along; III. iii. 4.

SHAPE; "to our s.", to act our part; IV. vii. 151.

SHARDS, fragments of pottery; V. i. 263.

SHARK'D UP, picked up without selection; I. i. 98.

SHEEN, brightness, lustre; III. ii. 172.

SHEETED, enveloped in shrouds; I. i. 115.

SHENT, put to the blush, reproached; III. ii. 430.

SHORT; "kept s.", kept, as it were, tethered, under control; IV. i. 18.

SHOULD, would; III. ii. 326.

SHREDS AND PATCHES, alluding to the motely dress worn by the clown, and generally by the Vice; III. iv. 102.

SHREWDLY, keenly, piercingly; I. iv. 1.

SHRIVING-TIME, time for confession and absolution; V. ii. 47.

SIEGE, rank; IV. vii. 77.

SIMPLE, silly, weak; I. ii. 97.

SIMPLES, herbs; IV. vii. 145.

SITH, since; IV. iv. 12.

SKIRTS, outskirts, borders; I. i. 97.

SLANDER, abuse; I. iii. 133.

SLEDDED, travelling in sledges; I. i. 63.

SLIPS, faults, offences; II. i. 22.

SLIVER, a small branch of a tree; IV. vii. 175.

SO, such; III. i. 69; provided that; IV. vii. 61.

SOFTLY, slowly; (Ff. *"safely"*); IV. iv. 8.

SOFT YOU NOW, hush, be quiet; III. i. 88.

SOIL, stain; I. iv. 20.

SOLE, only; III. iii. 77.

SOLICITED, urged, moved; V. ii. 380.

SOMETHING, somewhat; (Ff. *"somewhat"*); I. iii. 121.

SOMETIMES, formerly; I. i. 49.

SORT, associate; II. ii. 280.

——, turn out; I. i. 109.

SOVEREIGNTY; "your s. of reason," the command of your reason; I. iv. 73.

SPLENITIVE, passionate, impetuous; V. i. 293.

SPRINGES, snares; I. iii. 115.

SPURNS, kicks; IV. v. 6.

STAND ME UPON, be incumbent on me; V. ii. 63.

STAR, sphere; II. ii. 143.

STATION, attitude in standing; III. iv. 58.

STATISTS, statesman; V. ii. 33.

STATUTES, "particular modes of recognizance or acknowledgment for securing debts, which thereby become a charge upon the party's land" (Ritson); V. i. 118.

STAY, wait for; V. ii. 24.

STAY'D, waited; I. iii. 57.

STAYS, waits for me; III. iii. 95.

STAY UPON, await; III. ii. 117.

STICK FIERY OFF, "stand in brilliant relief"; V. ii. 279.

STIFFLY, strongly; I. v. 95.

STILL, always; I. i. 122.

STITHY, smithy; (F. 1, *"Stythe"*; (Ff. 2, 3, 4, *"Styth"*; Theobald, *"Smithy"*); III. ii. 93.

STOMACH, courage; I. i. 100.

STOUP, drinking cup; V. i. 69.

STRAIGHT, straightway; II. ii. 467.

STRANGER; "as a s.", *i. e.* without doubt or question; I. v. 165.

STREWMENTS, strewing of flowers

over the corpse and grave; V.
i. 265.

STRIKE, blast, destroy by their
influence; I. i. 162.

STUCK, thrust; an abbreviation of
stoccato; IV. vii. 162.

SUBJECT, subjects, people; I. i.
72.

SUCCESSION, future; II. ii. 378.

SUDDENLY, immediately; II. ii.
219.

SULLIES, stains, blemishes; II. i.
39.

SUN; "too much i' the s.", probably a quibbling allusion to the
old proverb "Out of heaven's
blessing into the warm sun,"
= out of comfort, miserable;
I. ii. 67.

SUPERVISE, supervision, perusal;
V. ii. 23.

SUPPLIANCE, dalliance, amuse-
ment; I. iii. 9.

SUPPLY, aiding; II. ii. 24.

SUPPOSAL, opinion; I. ii. 18.

SWADDLING CLOUTS, swaddling
clothes; (Ff. *"swathing"*); II.
ii. 414.

SWEET, sweetheart; III. ii. 240.

SWINISH; "with s. phrase," by
calling us swine; (a pun on
"Sweyn" has been found in the
phrase); I. iv. 19.

SWITZERS, Swiss guards; (Qq.
"Swissers"); IV. v. 97.

SWOOPSTAKE, sweepstake; (the
term is taken from a game of
cards, the winner sweeping or
drawing the whole stake); IV.
v. 144.

'SWOUNDS, a corruption of *God's
wounds;* an oath; II. ii. 625.

SWOUNDS, swoons, faints; (Qq. 2–
5, Ff. 1, 2, *"sounds"*); V. ii.
330.

TABLE, tablet; I. v. 98.

TABLES, tablets, memorandum-
book; I. v. 107.

TAINTS, stains, blemishes; II. i.
32.

TAKE ARMS AGAINST A SEA; an
allusion to a custom attributed
to the Kelts by Aristotle, Stra-
bo, and other writers; "they
throw themselves into the
foaming floods with their
swords drawn in their hands,"
etc. (Fleming's trans. of
Aelian's *Histories,* 1576); III.
i. 59.

TAKES, affects, enchants; (Ff. 1,
2, *"talkes"*; Ff. 3, 4, *"talks"*);
I. i. 163.

TAKE YOU, pretend; II. i. 13.

TARDY; "come t. off," being too
feebly shown; III. ii. 31.

TARRE, incite; II. ii. 380.

TAX'D, censured; I. iv. 18.

TELL, count; I. ii. 238.

TEMPER'D, compounded; (Ff.
"temp'red"); V. ii. 350.

TEMPLE, (applied to the body);
I. iii. 12.

TEND, wait; IV. iii. 50.

TENDER, regard, have a care for;
I. iii. 107.

TENDERS, promises; I. iii. 106.

TENT, probe; II. ii. 647.

TERMAGANT, a common character
in the mystery-plays, represented as a most violent tyrant; often referred to in as-
sociation with Mahoun, and
seemingly as a Saracen god;
III. ii. 17.

TETTER, a diseased thickening of
the skin; I. v. 71.

THAT, that which; II. ii. 7.

——, so that; IV. v. 220.

THEFT, the thing stolen; III. ii.
98.

THEREABOUT OF IT, that part of it; II. ii. 486.

THEWS, sinews, bodily strength; I. iii. 12.

THIEVES OF MERCY, merciful thieves; IV. vi. 22.

THINKING; "not th. on," not being thought of, being forgotten; III. ii. 148.

THINK'ST THEE, seems it to thee; (Qq. *"think thee"*); V. ii. 63.

THOUGHT, care, anxiety; IV. v. 191.

THOUGHT-SICK, sick with anxiety; III. iv. 51.

THRIFT, profit; III. ii. 71.

THOROUGHLY, thoroughly; IV. v. 138.

TICKLE O' THE SERE, easily moved to laughter; used originally of a musket in which the *"sere"* or trigger is "tickle," *i. e.* "easily moved by a touch"; II. ii. 348.

TIMBER'D; "too slightly t.," made of too light wood; IV. vii. 22.

TIME, the temporal world; III. i. 70.

TINCT, dye, color; III. iv. 91.

TO, compared to; I. ii. 140.

TO-DO, ado; II. ii. 379.

TOILS, makes to toil; I. i. 72.

TOO TOO, (used with intensive force); I. ii. 129.

TOPP'D, overtopped, surpassed. (Ff. *"past"*); IV. vii. 89.

TOUCH'D, implicated; IV. v. 210.

TOWARD, forthcoming, at hand; I. i. 77.

TOY IN BLOOD, a passing fancy; I. iii. 6.

TOYS, fancies; I. iv. 75.

TRACE, follow; V. ii. 127.

TRADE, business; III. ii. 358

TRANSLATE, transform, change; III. i. 114.

TRAVEL, stroll, go on tour in the provinces (used technically); II. ii. 353.

TRICK, toy, trifle; IV. iv. 61; faculty, skill; V. i. 101; habit; IV. vii. 189.

TRICK'D, adorned; a term of heraldry; II. ii. 497.

TRISTFUL, sorrowful; III. iv. 50.

TROPICALLY, figuratively; III. ii. 253.

TRUANT, idler; I. ii. 173.

TRUANT, roving; I. ii. 169.

TRUE-PENNY, honest fellow; I. v. 150.

TRUMPET, trumpeter; I. i. 150.

TRUSTER, believer; I. ii. 172.

TURN TURK, change utterly for the worse; (a proverbial phrase); III. ii. 295.

TWELVE FOR NINE; this phrase, according to the context, must mean "twelve to nine," *i. e.* twelve on one side, to nine on the other; V. ii. 179.

TYRANNICALLY, enthusiastically, vehemently; II. ii. 366.

UMBRAGE, shadow; V. ii. 128.

UNANELED, not having received extreme unction; I. v. 77.

UNBATED, not blunted, without a button fixed to the end; IV. vii. 139.

UNBRACED, unfastened; II. i. 78.

UNCHARGE, not charge, not accuse; IV. vii. 68.

UNDERGO, bear, endure; I. iv. 34.

UNEFFECTUAL; "u. fire;" *i. e.* ineffectual, being "lost in the light of the morning"; I. v. 90.

UNEQUAL, unequally; II. ii. 510.

UNGALLED, unhurt; III. ii. 291.

UNGORED, unwounded; V. ii. 272.

UNGRACIOUS, graceless; I. iii. 47.

UNHOUSEL'D, without having received the Sacrament; I. v. 77.

UNIMPROVED, unemployed, not turned to account; (? *"unapproved,"* i. e. "untried"; Q. 1, *"inapproved"*); I. i. 96.

UNION, fine orient pearl; (Q. 2, *"Vnice"*; Qq. 3–6, *"Onyx"* or *"Onixe"*); V. ii. 294.

UNKENNEL, discover, disclose; III. ii. 90.

UNLIMITED; "poem u.", i. e. (probably regardless of the Unities of Time and Place; II. ii. 432.

UNMASTER'D, unbridled; I. iii. 32.

UNPREGNANT, unapt, indifferent to; II. ii. 616.

UNPREVAILING, unavailing, useless; I. ii. 107.

UNPROPORTION'D, unsuitable; I. iii. 60.

UNRECLAIMED, untamed, wild; II. i. 34.

UNSHAPED, confused; IV. v. 8.

UNSIFTED, untried; I. iii. 102.

UNSINEW'D, weak; IV. vii. 10.

UNSURE, insecure; IV. iv. 51.

UNVALUED, low born, mean; I. iii. 19.

UNWRUNG, not wrenched, ungalled; III. ii. 260.

UNYOKE, your day's work is done; V. i. 60.

UP, "drink u." (used with intensive force); V. i. 308.

UPON; 'u. your hour,' i. e. on the stroke of, just at your hour; I. i. 6.

UPON MY SWORD, i. e. Swear upon my sword, (the hilt being in form of a cross); I. v. 147.

UPSHOT, conclusion; V. ii. 406.

UP-SPRING, the wildest dance at the old German merry-makings; I. iv. 9.

VAILED LIDS, lowered eyelids; I. ii. 70.

VALANCED, adorned with a beard; II. ii. 458.

VALIDITY, value, worth; III. ii. 204.

VANTAGE; "of v.", from an advantageous position, or opportunity (Warburton); III. iii. 33.

VARIABLE, various; IV. iii. 26.

VAST, void; (so Q. 1; Q. 2, F. 1, *'wast'*; Ff. 2, 3, 4, *'waste'*); I. ii. 198.

VENTAGES, holes of the recorder; III. ii. 386.

VICE OF KINGS, buffoon, clown of a king; alluding to the *Vice*, the comic character, of the old morality plays; III. iv. 98.

VIDELICET, that is to say, namely; II. i. 61.

VIGOR; "sudden v.", rapid power; I. v. 68.

VIOLET, emblem of faithfulness; IV. v. 187.

VIRTUE, power; IV. v. 157.

VISITATION, visit; II. ii. 25.

VOICE, vote, opinion; V. ii. 271.

VOUCHERS; "double v., his recoveries," "a recovery with *double voucher* is the one usually suffered, and is so denominated from *two* persons (the latter of whom is always the common cryer, or some such inferior person) being successively *vouched,* or called upon, to warrant the tenant's title" (Ritson); V. i. 119.

WAG, move; III. iv. 39.

WAKE, hold nightly revel; I. iv. 8.

WANDERING STARS, planets; V. i. 288.

WANN'D, turned pale; II. ii. 601.

WANTON; effeminate weakling; V. ii. 321.

——, wantonly; III. iv. 183.

WANTONNESS, affectation; III. i. 154.

WARRANTY, warrant; V. i. 259.

WASH, sea; III. ii. 171.

WASSAIL, carousal, drinking bout; I. iv. 9.

WATCH, state of sleeplessness; II. ii. 150.

WATER-FLY (applied to Osric); "a water-fly skips up and down upon the surface of the water without any apparent purpose or reason, and is thence the proper emblem of a busy trifler" (Johnson); V. ii. 84.

WAVES, beckons; (Ff. *"wafts"*); I. iv. 68.

WE; "and we," used loosely after conjunction instead of accusation of regard, *i. e.* "as for us;" I. iv. 54.

WEEDS, robes; IV. vii. 81.

WELL-TOOK, well undertaken; II. ii. 83.

WHARF, bank; I. v. 33.

WHAT, who; IV. vi. 1.

WHEEL, the burden or refrain of a song, (or, perhaps, the spinning-wheel to which it may be sung); IV. v. 174.

WHETHER, (monosyllabic); II. ii. 17.

WHICH, who; IV. vii. 4.

WHOLESOME, reasonable, sensible; III. ii. 339.

WILDNESS, madness; III. i. 40.

WILL; "virtue of his will," *i. e.* his virtuous intention; I. iii. 16.

WIND; "to recover the w. of me," a hunting term, meaning to get to windward of the game, so

that it may not scent the toil or its pursuers; III. ii. 375.

WINDLASSES, winding, indirect ways; II. i. 65.

WINKING; "given my heart a w.", closed the eyes of my heart; (Qq. 2–5, *"working"*); II. ii. 139.

WINNOWED, (*vide* "Fond").

WIT, wisdom; II. ii. 90.

WITHAL, with; I. iii. 28.

WITHDRAW; "to w. with you," "to speak a word in private with you" (Schmidt); III. ii. 373.

WITHERS, the part between the shoulder-blades of a horse; III. ii. 260.

WITHIN'S, within this; III. ii. 140.

WITTENBERG, the University of Wittenberg (founded 1502); I. ii. 113.

WONDER-WOUNDED, struck with surprise; V. i. 289.

WOODCOCKS, birds supposed to be brainless; hence proverbial use; I. iii. 115.

WOO'T, contraction of *wouldst thou;* V. i. 307.

WORD, watch-word; I. v. 110.

WORLDS; "both the w.", this world and the next; IV. v. 136.

WOULD, wish; I. ii. 235.

WOUNDLESS, invulnerable; IV. i. 44.

WRECK, ruin; II. i. 113.

WRETCH, here used as a term of endearment; II. ii. 169.

WRIT; "law of w. and liberty," probably a reference to the plays written with or without decorum, *i. e.* the supposed canons of dramatic art,= "classical" and "romantic" plays; (according to some,= "adhering to the text or extem-

porizing when need requires");
II. ii. 434.

YAUGHAN; "get thee to Y." (so
F. 1; Q. 2, *"get thee in and"*);
probably the name of a well-
known keeper of an ale-house
near the Globe, perhaps the
Jew, "one Johan," alluded to
in *Every Man out of his Humor;* V. iv.; V. i. 69.

YAW, stagger, move unsteadily;
(a nautical term); V. ii. 122.

YEOMAN'S SERVICE, good service,
such as the yeoman performed
for his lord;   (Qq. 2, 3, 4,
"yemans"); V. ii. 36.

YESTY, foamy; V. ii. 206.

YORICK, the name of a jester,
lamented by Hamlet; perhaps
a corruption of the Scandina-
vian name Erick, or its English equivalent; (the passage
possibly contains a tribute to
the comic actor Tarlton); V.
i. 206.

YOURSELF; "in y.", for yourself,
personally; II. i. 71.

STUDY QUESTIONS

By ANNE THROOP CRAIG

GENERAL

1. What was the story on which the outline plot of the play was based? Is the nature of the actual times of the story set forth in the play? To what period do the manners of the play belong?

2. What is the predominant nature of this tragedy?

3. Describe fully the character of Hamlet. Describe the condition of mind and feeling into which his circumstances have thrown him.

4. What is Hamlet's estimate of Polonius?

5. How does he treat the sycophancy of the courtiers? What does this tell of his character?

6. To whom alone does he show his true nature and mind?

7. Describe the character of Laertes. Does he seem an imperfectly constructed character, or is there something to explain or extenuate his final plot against Hamlet and to make it compatible with an originally noble nature?

8. What is the character of Claudius's penance? What impression is produced of his inner state of mind? Does he specifically express his feeling? Cite passages in explanation.

9. What seems to have been the root of Gertrude's behavior? What faults of nature are set forth in her?

10. Describe the experiences of mind and emotion that cause Ophelia's madness. What passages make the character of her love apparent?

11. How is the character of Horatio expressed? In

what passages are his qualities especially manifest? Cite Hamlet's expressions of feeling for him.

12. Does any important action of the plot hinge upon an element of Polonius's character? What element is it? Is this use of personal traits in the persons of his dramas characteristic of Shakespeare?

13. In what way is the Fortinbras and Norway situation important to the action?

14. What passages are characterized by particular technical excellence, beauty, and simplicity, throughout the play?

15. What causes Hamlet's delay of action against the king? What elements of the situation if thoroughly known to him, would have made restraint just and rational? What would it have bespoken of him, if he had acted on impulse of the Ghost's revelation? What does his restraint in this matter indicate regarding his character and state of mental control?

16. In what different ways does Hamlet's suffering lead him to express himself? How does his initial grief effect his relations in other directions? Explain the psychological impulse for such varying manifestations in the several cases.

17. What is the main difference in being overwrought in nerves and emotions and in being actually insane, even temporarily? Compare the final uncontrol of Laertes with the action of Hamlet throughout.

18. In applying their hypotheses and diagnoses might pathologists sometimes charge insanity even upon strong and sane men whose tenor of behavior is characterized by consistence and control, however overwrought they may be on occasions from strain of nerves and feeling? Do these overwrought states of nerves necessarily suppose or produce unbalance of a strong intellect. Apply your conclusion to Hamlet's case.

19. What is the striking characteristic of scene i?

20. What is the dramatic value of the Ghost's reservation of its speech for Hamlet?

21. What lines bring out most the tragedy and pathos of Hamlet's feeling, in his speech with the Ghost of his father? What do they show of his character?

22. By what means do Hamlet's speeches to the king and queen convey the impression of the undercurrent of his feeling and his secret knowledge?

23. What is the dramatic effect of placing Horatio's tale of the Ghost's appearance immediately after Hamlet's soliloquy in scene ii?

24. What characteristics does Polonius display in his talk with Laertes?

25. Is it natural for Laertes to warn his sister against Hamlet's protestations of love? What lines of Laertes' make his warning compatible with respect for Hamlet?

26. What is the dramatic treatment of Hamlet's distraught state after his experience of grief and supernatural conference, in scene v?

27. Explain the psychology of his state of mind and feeling in this instance?

28. What is the general dramatic effect of the scenes in which the Ghost appears? What characterizes the preliminaries to the appearances?

29. How does the character of Polonius further display itself in scene i?

30. What aspect of character is exhibited by Rosencrantz and Guildenstern in scene ii?

31. How does Hamlet's behavior help the impression that he is mad?

32. What is the technical distinction between the lines recited by Hamlet and the players as quotations,—and the lines of the characters in their proper persons?

33. Trace the dawning in Hamlet's mind of the suggestion for his use of the players.

34. What is the feature of Hamlet's final soliloquy in scene ii?

35. Why does he still doubt his suspicion of Claudius?

ACT III

36. To what state of mental distress has Hamlet arrived in scene i?

37. How is it reflected in his passage with Ophelia? Explain the emotional and intellectual process that could lead him to talk thus to Ophelia.

38. Cite the beauties of Ophelia's soliloquy after Hamlet leaves her. What state of feeling does it express?

39. Where does the impression of Claudius's fear of Hamlet begin? Why was it to his advantage to try to have Hamlet diverted?

40. What does Hamlet's talk with the players in scene ii make evident of the Poet's ideals of good acting?

41. Wherein is the pathos of Hamlet's choosing to sit near Ophelia during the enactment of the play in scene ii?

42. In what lines in this scene is the bitter irony of Hamlet's sentiment especially poignant?

43. Is it natural that the play-scene should produce the effect it does upon the king? Give your reasons.

44. What is the mood of Hamlet's talk with Horatio after the play?—Explain the mood and thought of it as carried over into the passage with Rosencrantz and Guildenstern.

45. What characterizes Hamlet's talk concerning his mother?—and to her, in their interview?

46. Does the passage between the Ghost and Hamlet voice Hamlet's own conflicting feelings about his mother? What constitutes the subtlety of Shakespeare's use of apparitions?

47. Is it clear whether or not Gertrude knew of the murder of her husband? Is there an effect gained by its

doubtfulness? How did the earlier versions of the
play treat Gertrude's relation to the murder?

48. Why does the death of Polonius give the king
further alarm?

49. Why was the King afraid to harm Hamlet openly?

50. What dramatic application is made of the information the Captain gives Hamlet in scene iv?

51. Why does Gertrude not want to see Ophelia?

52. What lines through Ophelia's mad scenes are remin-
iscent of her love and griefs? Describe the dramatic expression of her madness.

53. Characterize the spirit of Laertes' lines throughout
his passage with the King. His expression of sentiment
over Ophelia's madness.

54. Comment on the effect of the king's villainy upon
Laertes.

55. What constitutes the dramatic perfection of scene
i in the process of its development?

56. How has the psychology of presentiment been employed for dramatic purpose in this act? Cite other instances.

57. To what specifically does Hamlet apply his figures
in lines 60–62, scene ii?

58. Does Hamlet feel any foreboding concerning the
sword play? What does Horatio urge? What is the
nature of Hamlet's reasoning in reply?

59. What in the dramatic method gives the superbly
convincing effect of fatality in the final resolution?

60. What is the climax and end of the play? What
constitutes an anti-climax?